CW01631619

There's No Place Like Home

By Peter Haworth

DEDICATION

Who else could I dedicate this, the third book in the series to, but once again my wife Julie!

After another season of gut wrenching, nerve shattering weekends, get ready the next one starts soon!

ACKNOWLEDGEMENTS

Once again, I owe a massive debt of gratitude to my friend, ex work colleague and now author in his own right, Ed Skingsley. Not a page has been written on which Ed has seen fit to spare the red pen. I would not have believed it possible that so many errors could creep into such a small piece of writing had it not been for Ed's proofreading diligence. I thank him most sincerely for his time, patience and understanding. It's bad enough having to write this stuff let alone having to read it! It has been for him a labour of love, for which I know he would not seek monetary recompense. I will therefore not embarrass him by offering any.

Similarly, my old 'mucker' Steve Calderbank, a man with whom I have shared many pints, most of which paid for by myself. Steve, now an émigré to the Lincolnshire wastelands, has once again used all his technical skills and keyboard wizardry to convert this collection of written ramblings into the fine piece of literature you now have in your hands. He is a modest man, living a frugal existence who would not want all the trappings associated with wealth. This is probably just as well as he has also donated his services, 'free of charge'. What a magnificent gesture.

Thanks are due to Jim Thomson for his contribution of a brief foreword. Jim joined the club in 1968 making the move from Chelsea to Burnley for a fee of £40,000, a not inconsiderable sum in those days. A stalwart of some 363 appearances (360 starts) and six goals in all competitions, he is a true Claret.

Special thanks to Amber Corns of Burnley Bondholders for providing the excellent cover photograph of Turf Moor. A special mention here for fellow author Dave Thomas for his assistance in this matter.

John & Judy Weir and John Greenwood, my fellow long-suffering Clarets. For far too many years to recall these hardy souls and myself have followed the many 'ups and downs' of our beloved team. Celebrating the good times, moaning like hell about the bad times, but always there. Matchdays, without pre-match pints at the Talbot with these friends of old, would just not be the same.

My many walking buddies in the Lancashire Dotcom Walkers and the Burnley Contingent. Special thanks here to Bob Clare who selflessly invests a great amount of time and effort ensuring interesting and amiable walks are planned every week (barring school holidays - don't ask!) Bob has a wicked sense of humour and is never shy at putting words into other people's mouths. Yes Bob, you know what I mean! These walking groups continue to grow in numbers, surely a testament to the pleasure obtained from healthy exercise, good company and lovely countryside. Long may they continue.

How could I fail to acknowledge the magnificent efforts of all concerned at Burnley Football Club? Directors, managerial staff, coaches and of course the players have again defied all the odds and pulled off perhaps the biggest miracle of all, Premier League survival. In the 1959/60 season, when Burnley were crowned English League Champions, I saw my first ever game at Turf Moor and was hooked. Now all these years later, after a roller coaster ride that has seen us hit rock bottom and rise again, the magic still lives on. What a poorer place Burnley would be without its football team, the heart and soul of the town. Thanks once more to Sean Dyche and his team for restoring the **PRIDE** to this small corner of East Lancashire.

Table of Contents

FOREWORD

In 2015/16, they said it was a miracle when Leicester City lifted the Premier League trophy. At Turf Moor the Burnley fans said 'What's new? We've been pulling-off these minor miracles for decades.'

So how does this small town, more like a small village in footballing terms, continue to defy all odds and survive in the biggest and most profitable sports business on the planet, the English Premier League?

Let me tell you the secret, which Jimmy Adamson shared with his teams of the 1970's when I was proud to be a part of the first eleven. All you need is a good squad who will work hard, a stable board most of whom were taken to Turf Moor as children, a great set of loyal supporters who understand Burnley's winning formula and an incredible manager.

The 2016/17 was a classic Burnley FC experience. We had the lowest wage-bill in the league (c £33million when the top wage bill in the Premier League was £225million), we were odd's-on to be relegated and yet we finished with 40 points, fifth from the bottom, putting another £250million+ in the coffers.

We didn't have many Ferrari's or Rolls Royce's on the player's car park, but we did have some big hearts who excelled at Turf Moor. If you don't believe me ask Liverpool, Everton, Watford or Crystal Palace ....

Read on and let the story unfold.

Jim Thomson - Burnley FC 1968-81

INTRODUCTION

On May 2nd 2016 Burnley Football Club defeated Queens Park Rangers at a crowded Turf Moor to secure promotion once again to the Premier League. Having previously achieved this in 2009, via the play-off route, it was a feat considered *unbelievable*. To repeat this success in 2014, this time as runners-up to Leicester City it was *incredible*. For a town with a population of under 100,000 (and falling), to pull the rabbit out of the hat for a third time in seven years, was *beyond the comprehension of man.*

Yet somehow, thanks to manager Sean Dyche, the epitomy of positivity and self-belief, and a team of players totally buying in to the all for one and one for all mentality, the impossible had once again been achieved.

This achievement fellow Claret, and lover of a triumph of the underdog, leads you to exactly where you now sit. Back in 2009 after the magnificent play-off victory at Wembley Stadium, I vowed to mark the event of Burnley's Premier League debut season in print, and duly published 'A Season In The Sun'. At the end of that journey, unfortunately ending in relegation, I rashly promised to write a second diary should the opportunity arise. That led to the publishing of 'With Heads Held High', the second in the series of Premier League Diaries. Now as I sit here in early May 2016, basking in the afterglow of another magical season, I am compelled to once again commit the forthcoming season to print in the as yet untitled, third in the series. How many more will there be? Who knows? At this club anything can, and usually does, happen.

Any reader who has experienced either or both of the previous diaries will appreciate that they are not wholly confined to football. In an attempt to give the books a wider appeal, I have also tried to encompass other facets of my humble existence, which often interrelate with the 'glorious game'. These usually consist of amusing (hopefully) anecdotes and reminiscences often gleaned from outings and conversations with my walking buddies.

Many of you may recall my ongoing friendly (?) rivalry with other members of a walking group, Lancashire Dotcom Walkers. This hardy band of amiable retirees assemble most Tuesdays throughout the year for a seven or eight-mile ramble, sometimes if we are lucky, topped off with a pub lunch. This group which over the years has risen from a small band to now in excess of thirty souls, is made up of people from mainly Preston, South Ribble and Burnley areas with a few unfortunates from Mellor in the Blackburn area, but we try not to mention them.

Among the group are, as one would expect, a sizeable number of fellow Clarets, followed by an enthusiastic but misguided bunch of Preston fans. We have also attracted one or two other exotic species such as a Liverpool, Manchester United, Derby County, and bizarrely an Oldham Athletic supporter and one Blackburn Rover, but we will pass quickly over him.

During our second Premier League season, I was goaded in to taking a bet with one of our PNE friends, retired Police Officer Jim Skipper (of the Yard). The wager agreed was that both PNE and Burnley would start the 2015/16 season in the same division. At the time we were of course PREMIER LEAGUE, whereas PNE were League 1.

Unfortunately, our relegation and Preston's victory in the very last match of the season meant that Jim had won the bet.

This meant that I had to suffer the ignominy of handing over the £5 stake (a not inconsiderable sum to a pensioner!) in a photo shoot in front of the Tom Finney statue at Deepdale. As Jim (Skipper of the Yard) had decided to donate his ill-gotten gains to the local Hospice, I felt in my weakened and confused state, obliged to double the stake.

Imagine my joy this time round as at the commencement of this glorious season, we once again struck the same bet. Jim would be the victor if both teams were in the same division for 2016/17, but our promotion back to the Premier League meant the victory spoils were mine! Curiously Jim failed to appear for the walk on the Tuesday following the clinching of our elevated status. Not to worry I have a whole summer to catch up with him!

Obviously this time there will be no humbling and degrading ceremony for me on enemy territory. No this time it will be on home turf, literally! Now for me just the tricky decision whether to reciprocate by handing over the dosh to charity, or aiding local beer hostelries and protecting jobs at Moorhouse's brewery by drinking the winnings. Keep reading to find the outcome.

As a result of our success in reaching once again the 'Promised Land', I find myself in the strange position of being the subject of congratulations from all sorts of people. Why are they congratulating me? I have neither kicked a ball, nor been involved in team selection and tactics. In the aftermath of victory over QPR to secure the promotion, texts arrived thick and fast.

Even the North Enders managed, through gritted teeth, to extend their best wishes. My ex work colleague Alison (a lapsed Bolton supporter; who wouldn't be - who is now 'glory hunting' with Manchester City), and former work associate, Rob Waterworth a staunch Huddersfield Town fan, joined in the celebration. My sister in the deep south (Isle of Wight) along with her son (Arsenal fan) were also swift to the Smartphone and Tablet keyboards. Best of all was the email from my good friend in Germany, Heiko Ketzler the self-proclaimed sole member of the Borussia Moenchengladbach branch of the Burnley Supporters club, who wrote:

Dear Peter. Again your dream comes true!!! Up the Clarets!!! Congrats to my team in England!!!

The one question all these people and countless thousands more had in common was... Will there be a Volume 3 of Burnley FC, The Premier League Diaries? In view of such a clamour, I felt I had no option but to oblige.

Sit back, relax, pour yourself a stiff drink (you'll probably need it, I know I will!), and enjoy if you can our third epic saga of the 'Clash Of The Titans'.

But before we get to that let's take a few pages to review our sometimes happy, sometimes sad, mostly nerve wracking but certainly never boring, route to El Dorado.

2015/16

Burnley FC's second joust with the Premier League in 2014/15 ended with the same outcome as their first (2009/10) in relegation. However, this time it didn't end with the same bitter taste as first time around. There was no mass defection of manager and backroom staff halfway through the season, and none of the alleged unrest in the squad as on the first occasion.

This time despite the disappointment of the final outcome there was still a strong feeling of unity. Buoyed by a good end to the Premier League season, two away victories and a home draw in the last three fixtures, hopes were high of a decent shot at a quick return.

Inevitably key players were lost as they pursued their options of furthering their careers in the Premier League. Danny Ings departed to Liverpool with a compensation fee looking likely to be decided by tribunal, whilst Kieran Trippier headed south to Tottenham. Surprisingly Captain Jason Shackell also left, returning to Derby County for a substantial fee for a player the wrong side of thirty.

However, the most important part of the jigsaw, in the eyes of most fans, was manager Sean Dyche and it was imperative that his services were retained. Rumours were rife of interest from Premier League and ambitious Championship clubs, but as vacancies were filled a collective sigh of relief echoed round the town. August saw the start of the new campaign with Sean still firmly in place.

Obviously there were some significant gaps to fill on the playing side, but armed with incoming fees, parachute payments, and presumably some unspent funds from the Premier League war chest, the fans looked forward to some frenetic activity.

The first priority was to replace the outgoing players, and also with an eye on a number of long term injuries, recruitment began in earnest. The first signing was an experienced and relatively young Premier League full back, Matt Lowton from Aston Villa, generally seen by the fans as a good replacement for Kieran Trippier. Next to arrive was the Belgian striker Jelle Vossen, presumably as 'the new' Danny Ings. However, the newlywed Jelle never looked settled and was on his way back to Belgium within a period of about eight weeks. We don't seem to have much success with overseas recruits!

Another incoming striker was the highly rated youngster Chris Long who had turned down a contract offer from Everton in the hope of furthering his career with more first team activity. Ahead of the season's opening game - a shock arrival, full back Tenday Darikwa from Chesterfield. A bit of a surprise this as he had looked destined to join newly promoted Preston North End for most of the summer.

The striking department appeared well loaded now with Jutkiewicz, Vossen, Vokes, Sordell, and Long, plus the long term injured Ashley Barnes. However not long into the season, another surprise arrival with the German Rouwen Hennings, top scorer with Bundesliga 2 side Karlsruher, joining for a substantial fee.

Raised eyebrows all round but stranger was still to come. Brentford striker Andre Gray reportedly on his way to

Bristol City, rejects the deal and signs in at Turf Moor in a rumoured staggeringly large £9m deal! What the hell is happening? The world has gone mad, and normally penny wise Burnley have gone with it! Now with seven strikers on board we are definitely top heavy, but within days Vossen returns to Belgium, and Sordell has his contract cancelled by mutual agreement. Ironically Jutkiewicz then becomes yet another victim of the Clarets cruciate ligament curse and faces a long spell on the injured list.

Still no cover for the seriously undermanned centre midfield positions, but following an unbelievably long on/off saga concerning Nottingham Forest midfielder Henri Lansbury, another shock! Joey Barton, 'enfant terrible', signs for Burnley on a one-year deal. Released by QPR and reputedly on wages of £90k/week, this stuns the town!

There's no doubt that Joey can play and may just be the midfield general we are crying out for, but would he be able to control his temper and stay on the pitch! Time would tell.

So a most unusual transfer window for Burnley and a big change in spending patterns. Would it work? Nothing for it, but to just wait and see.

The season kicked off with a tricky fixture away at Leeds and we came away with a hard fought point courtesy of a late Sam Vokes equaliser. The first home game saw the Clarets trailing twice to Birmingham but levelling on both occasions. Next up was another tough away fixture resulting in a 2-0 loss at high flying Ipswich. Not too impressive a start, two draws and a defeat in the first three. However normal service was resumed and the Clarets won the next three, not convincingly, but at least some momentum was starting to build.

After six games we sat 5th in the table, joint third on points, and with injured players starting to return and new man Barton approaching match fitness, optimism was building. Andre Gray had scored on his home debut, always a good sign, and looked just the kind of striker we had been looking for.

The seventh game, home to newly promoted MK Dons, again resulted in a victory, the fourth consecutive one. This gave the Clarets the identical start to the last Championship promotion season, four wins, two draws and one defeat in the first seven fixtures. Was it an omen?

A creditable if somewhat tedious 0-0 draw in the televised fixture at Derby County ends the winning run. This is then followed by a disappointing home reverse (1-2) to a rapidly improving Reading side. This fixture sees the much awaited entrance of Joey Barton, introduced as a second half substitute, with some promising effect.

For the fourth time in the opening 10 fixtures the Clarets are featured as the live TV game in the away fixture at Rotherham. Normal service is resumed with a 2-1 victory, goals coming from both strikers Andre Gray and Sam Vokes. Joey Barton makes his full debut and earns a 'Man of the Match' accolade for his efforts. Promising signs indeed and with injured players returning optimism is rising.

After the Rotherham game there is a two week break as international fixtures come into play. We enter the break in sixth position, joint third on points, and handily placed after a sluggish start.

A black cloud appeared on the horizon with the prospect of losing manager Sean Dyche to Premier League relegation strugglers, Sunderland. The Wearsiders, manager-less following the resignation of Dick Advocaat, rumoured to be strong admirers of Dyche. Fortunately, the job is quickly filled by the appointment of 'firefighter general' Sam Allardyce.

Following the meaningless, in terms of both qualification and standard of opposition International break, momentum was maintained with a scrappy home victory over Bolton (2-0). This was followed by a somewhat fortuitous 1-1 draw at Nottingham Forest, Matty Taylor grabbing a late equaliser. Ironically this result being assisted by the sending off of Forest captain and long term summer transfer target, Henri Lansbury. Silly boy!

These results cemented our place in the leading pack chasing early leaders Brighton, who after 12 games had a six point advantage on us.

Next up was a magnificent if undeserved victory at the old enemy Blackburn Rovers, the winner coming from a superb Scott Arfield strike that arrowed into the Rovers net from the edge of the box. Needless to say this was greatly appreciated by the Claret hordes, and Scotty earned himself a place in Burnley history.

A highly successful October was rounded off with a home victory over Huddersfield, both goals coming from Andre Gray, quickly establishing himself as a key player. The month ended with the Clarets in third position (joint second on points) and just two behind leaders Brighton.

November started in similar fashion with a highly entertaining 3-1 home win over upwardly mobile Fulham. Once again Gray bagged a brace and with a bit of luck would have had the 'hat-trick'. A real sense of belief was beginning to grow at the Turf, and not surprisingly on the strength of recent results. The last 12 games had seen nine wins, 2 draws, and only the one defeat reaping 29 points from a possible 36.

A not so entertaining, in fact rather dour 0-0 away at Wolves followed, but again a hard earned point at a difficult venue.

Again another International break interrupted the season in mid-November but perhaps a chance to rest weary legs and recover from some of the minor knocks.

Away from the football for a moment, readers of my previous diary 'With Heads Held High' will be aware of the ongoing battle for superiority in the Lancashire Dotcom walking group. Tuesday November 10th gave the Burnley Contingent the opportunity to regain their crown, lost in 2014, in the annual Dotcom Walkers quiz. This time in a contest held over an excellent lunch at the Clog and Billycock pub in Pleasington (enemy territory!), we came out victorious in the battle against the Rest of the World (ROW) team. A tremendous effort for the six 'Sons (and daughters) of Claret' to overcome three opposing teams selected from the ROW.

Not wishing to take too much credit for this achievement, but conscious of the fact that the title was lost in my absence last time, I believe the success on this occasion was down to the reduced number of former school teachers in our line up. What a sad indictment of our education system!

Another draw followed, this time 1-1 at home in front of Sky TV cameras, against the still unbeaten Brighton. This result saw us drop to fifth in an increasingly crowded top end of the table. Two points separated the top five clubs with all the fancied contenders, Hull, Derby, Middlesboro, Brighton and ourselves, all going strongly.

Rapidly becoming the draw specialists, November ended with the Clarets still in fifth position, four points behind leaders Brighton but only two adrift of the second automatic promotion spot. An eventful 2-2 draw at a never easy place for us Cardiff, coming back from 2-0 down with two late, late goals, including a first for German import Rouwen Hennings, maintained the unbeaten run. An afternoon that looked as though it would be ruined by some very poor refereeing decisions ended in smiles for the Clarets who witnessed it, but disbelief for the doubters who had left the stadium early.

Next match up, and I'm sure any readers who read Volume 2 (With Heads Held High) will appreciate the special significance of the game, Preston North End! Bragging rights among the Dotcom Walkers up for grabs, time for a return to winning ways?

A foul day in terms of weather and result! Defeat to arch rivals 0-2, and precious points lost in the promotion chase. A bad day at the office indeed! A tricky run of fixtures was now looming and we had no wins in the last four games. Are the wheels coming off?

The next two difficult away games resulted in a 0-0 draw at QPR, and a 0-1 defeat at new leaders Middlesbrough. The results meant we remained fifth, but the gap was closing below and opening above.

There were the early signs of rumblings of discontent among the fans, primarily concerning Sean's reluctance to change the team and/or the formation. Not one to make wholesale changes Sean did opt for the recovering Dean Marney, and Matt Lowton to replace David Jones and Tenday Darikwa for the next home fixture.

Bingo! The team responded to give Dyche his biggest ever Burnley victory with a thumping 4-0 victory over a very poor Charlton Athletic. It was a pleasure to see the marauding Marney back to full fitness following his cruciate ligament injury and looking none the worse for it. There was also an impressive contribution from Lowton, and the fans went home happy to enjoy the Christmas festivities. Had Sean found the winning blend?

Unfortunately, apparently not. Boxing day 2015 brought a heavy defeat at rivals Hull City, a ground where our record had previously been excellent. A black day all round after persistent rain throughout December, torrential overnight rain left Padiham, Whalley, Todmorden and Hebden Bridge with serious flooding issues. The 3-0 defeat doing nothing to lift the gloom!

The Hull game marked the half way point in the season, the team remained in fifth place but were tailing off badly. A big improvement was going to be required in the second half of the season if we were to once again reach the Promised Land.

Two days after the Hull defeat the Clarets brought the curtain down on 2015 with another emphatic 4-0 win at the Turf. A team that for much of the first half season had struggled for goals had suddenly gone goal crazy. To be fair once again the standard of the opposition left much to be desired as Steve Cotterill's Bristol City were put to the sword. The game produced a first Football League hat trick for Andre

Gray, and the fans forgot the disappointment at Hull to once again go home in celebratory mood.

December ended with the Clarets still in fifth position and another home fixture to start the new year. This time a hard fought encounter with sixth placed Ipswich Town ended 0-0. A sound enough defensive performance but once again lacking attacking penetration against the stronger sides.

The transfer window reopened in January and once again we awaited our usual torture as our rivals sign everyone in sight and we miss out on our wish list.

A break from league action saw us drawn away to Middlesbrough on FA Cup 3rd round day. This was to be the first of three consecutive away fixtures in six days. Our hosts topped the Championship and were in a run of serious good form, not a tie we would have wished for.

We are comprehensively outplayed in the first half but a combination of poor finishing and good goalkeeping limits the Boro to one first half goal. A flash of inspiration on the stroke of half time from Sam Vokes sees Rouwen Hennings equalise from close range and we are suddenly back in it. Buoyed by that goal we are much more competitive second half and Stephen Ward scores his first Burnley goal to give us an unexpected cup victory. On the following Monday evening we learn our reward, an away tie at FA cup holders Arsenal...

However, the result is a great confidence booster ahead of two away league games coming up in rapid succession. The momentum is carried into the first game on the Tuesday and results in a resounding 5-0 away win at MK Dons. The result never in doubt after Joey Barton's opener for the Clarets, the team goes nap with goals from five different scorers, including a first for Matt Lowton.

The game is then followed by another long away journey for a Friday night televised fixture at Brentford. A supremely dominant first half has the Clarets 3-0 up at half time, all the goals scored from outside the penalty area, and again with three different scorers. The shell shocked hosts find a better second half performance but despite a spirited fightback, the Clarets close the game out 3-1.

A great start to the new year and we are up to fourth position, seven points behind leaders Boro, and five behind second placed Hull who both have to come to Turf Moor. At last the confidence seems to be growing within the team and the supporters. A tremendous week on our travels with three victories, ten goals scored and only two conceded, that's more like it! Next up another 'six-pointer', home to much fancied Derby County who lie third one point ahead of us.

We certainly seem to have the 'Indian sign' on poor old Derby and Monday the 25th of January's televised fixture is no exception. A strange night at the Turf ends with the Clarets again big winners over our free spending promotion rivals.

A first half lead, much against the run of play comes courtesy of Derby centre back Keogh's headed own goal from a Matt Lowton cross. This is followed by an almost instantaneous equaliser for the Rams from a thunderous volley from 20 yards. The score remains at 1-1 at the break with our visitors still in the ascendancy.

It makes for an uneasy half time interval as we anticipate a difficult 45 minutes to come. How wrong we are, bizarrely two penalties in a three-minute spell early in the half stand the game on its head. First as Gray wriggles in the box he is upended by Keogh and duly despatches the resulting spot kick. A handball by none other than returning ex skipper, Jason Shackell followed quickly, resulting in a second penalty. Surprisingly it's not taken this time by Gray but by his strike partner Vokes but with the same end result.

Unbelievably we are suddenly 3-1 ahead but still not finished. From a flowing passing movement, Arfield bears down on the Derby goal, his shot from 25 yards deflects off the foot of the hapless Shackell and over keeper Carson to nestle in the back of the net. Game over and another four goal haul for the now rampant goal scoring Clarets.

A nightmare evening for the Derby centre backs ends with us leapfrogging them in the table as we go third and they drop to fifth. January's league form has been nothing short of phenomenal with a draw and three victories in the league. Twelve goals have been scored in these games and only two conceded resulting in a vastly improved goal difference. More importantly I feel the growing sense of belief that promotion can once again be achieved has returned. With eighteen games to go in the season, and ground still to be made up on the leaders, it will be a tough but not impossible ask.

January ends with an FA Cup exit, albeit not unexpected, as we go down bravely to Arsenal at the Emirates stadium. A battling performance as Sam Vokes equalises Arsenal's early lead, but in the end a second half goal from Alexis Sanchez seals the tie. As a fan I am not too downhearted by the result, as all losing teams say after a cup tie defeat, we can now concentrate on the league.

As a rule any of our incoming transfer activity in the January window was likely to be conducted on the last day!

This year again ran true to form with just one major signing, that being James Tarkowski, the Brentford centre back. The saga with this particular player had rumbled on for some time and was probably not helped by his refusal to play against us in the recent fixture. With a fee rumoured (but undisclosed) to be £6m this represents another significant outlay for the club. It's thought the deal was more likely £3m upfront with a further £3m in add-ons. Welcome aboard James.

The first fixture in February looked set to be a stern test of our unbeaten run in the league in 2016. Our opponents were promotion chasing Sheffield Wednesday, lying in seventh position and unbeaten at home in a run stretching back to August and encompassing 14 games. Once again a flying start for the confident Clarets as Andre Gray fires us ahead on three minutes. However, a more spirited second half showing by our hosts means we have to settle for a very creditable 1-1 draw. The run continues…

Next up came league leaders Hull City at the Turf and after our defeat to the Tigers on Boxing Day surely time for revenge. It was also a game with special significance for myself as readers of my second Premier League diary, 'With Heads Held High', will appreciate. This being down to the fact that an old mate of mine who had recently relocated himself in the 'badlands' of Lincolnshire, seems now to consider himself to be a Hull fan. Now I know for a fact that he has never seen them play and probably couldn't name one of their players, nevertheless he likes to gloat over their current temporary superiority over the Clarets.

A tight game played in once again terrible weather conditions of gusting wind and driving rain was heading for a goalless draw. Burnley shaded the first half, whilst Hull edged the early part of the second. Then on 77 minutes a Joey Barton shot is spilled by the Hull keeper and turned in by Sam Vokes. Revenge they say is a dish best served cold, and on a bitterly cold day, it certainly tasted sweet! All three points to the Clarets, third position in the table, and the gap cut behind the top two to a single point, albeit they have games in hand. A thoroughly satisfactory day's work and bragging rights re-established in my favour, boy would my mate suffer!

Another away point garnered from the next fixture at Reading maintained third position but our 'friends' at Ewood could do us no favours losing at home to Hull. Brighton won their fourth consecutive game to confirm the end of their mini slump as things tightened up near the top. A gap of eight points between ourselves and seventh spot looked like a play-off place was becoming a distinct possibility, but automatic promotion had to remain the real goal.

A so far highly satisfactory February continued with a scrappy but thoroughly deserved home victory over Neil Warnock's relegation threatened Rotherham United. The points haul from the four games so far in the month stood at eight from a possible twelve. The unbeaten league run now stood at nine games extending back to the Boxing day defeat at Hull. The win took the Clarets into second place with neither leaders Hull City nor second placed Middlesbrough in action. With a further home game against Nottingham Forest following swiftly it was another good opportunity to pressurise the front runners!

Forest provided result number ten in the unbeaten run as we ran out 1-0 winners, with an impressive first half performance but with no goals to show for it. A slower start to the second period but then a Sam Vokes goal, his sixth in the last nine games, and a relatively untroubled end to the game safely netted maximum points. A good job too as our three nearest rivals all recorded victories in what was becoming a very competitive chase for the automatic promotion spots.

On Saturday 27th February a brilliant month for the Clarets concluded with the team going top of the Championship! From six games played 14 points were gained from a possible 18 with four wins and two draws. A draw at home on Friday evening for Hull City meant that victory for the Clarets at lowly Bolton would lift the Clarets into top spot. This would be easier said than done as our relegation threatened hosts waged what one Sunday newspaper described as a 'physical slanging match'.

Goalless at half time, but then one down on 69 minutes meant our coveted 'top dog' position looked decidedly unlikely. However, the never-say die Clarets had other ideas as top scorer Andre Gray returned to form with a stunning late brace to take the Clarets clear.

Middlesbrough had a comfortable away win at Fulham whilst Derby went down at Wolves on a great day for all of the Claret and Blue persuasion. With 12 games to go we led on 65 points, Hull and Middlesbrough were on 64, Hull having one game in hand with Boro having two. Brighton were on 60 points with a home game to come on Monday night against Leeds United, and the top six were competed by Derby on 57 and Sheffield Wednesday on 55.

The first week in March featured midweek games for all our closest rivals but not for ourselves. On the Monday night Brighton steamrollered Leeds to move within two points. Better news on Tuesday though as the old enemy Blackburn did us a monumental favour beating

Middlesbrough who would have gone top with anything bar a loss. More encouragement as similarly placed Hull lost at Birmingham City and we surprisingly remained top. However, this position was relinquished on Friday night as the Boro beat a poor Wolves side 2-1 to go two points clear at the top.

Would February's excellent form continue into March for the Clarets? First up in March none other than the accursed Rovers! Our last victory over them at the Turf was as far back as 1978 but with two recent victories at 'Deadwood Park' this remained the only wrong to right. Sean Dyche up to this point had not lost an East Lancashire derby in his previous five attempts. A dour affair settled by an early penalty for the Clarets, scored by Andre Gray, preserved his unbeaten run. Top spot regained, a double completed over the now not so mighty Rovers, could it get any better? Eleven games to go now, including two away fixtures in the following week at Fulham and Huddersfield. Points would be very welcome from these as we really got into the business end of the season.

Fulham away, with Burnley top scorers in the division and Fulham next, did we expect a no-score draw? Not really. Did we get a goal drought. No way. The Clarets ahead on nine minutes, trailed 2-1 by 22 minutes. A combination of good defending and great goalkeeping kept that score till half time. Level on 49 minutes and ahead again on 62 kept the nerves jangling in a pulsating game. We held on to close the game out 3-2 and amass another invaluable 3 points.

Defeat for Middlesbrough at lowly Rotherham, and no victory for any other team in the top six, meant we opened a four point gap over Boro at the top, six over Brighton, and seven over Hull. With Middlesbrough one game in hand and

Hull two, victories in these games would still leave them short of us. Another great night to be a Claret. The unbeaten run now at 13 games with the last five all won, could we keep it going with just 10 to play. Bring on Huddersfield!

Ahead of the away fixture at Huddersfield Sean Dyche was confirmed as Manager of the Month for February. Would the curse that usually accompanies this accolade strike?

Did I say curse? Of course Sean Dyche doesn't do curses and the Clarets continued along the relentless path ending hopefully at the 'Promised Land'. Huddersfield were systematically dismantled in a first half demolition that took us to the break 3-1 ahead. As expected a more spirited show from the hosts in the second period, but steady nerves meant we closed the game out without too much discomfort. The magnificent run continued and now read 14 games unbeaten of which incredibly 11 were won, including the last six.

Our rivals, not surprisingly, were finding this sort of form difficult to live with. By the end of the weekend we had established a seven-point gap over Boro (one game in hand), nine points over Hull (two in hand), and nine over Brighton (one in hand). I hesitated to say it but the atmosphere was akin to the sort of momentum that built in our last promotion push in 2014. Our nearest competitors Middlesbrough also appeared to be falling apart at the seams with a fall out between manager Aitor Karanka and his players resulting in his departure from the club, then subsequent reinstatement! Similar friction was also evident at Derby, now 13 points adrift of the rampaging Clarets as their caretaker boss came under fire from senior players. Meanwhile at Turf Moor it was business as usual as Dyche maintained a calm but resolute manner.

After the two successful and profitable away trips it was back to earth with a bit of a bump. The home game against Wolverhampton Wanderers was seen by many as eminently winnable, but as is so often the case, it proved not to be the case. Amongst the fans too many chickens had been counted before the eggs hatched.

A difficult game saw the Clarets well on top for the first 20 minutes but failing to unduly trouble the Wolves keeper. This gave the visitors confidence and they grew more into the game. Goalless at half time but then the visitors sensing something to be had started to take the game to us. However, on 68 minutes and against the run of play a magnificent Sam Vokes header put us in front and heading for a seventh consecutive victory. As the fourth official signalled four minutes added time we sat on the edge of our seats awaiting the final whistle, then tragedy... From a late corner (92 minutes) a headed equaliser and a stunned Turf Moor crowd left the ground with two vital points snatched away.

Other results saw Brighton, our next opponents, leapfrog Middlesbrough into the second automatic promotion spot, whilst Hull's defeat at Boro on the Friday evening left them in fourth. Points gap narrowed but still in the driving seat, the position was now Burnley 75 points (38 games), Brighton 71 (38), Middlesbrough 70 (37), Hull 66 (37).

Sean Dyche summed it up with his after match comments. *"People need to remember that despite our position, nobody comes here just to lay down and roll over.*

"Nothing ever comes easy for us here or when we're playing away from home.

"We're still clear at the top and we're still on a long unbeaten run. As long as we don't put too much pressure on ourselves then we'll continue to be OK.

"There's pressure everywhere in football, but we're not feeling any here."

After an enforced two week break to accommodate International friendlies, battle recommenced with a decidedly juicy contest away at Brighton. Ahead of the game the club announced a net profit of a staggering £30.1m, a legacy of the previous Premier League season. Everything in the Claret's garden was unbelievably rosy. However, 55 plus years of watching our heroes still had me racked with doubts and praying for a successful conclusion to the season.

As expected Brighton proved a stern test! Urged on by a partisan home crowd of almost 30,000, (including 1633 Clarets, having made the long journey for a 12.30 televised kick off) they were soon at our throats. Our old nemesis of poor defending at corners reappeared leading to a setback on 30 minutes, but by 33 minutes equally inept corner defending by our hosts handed Andre Gray the equaliser. On the stroke of half time Albion regained a precious lead when the tricky but unpleasant Knockaert twisted and turned the defence before firing home.

A third goal for the Seagulls in the second half would no doubt have sealed our fate but was not to be forthcoming. As time ran out Sean Dyche rang the changes throwing Matty Taylor, Dean Marney and the returning Ashley Barnes into the fray. As the Clarets upped the pressure there occurred a moment of real controversy. On 88 minutes a Keane header from a Taylor corner clearly crossed the Brighton goal line before being cleared. Unfortunately, not clearly enough for the referee and his assistant who waved play on. As the BBC Radio Lancashire commentators noted, a wrong decision that could cost the Clarets £100m if it meant we missed promotion. Then unbelievably in this unbelievable season the trick was repeated in the third minute of added time. Taylor corner, Keane header, 2-2! Now Brighton, obviously masters of poor corner defending, must know how we felt with the late goal coming from Wolves in the last match.

So an often bad tempered and controversial encounter ended all square and we maintained our four-point advantage over a team who are serious challengers for an automatic promotion spot. Brighton indeed dropped to third as a result of Boro's 2-2 away victory at QPR on the previous evening. With Hull thumping Bristol City 4-0 at home the table now read:

Burnley - Points 76 (39 Games)
Middlesbrough - 73 (38)
Brighton - 72 (39)
Hull - 69 (38)

So, still ahead but a big week to come with a midweek home game against play off chasing Cardiff, followed by a televised home 'derby' with old adversaries Leeds.

It proved a difficult night at the Turf against play-off chasing Cardiff. Our visitors in no mood to make life easy threw up an Iron curtain defence and looked to catch us on the break. It damned near worked but with resolute defending and a bit of luck we stayed firm. At the other end not many chances and some immaculate saves by the Cardiff keeper ensured the game ended in a 0-0 stalemate. In truth not a result that did either side any favours!

With a straightforward home win for Middlesbrough, and a vital away win for Brighton, our lead at the top dwindled to one point. With in-form Boro in second and with a game in hand, our grasp on the title was slipping fast. Brighton had now closed to within two points but with much inferior goal difference. The one bright spot on the night was the 4-0 thumping fourth placed Hull took at Derby, leaving them now eight points adrift of the Clarets.

My nerves, by now already frayed, were in danger of being shattered, and with six games still to play it was becoming torture. Not a single Claret's fan I knew relished the prospect of the play-off lottery, which was rapidly becoming a distinct possibility.

The second home game that week once again saw the Clarets open the round of Championship fixtures with the 12.30 televised kick off against Leeds. And what a start! Within a minute Scott Arfield fired us ahead and we looked forward to a more relaxed ninety minutes at the Turf - but no not for us that luxury. As the second goal failed to materialise the crowd and then the players became increasingly edgy. The visitors smelling the scent of an upset went for it, fortunately spurning two golden chances in the process. A fine chance to wrap up the spoils in added time was fluffed by Ashley Barnes failing to hit an open goal. However, once again we hung on grimly to the death for a much needed three points.

The result ensured we stayed top of the division taking us four points clear of Boro and five clear of Brighton at the game end. Unfortunately, our pals from Preston could not assist us, going down 1-0 at Middlesbrough in the afternoon fixture, reducing the lead to one point again. Brighton were scheduled to play at Nottingham on the Monday evening and we prayed, albeit not too hopefully, for a shock Forest victory. Hull could only manage a draw at Huddersfield and dropped to ten points behind with a game in hand.

As expected Forest too proved incapable of aiding our cause going down 2-1 albeit to a late winning goal in the first minute of added time. With no midweek fixture for us it gave Middlesbrough the opportunity to take top spot if they could win their game in hand at home to Reading. In what was turning out to be a bad week for us this they duly did, with once again a very late winner coming in the 93rd minute, 10 seconds from the end of the game!

So, down to second and trailing by two points, but worse was still to come. The weekend round of fixtures commenced with Brighton at home to Fulham on the Friday night. No need for late goals in this game as the Seagulls blitzed the Cottagers 5-0 to leapfrog the Clarets and claim second spot one point ahead. Essential now that we were to get at least a point in our game at Birmingham to reclaim the automatic promotion position if only on goal difference.

Middlesbrough had on paper what looked a fairly comfortable away game at already relegated Bolton. A win here in the lunchtime kick off would take them five points clear of the Clarets with the 'Clash of the Titans' to come at Turf Moor on the following Tuesday evening. Tense times indeed for all of the Claret and Blue persuasion!

Well to round off a very uncomfortable week, Bolton contrived to snatch defeat from the jaws of victory going down 2-1 after leading. Would you believe it Boro's winning goal coming once again in added time!

It was enough to dampen the spirits of any man, but not those of Sean Dyche and his fast becoming team of invincibles. In a typical battling Clarets performance once again demonstrating Sean's oft quoted term 'resilience' our heroes emerged 2-1 victors at Birmingham's, St Andrew's. A first half opener from George Boyd was cancelled out early in the second half by a Blues equaliser, only for the Clarets to come roaring back to take all three vital points with a winner from who else, Andre Gray.

The unbeaten run stretching back to Boxing Day 2015 now stood at 19 games. Could the Clarets see out the remaining four fixtures to go a full half season undefeated? Four points now separated the top three teams Middlesbrough (85), Burnley (83), Brighton (81), and the rest also rans. Now came a massive game at Turf Moor on Tuesday with the visit of the leaders. Who would hold their nerve?

A no holds barred encounter at the Turf in front of an extremely fired up 20,000 crowd ended all square with yet another late goal, this time for our heroes. Middlesbrough came brim full of confidence from a five match winning run and a real gritty skirmish ensued. Boro shaded the first half but with only one thumping shot off the crossbar to show for it. The Clarets had the upper hand in the second, but fell behind around the 70-minute mark from a disputed free kick tucked away at close range by arch enemy Jordan Rhodes.

The visitors appeared well content with their slender lead and retreated to deep defensive positions in an attempt to see out the game. A big mistake as the Clarets seized the initiative and launched an aerial bombardment not seen since Dresden. Several close efforts came and went before the assistant referee signalled an additional six minutes. Roared on by the crowd a final assault was launched and in minute two of the six, we are LEVEL!!! Taylor's corner falls in the box to Keane who prods home from close range. Cue scenes of absolute ecstasy in the stands, and a roar the likes of which had not been heard at the Turf since Robbie Blake's winner against Manchester United.

With Brighton once again demolishing their opposition, this time by 4-0, what an absolutely vital point that was. Middlesbrough looking likely to have gone five points clear of ourselves, Brighton would have gone one point above, are both pegged back in added time. What a nail biter now! Boro lead by two points, Burnley second, and Brighton third on the same points as ourselves but with a poorer goal difference. Three games to play and still Middlesbrough have to meet Brighton on the last day of the season.

For us it's simple, win the last three games and we are up. First of the three is Preston away in a televised Friday night fixture. We certainly owe our local rivals one after their victory at the Turf, but for sure we could expect no favours from them.

A tremendous following of over 5000 for an away fixture on a Friday evening saw the Clarets come home once again triumphant and with the unbeaten run now at 21 games. A sixth minute free kick from Joey Barton, with the aid of a massive deflection was enough to see us home and dry in a game that could have been won more comfortably.

That took the Clarets back top of the table and heaped the pressure back onto Middlesbrough and Brighton. Their respective Saturday fixtures were, Boro home to mid-table Ipswich, and Brighton away at already relegated Charlton. As expected Brighton won their fixture 3-1 with the aid of a late penalty, but Boro could only conjure a draw from their game.

This left an intriguing picture at the top with three teams all on 87 points only separated by goal difference! Burnley (+33), Middlesbrough (+32), Brighton (+30), could it be any tighter? With Middlesbrough to play Brighton in the final fixture of the season, an intriguing end was guaranteed.

Still just in the driving seat we had two remaining fixtures, Queen Park Rangers at home and Charlton away. Just two more wins and we were untouchable, could we get over the line? Both our rivals would play trickier opponents before we entertained Queens Park Rangers in yet another televised game scheduled for Bank Holiday Monday 2nd May at 4.45. We prayed that one or the other would drop points but whatever the outcome we would know exactly where we stood before we kicked off.

The penultimate round of fixtures kicked-off with Boro away to Birmingham in a Friday evening fixture. The Blues took the lead but were overhauled and trailed 2-1 before a scrappy equaliser shared the points. A good start for us, but not so good for Middlesbrough who had now drawn three consecutive games.

With neither Brighton nor ourselves scheduled to play till the Bank Holiday Monday it meant another anxious weekend for the fans. Brighton got things underway at 14.30 on the Monday with what looked a tricky fixture at home to play-off contenders Derby, who were running into good form. The game certainly turned out that way and to the delight of many thousands of Clarets making their way to Turf Moor, the Rams took the lead late in the second half. However, as had so often happened in the run in, a late goal for Brighton restored them some hope but a draw was not what they would have wished for.

These results meant a Burnley victory over QPR would see us promoted, and an expectant but nervous crowd packed the Turf. There was good reason to be edgy as our visitors, with a stiff breeze behind them gave us a difficult 45 minutes, but we got off level at half time. With the benefit of the wind in the second half we started to grow into the game. Cue bedlam on 61 minutes as Sam Vokes rose to glance a vicious whipped free kick from Dave Jones into the visitor's net. A huge collective sigh of relief and belief swept the ground. Despite one stinging shot against our post QPR could not muster an equaliser and after three agonising minutes of added time, the prize was ours. PROMOTED to the Premier league for the third time in seven years, you couldn't write the script!

A massive outpouring of joy at the end as Sean Dyche led the team out after the game to thank the fans, and many sore heads to follow the partying that ensued. An incredible feat achieved by a solid sense of belief and professionalism, Sean was a picture of both happiness and pride. Now just the small matter of clinching the Championship with a result at relegated Charlton remained, whilst Middlesbrough and Brighton had to battle it out at the Riverside to avoid the dreaded play-offs. Avoiding defeat at Charlton would mean a full half season played with no defeats, what an achievement that would be, and who would bet against it.

On Saturday May 7th we duly completed the one outstanding task by claiming our position as Champions with a comprehensive 3-0 away victory at Charlton. Goals by Sam Vokes, George Boyd and Andre Gray finally put the icing on another remarkable season. Boro and Brighton fought out a 1-1 draw at the Riverside leaving the home side to celebrate promotion whilst the Seagulls faced up to the tortuous play-off battles.

The results from the final round of fixtures left us four points clear of our nearest rivals and a with a superior goal difference. How could we have ever doubted the outcome?

Bizarrely the Football League decided that the Championship Trophy would not be presented at the Valley, quoting the vague excuse of anticipated crowd protests from the relegated Charlton fans. Instead they paraded the Trophy at the Riverside stadium in Middlesbrough, hoping to hand it to one of the sides which Joey Barton disdainfully dismissed as 'never going to win it'.

What an amazing season we had witnessed, with uncanny parallels with our last promotion season. Both times we finished on 93 points, both times with 26 wins, 15 draws, 5 defeats, the same number of goals scored (72) and two goals less (35) conceded this time. The difference this time, we were the CHAMPIONS. We had made the natural progression, first promotion as play-off winners, second time as runners-up, and this time at the top of the pile.

In truth it all felt a bit harder this time round, a slightly stuttering start to the season a disappointing December, then the magnificent second half season with zero defeats in the league and only one in the FA Cup going out away at Arsenal

2-1. In 23 games after the Boxing Day defeat at Hull City, we had the unbelievable statistics of:

Played 23, Won 16, Drawn 7, Goals for 42, Goals against 12!!!, Points 55.

Without doubt key to the second half season's dramatic improvement was the switch of Ben Mee to Centre Back, and the introduction of Matt Lowton and Stephen Ward at Full Back. Not only was the defence stabilised but we then carried a more potent attacking threat down the flanks.

It could be said that the inspirational signing of Joey Barton was the catalyst, or that the expensive capture of Andre Gray with his 25 goals (23 for the Clarets) was the masterstroke. However, the truth is that as with all Sean Dyche's successes, team spirit and teamwork were the most important factors. Once again up against more fancied squads and teams with more cash at their disposal, little old Burnley had again come up trumps!

Oh, and let us not forget the invaluable contribution made by match day 'lucky charms', which are now becoming too numerable to list - more of that to come later.

Now it was time to PARTY, and boy was the town of Burnley going to do that. The daunting prospect of playing in the Premier League could wait for a couple of months; we had some serious bragging and gloating to do. Bring it on.

MAY

In the final game of the Championship winning season, a nice gesture was made by Sean Dyche in respect of long serving defender Michael Duff. With the game won and time running down, Duffer was introduced for a last cameo appearance as a Clarets player. Tom Heaton duly handed over the Captain's armband and our popular hero of many a battle brought down the curtain on his playing career.

Shortly after the match, Duffer announced his retirement from the game ending a long playing career with the Clarets stretching back to July 2004. Rarely in this day and age do we see players notching up such longevity with one club. A bargain buy from Cheltenham, Micky has repaid the outlay for him many times over, and there is not a single fan who would not wish him well. Fortunately, in pretty quick time the club announced that he would be taking up a position with the Development squad, thereby allowing him to continue his association with Burnley FC. Thanks and best wishes Duffer!

Promotion back to the Premier League ensured us of an almost mind boggling financial windfall. Various figures have been bandied about concerning the minimum value, one of the more realistic one's being £187m. This figure being made up of TV money in the region of £100m in the first year, and parachute payments totalling £87m spread over three years should we once again fall at the first fence. This of course ignores any additional funds coming in from gate receipts, sponsorship and advertising revenues. Now that is a not inconsiderable sum!

Add to that the £30.1m profit declared in the last set of accounts, and the Danny Ings compensation money (£6.5m rising to £8m with add-ons) and it is obvious that the club has never been in a sounder financial state.

Clearly there are increased costs associated with our new status, not least of which are promotion bonuses and wage costs. However, that should still leave a tidy sum in the kitty for incoming transfer activity in order to build a squad hopefully capable of retaining our Premier League status. Of course it's not long before the fan's website messageboards are full of speculation as to who the incomers may be. One major criticism made by the fans in the last Premier League campaign was of a lack of investment in quality signings. What and who will this time bring? We wait with bated breath!

On Sunday May 15th a giant mural of Sean Dyche, resplendent in Claret & Blue appeared on the wall of a building adjacent to the long closed and derelict Mitre Pub – a fitting tribute to this heroic adopted 'Son of Burnley'. The artwork was highly visible on a major gateway into the town and I must say did go some way to brightening a rather dismal approach to the town centre.

The season may well be over for us the fans, but it certainly isn't for a number of our squad. With the Euro 2016 Finals about to get underway in France in June, several players were already being called up for their respective national training camps. First calls went to Danny Lafferty to join the Northern Ireland squad, quickly followed by Sam Vokes for Wales. Following quickly on their heels was Stephen Ward's call up for the Republic of Ireland, and on Monday 16th May, Tom Heaton for England. Hopefully all will make it successfully through the training camps and progress on to make the final squads

It didn't take long for transfer speculation to start doing the messageboard rounds. Sky reported that Joey Barton was in talks with Glasgow Rangers about a possible move to the Glasgow giants. There seemed to be some foundation in this one as Joey was reported to be a pal of Frank McParland, who seemed to be instrumental in bringing him to Burnley before departing to Rangers. Joey's desire for a two-year contract, coupled possibly with Burnley's reluctance to offer a player turning 34 in September more than one year, may tempt our Scouse hero to opt for a Scottish career finale. We will just have to wait and see.

Our old favourite Henri Lansbury, he of many recent transfer window sagas, quickly reappears as a rumoured target. This one arising once again from journalist Alan Nixon in a column in the Sun on Sunday. This one may well have more than a grain of truth in it. Sean Dyche is a well-known admirer of the player who we have pursued vigorously in recent transfer windows. It is thought that the player has a release clause in his contract triggered at £3m for interested Premier League clubs, and we are rumoured to be about to test this.

May and June are traditionally slow months for news coming out of football clubs. Players and managers are usually taking holidays, and contracts don't normally expire until the end of June. I guess it's a time for agents to be touting players and setting up deals ahead of the July transfer rush.

Fortunately, this gives me the opportunity dear reader to update you with some of my recent developments.

It has long been a cherished ambition of mine to learn to play a musical instrument. Inspired by my late father's collection of George Formby classics, played on a wind up gramophone with a pin for a stylus, I decided the Ukulele was the instrument for me. Now before you purists start I know that George played a Banjolele not a true Uke, but I had to start somewhere.

Interestingly my old mate John W (of Volumes 1&2 infamy), expressed a similar desire. John had decided to explore the Ukulele as an alternative to the guitar with which he was proficient. His reason being that on his long haul camping trips across darkest Europe, in an already 'stuffed to the gunwales' prehistoric Ford Mondeo Estate car, space saving was the uppermost consideration.

John W, not being a man to risk his capital, hit upon the idea of making a modest outlay on the smallest member of the Ukulele family, a Soprano Uke. He decided that after a trial with the instrument, if he liked the experience, he would purchase a bigger and better Concert Uke. Knowing of my intentions he then reasoned that he could sell the Soprano Uke to me in order for me to commence my musical career. Within a matter of a few weeks John had approved the instrument, purchased its successor, and sold the original (at cost price plus Handling fee!) to myself.

So, I am now the proud owner of a lilac coloured Soprano Ukelele, which my daughter Stephanie described as 'girlie'. With no ability to read music, and arthritic fingers at least three sizes too big for the fretboard, I was about to embark on my musical journey. I thought it prudent to purchase some sort of Idiots guide to learning the Ukulele and duly obtained the cheapest one I could find from Amazon. At the moment I can only describe my status as a 'work in progress'.

My tuition book is obviously aimed at children of about five years of age, which seems to be about the correct level for myself. Consequently, most of the tunes in the book are of the nursery rhyme variety. Suffice it to say at this point I have just about mastered 'London Bridge is Falling down', and an almost recognisable 'When the Saints go Marching in'. Ah! I hear you say, that's not much of a repertoire to earn a living. However, I have a cunning plan.

I intend to get myself a dog (preferably with a sad face), a hat (for collecting coins and **notes**) and a prime pitch outside M&S Burnley (all the posh people shop there) in time for Christmas. Hopefully by then I will have also mastered 'Jingle Bells' to add a seasonal flavour. I hope I am not getting over ambitious, but having heard the worst Recorder playing in the world by a guy in Bolton shopping centre, I am optimistic that a living can be made. Anyway there's more chance of getting rich from that than by writing these books! Stay tuned (get it?) for further updates on my mastery of the instrument.

Those of you who are familiar with Volume 2 of the diaries, "With Heads Held High", will be aware of my association with a walking group, Lancashire Dotcom Walkers. This merry band of souls meets every Tuesday (excepting school holidays, don't ask!) to enjoy the Lancashire countryside whilst getting some gentle exercise of the body and mind.

At last year's annual awards ceremony, I had the honour of being inducted into a very select band, the Dotcom walkers "Hall of Fame". In walking circles, which incidentally is not a good idea in that it gets you nowhere and makes you very dizzy, is akin to becoming a Rock & Roll Legend. In the coming months I will attempt to keep you abreast of any interesting snippets that invariably arise from my rivalry with supporters of some of our group's lesser teams, notably Preston, Oldham, Derby, Manchester United, Liverpool, and least (not last) Blackburn (spit).

One thing to mention at this stage is some increasingly bizarre behaviour of group leader Bob Clare. Now Bob is a well-respected ex Burnley schoolteacher currently living in Penwortham, but hailing from the deep South. Through his leadership of the group he has established contacts with local newspapers and Radio Lancashire. Frequently the Lancashire Evening Post, and the Blackpool rag feature reports of some of our weekly walks.

One such report covered a May walk from Penistone Hill to Bronte Falls and Top Withins. The more educated among you will now be screaming out that this is in fact not a Lancashire walk, but I must point out that occasionally we are allowed to stray into neighbouring counties. These ventures are referred to as trips to TOP, i.e. That Other Place, our members being unable to bring themselves to say the word Yorkshire.

In the said report were some interesting comments attributed to two PNE stalwarts Chris McCann (no not that one!) and Steve Glover.

"We usually go to Yorkshire with a great deal of reluctance because we are so deeply rooted in our Red Rose heritage. However, we made an exception for Charlotte Bronte who besides being a very charming lady wrote some great books."

Well I think I can say with some certainty that these remarks were never made by Mr McCann, who for one I have never known speak so eloquently. Secondly I doubt that Chris has ever read any of Ms Bronte's books never mind knowing her as a charming lady.

The report goes onto say that the Walking group has three published (yes including yours truly) authors among its members. Steve Glover of Fulwood is then reported as having said.

"I think this explains why we feel we have such a clear affinity with the Bronte sisters. I suppose you could describe us as a literary club that walks."

A quick text to both 'quotees' confirmed my suspicion that neither had ever said anything of the sort! I fear that Mr Clare's mischief will in future have to be watched very carefully and any media reports closely monitored. Of course he does have 'past history' on one occasion having attributed quotes to Scouse Brian, who had not even been on the walk in question.

Anyway, time now to get back to the main matter, football. On Monday May 23rd the club announced that three out of contract players would be leaving the club. These being, Matty Taylor, Matt Gilks, and Lloyd Dyer. New contracts had been offered to Joey Barton, and Goalkeeper Paul Robinson. However, strong rumours, fuelled by his own 'tweets' suggested that Barton would not be taking up the offer.

No real surprises in that lot. Matty Taylor had been a valuable member of the squad but had been limited almost wholly to substitute appearances. He had scored four goals and made some telling contributions from the bench in the last season. However, his age probably now ruled him out of a further contract in view of the increased physical demands a Premier League season would bring.

Matt Gilks had been with us for the last two years but had not made one league appearance in that time. As second choice to Tom Heaton what chance did he have! Lloyd Dyer couldn't even really be described as a bit-part player. Having been brought in to assist with the final push over the line, he enjoyed precious little game time and at his age it was no surprise he was released.

On the 24th May Joey Barton confirmed verbally that he would be taking up the offer of a two-year contract with Glasgow Rangers. Our brief love affair with Joey was over. Our potential 'enfant terrible' had turned out to be nothing of the sort and proved to be an inspirational signing. His drive and energy, and motivational qualities both on and off the field had proved invaluable in our quest. We had for a short while been good for each other, and now hopefully after all that had been achieved, parted good friends.

Best of luck Joey, but for us it had to be onwards and upwards! There must be more midfield maestros out there, let's go and get some.

Thursday 26th May's Burnley Contingent ramble brought us into contact with an interesting gentleman with whom we have had previous acquaintance. On an earlier outing after stopping for our picnic lunch outside the church of St Nicholas in Sabden, (we like to eat staring at gravestones), we had been accosted by a gentleman who appeared to be doing renovation work on the nearby Sabden House. This person, obviously missing the company of human beings in this deserted backwater, exchanged pleasantries and then asked if we would like to hear some poetry. Not being in any particular rush, and to be honest glad of the rest, we agreed.

He then asked us if we would like a poem about Burnley FC, he had clearly a good eye for an intelligent listener. He then went on to recite a very complimentary ditty about the Clarets. Impressed by our enthusiastic response, he promptly continued with a further offering, the subject of which at the moment escapes me. Wishing him all the best we then continued on our weary way in search of the end, and a pub!

On this Thursday, knowing that our route would again take us by this road, there was much conjecture as to whether we would encounter him again. On reaching the self-same spot as last time, he appeared as if by magic. Same question, would you like to hear some poetry? Same answer, yes can we have the one about Sean Dyche. No sooner said than done, and for good measure a further piece from his repertoire concerning the Trough of Bowland thrown in.

Our new friend then went on to explain that although he was a very much a manual worker he had something of a penchant for writing poetry. The chaps name is William Michael Neary, whom we have christened the 'Bard of Sabden', although more correctly it should be of Chipping as this is from where he hails. When we suggested he should have his poetry published he replied that he had, and would we like to purchase copies of his booklet (which he just happened to have with him). Having relieved us of a small amount of our cash we again went merrily on our way.

An interesting fellow is William Michael Neary or Mick as he prefers. His blurb reads:

"Composing poems out in the fields whist working on the old field tile drainage systems or dry stone walling 'the words just come to me' he says. His mischief with random recitals to unsuspecting hikers and generally anyone who crosses his path are "so much fun". He draws his inspiration from the people he meets and the stories they tell him, his renewed Christian faith, The Forest of Bowland, his Father's homeland in the West of Ireland, Cleveland or California.

If you do chance upon him, ask for the Clarets poems and make his day. Look him up on Google, under William Neary poet, or contact him on **williamneary@yahoo.co.uk**.

Friday 27th May saw finally, after much waiting and bench warming, an England debut for Goalkeeper Tom Heaton. I believe the first Burnley player to represent England at full International level since Martin Dobson in the 1970's. What's more a clean sheet for Tom on his debut, albeit he only got on the pitch for about five minutes as a late substitute!

On the following Tuesday he is confirmed as one of the three Goalkeepers to travel to France as part of the England squad for the Euro 2016 finals. A great honour for Tom and richly deserved, as are the call ups for Sam Vokes and Stephen Ward, for Wales and Republic of Ireland respectively. Wardy celebrates his inclusion with a goal for the Republic in a friendly with Belarus but unfortunately they go down 2-1. Danny Lafferty misses out on a final place in the Northern Ireland squad, but is promised by his manager that he still has a future at International level. We wish all three of our heroes 'bon chance' en France.

JUNE

In the words of the inimitable Jimmy Greaves, 'It's a funny old game!' It certainly seems that way after the events of Thursday 2nd June concerning managerial appointments at two of our neighbouring Lancashire clubs.

Firstly, Gary Bowyer (ex manager of Blackburn Rovers), he of the 'hang-dog' look and boring monotone voice, was confirmed as manager at the fast sinking ship HMS Blackpool. This 'car-crash' of a club recently relegated to League 2, and with the most despised owners ever, seem intent on continuing their downward spiral. Why would anyone want to take the reins there? Of course Mr Bowyer might be a bit short of 'readies' since his departure from our friends at Deadwood Park, but surely not that desperate! To be fair, Gary did steady the ship somewhat at Blackburn before his masters in Pune got impatient for success, which he was never going to be able to bring.

That brings us to the second appointment, who would the Indian Chicken magnates of Blackburn turn to following Paul Lambert's retreat from the mayhem. Who could guide the hapless Rovers back to the top flight? In the eyes of the powers that be there could be only one man, Owen Coyle! Yes, Judas as he is commonly known on the streets of Burnley would be returning to East Lancashire, his spiritual homeland. Many of you may remember Coyle's greatest moment in football as he guided unfancied Burnley spectacularly to the Premier League, winning the Championship Play-off Final at Wembley on the 25th May 2009.

What happened over the following months as the Clarets promising start to life at the top, four successive home wins from the start of the season, is history. As the early season momentum started to fade, the club were still in a reasonable position to fight a relegation battle at Christmas. However, our would be Messiah had other plans and jumped ship to take over the vacant managerial post at near neighbours Bolton Wanderers. Taking with him the entire backroom staff and also hijacking the transfer deals set up for the January window, he effectively crippled our effort and broke the hearts of the club and supporters. An action that will never be forgiven on the 'mean streets' of Burnley.

Suffice it to say that despite a half season of limited success at Bolton, managing to preserve their Premier League status, he quickly suffered the fate of all villains. Relegations with Bolton Wanderers, followed by a short stay at Wigan Athletic and the attendant dismissals soon destroyed Coyle's reputation as a young manager going places. Or did it, he certainly went somewhere but it wasn't to a top side in the English Leagues, no he was banished to the soccer wilderness of the USA with Houston Dynamo! Again a short reign and the termination of contract by 'mutual consent', finds Owen back on the jobless ladder. Until... yes, irony of ironies, the arch villain pitches up with the arch enemy! Truly a marriage made in heaven.

I would like to say that I wish him well in his new job, but I don't so I won't. Suffice it to say that I hope both parties get what they deserve.

On the transfer news front as is always the case, precious little was actually happening. That didn't stop the rumour mill getting into full swing however. On 6th June

ClaretTony led with an article on the Up The Clarets website entitled 'Clarets looking for more internationals'. This was basically a review of some of the recent transfer speculation particularly with regard to interest in recently linked players with full International status.

One prominent rumour surrounded local Burnley lad Oliver Norwood, currently playing his international football with Northern Ireland and League action with Reading in the Championship. A centre midfielder in his mid-20's he was the type of player who might fit the bill. Recent pronouncements from the player had not ruled out his desire to at some point play for his home town club.

Another rumour surrounded Henri Bedimo, a Cameroon international left back, currently employed by Lyon in France. It's possible as left back may well prove to be an area we are looking to cover.

Two more names were added to the list in Tamas Kadar, and Paulus Arajuuri both currently featuring for Polish side Lech Poznan. Kadar is another left back like Bedimo and an established Hungarian international, whilst Arajuuri is billed as a 27-year-old centre back playing for Finland.

These players join a growing list of would be's, maybe's and won't be's, now including:

Nick Pope - Goalkeeper - Charlton Athletic
Daniel Bentley - Goalkeeper - Southend United
Henri Lansbury - Centre Mid - Nottingham Forest
Graham Dorrans - Centre Mid - Norwich City
Ashley Westwood - Centre Mid - Aston Villa
Gary Gardner - Centre Mid - Aston Villa
Jeff Hendrick - Centre Mid - Derby County
Jordon Mutch - Centre Mid - Crystal Palace

Tuesday 7th June seems to confirm some truth in the Nick Pope rumour with the South London Press reporting Charlton rejecting an offer from Burnley. The report however believes a further offer will be forthcoming.

The same day also sees a paragraph in the Daily Express saying that Sean Dyche has been given a £60m transfer budget! Hells teeth! Why are we bothering with these lads, we should be getting in for Ibrahimovich, and Messi, or Vardy at least.

The Burnley Express of Friday 10th June runs with a Sports page story that Burnley have indeed had an offer for Nick Pope rejected. They also suggest an offer of €1.5m (£1.2m) has been made for Tamas Kadar who is currently in France representing Hungary at Euro 2016. We should hopefully therefore be able to get a preview of what we might be getting.

Speaking of Euro 2016, for a little light relief I have joined a league in the BBC Predictor League created by my daughter Stephanie's partner, Tom. Now Tom is a North Easterner by birth, son of a Sunderland supporting Father. However, he has been brought up in the soccer wastelands of Cumbria and has therefore struggled to discover his true football allegiance. After a dalliance with Liverpool (why?) I am attempting to subtly convert him to Claret-ism by taking every opportunity to bombard him with tales of our glorious past and glittering future. At the moment I am unsure whether it is working, I have even heard him mention that he may adopt Carlisle as his club! The impetuosity of youth! I sometimes worry for my daughter. As they are currently living in Darlington, I can't see this as a realistic prospect.

Anyway, tonight (10th June) sees the start of the tournament with hosts France v Romania. I have gone, under my pseudonym of 'Claret Avenger', for a 3-0 victory for the Gauls and am confidently expecting plenty of Predictor League points. Taking a sneaky peek at the League I see I am not alone, and am joined by 'Claretforever', so it looks like a one-two finish for the Burnley Boys. Daughter Stephanie also features as 'Miss Chatterbox' how appropriate! Wonder what odds I can get on her finishing bottom of the table?

Tuesday June 14th a walk planned from Clowbridge to be led by yours truly, gives the opportunity for the hand-over of the previously mentioned annual Dotcom wager. Yes, this time the North Enders must make the humiliating trip to Turf Moor to hand over the 'dosh'. Not having the luxury of a statue like the Sir Tom Finney one at Deepdale, I opt for photos in front of the next best thing. The 'filthy lucre' will be handed over under the watchful gaze of Clarets legend, Jimmy McIlroy's portrait on the stand bearing his own name. Touché, North Enders.

Well at least that was the plan, but like all the best plans it was scuppered, this time by building contractors. Turf Moor this mid-June was a hive of activity with work going on to higher the floodlights, and major building work on the new offices and store on Brunshaw Rd. Poor old Jimmy Mac's portraits were almost totally obscured by contractor's vehicles. However, on meeting up with the Preston Mafia we fortuitously spotted a small gap in the defences near the electronic scoreboard. We were through it in no time, like Andre Gray through the opposition, and almost onto the hallowed Turf. Not wanting to spoil the lush new grass we opted for some quick snaps just outside the playing area. Sean the Gnome (my lucky charm) made his Turf Moor debut whilst his North End counterpart Nobby, looking rather sheepish and overawed, also got to grace the scene.

Jim (Skipper of the Yard), duly handed over the cash with as much good grace as he could muster, and Pendleside Hospice became the beneficiaries. Mischievous suggestions by Bob Clare, Dotcom walks group leader, that the wager would be doubled year on year were quickly rebuffed by both parties. As was his suggestion that I would be treating all the walkers following our Clowbridge ramble to Champagne in the New Waggoners!

Wednesday 15th June was publication day of the Premier League fixtures for the upcoming season. Always eagerly awaited I was glad to see that we would kick off our third assault on the league with a home fixture. Swansea City at the Turf would be the first fixture followed by two tough away trips to Liverpool and Chelsea. Home games on Boxing Day and New Year's Eve were another plus against Middlesbrough and Sunderland respectively. All in all, the fixture list seemed to have been as kind as it could have. The only real downer for me was that I would miss the Arsenal home game whilst away on holiday in Madeira.

Following closely on the heels of the new season's fixtures was the announcement on 16th June of a new shirt sponsor, Dafabet. The deal said to be worth multi million pounds would run over the next two seasons and was the biggest in the club's history. It would appear that Dafabet (or daft to bet) were also sponsors of Sunderland and Blackburn Rovers (spit). Let's hope they bring us a bit more success than our illustrious partners.

June 20th and it's still all quiet on the incoming transfer front, but more worryingly are increasing reports of imminent bids for one of our most important players. New Premier League Champions Leicester City are said to be about to table a bid of £10m for central defender Michael Keane. I wouldn't want to see this one happen as the player is a key component of our season's survival plan. With reported interest also from Everton and Stoke, a bidding war may well be about to break out.

Friday June 24th Burnley Express lead on their Sport page with the Michael Keane story but apparently the offer now at £12m has been rejected by the Clarets. The newspaper also runs a story linking us with Stoke midfielder Charlie Adam, late of Blackpool and Liverpool. Two other names entering the speculation are Sheffield Wednesday central defender Tom Lees, and Crystal Palace's Welsh midfielder Joe Ledley. In view of Wales's continued involvement in Euro 2016, this interest if indeed there is any, will inevitably remain on the back burner.

Out of the blue comes a rumour that our very own central defender, and 'Player's player of the Season' Ben Mee is wanted by West Bromwich Albion. All this speculation about players leaving is not what we are wanting to hear right now!

England meanwhile have managed to stumble their way through the Group stage of the Euro 2016 finals finishing Runners-up to the mighty Wales in Group B. Fortunately for them they narrowly avoid an encounter with Ronaldo's Portugal in the last 16 tie and face an on paper easier tie with minnows Iceland. I say on paper, but the Cod Fishers have proved themselves no slouches in this tournament and emerge from the Group phase unbeaten. Rapidly becoming everyone's favourite second team the forthcoming tie on Monday 27th has the makings of a giant banana skin for the currently misfiring England team.

Mention of the Euro 2016 finals prompts me to give an update of my own faltering progress in the BBC Predictor League set up by daughter Stephanie's partner Tom. After the Group phase I am lying joint 6th of 17 in the Goon Boys League. A poor first round of predictions, had me well behind even Miss Chatterbox, but an improved second phase saw me leap into joint second with eyes on the prize. Unfortunately, a poor third round has me slumped to joint 6th, 120 points adrift of runaway leader Eduardo. I suppose it's my own fault really for inviting Eduardo to join the league at the last moment. There have been suggestions made that Eduardo has been involved in some form of 'insider dealing' but I am more inclined to believe he has just been plain lucky. I look forward to the knock out stages of the competition confident in the knowledge that things can only get better.

Friday the 24th June is a monumental day in Britain's history as we learn the result of the referendum on European Union membership has resulted in triumph for the Brexit camp. Yes, those political giants Boris Johnson, Michael Gove and Nigel Farrage have trumped the elected Government and started the process to take Britain out of the EU. We live in dangerous times brothers and sisters.

A whole nation is about to set sail in 'uncharted waters', and soon to be Skipperless as Prime Minister Cameron commits Hari Kari following his failure to carry the vote. There's panic in the boardrooms, meltdown in the financial markets, and murder on the dance floor. Armageddon is nigh! The lunatics have finally taken over the asylum. But, amongst all this there is still no answer to the BIG question! **When are Burnley FC going to announce some signings?**

June 27th is departure date from Manchester Airport for a flight to Rome to join a cruise ship in the Italian Port of Civitavecchia and commence my annual escape to the sun. On the BBC Predictor League I am enjoying a more successful knock out round and lie in second place only 30 points off leader Eduardo.

My prediction for tonight's England walkover against 'minnows' Iceland is 3-0, and I confidently emerge from an excellent dinner expecting a comfortable half time lead. Finding a seat facing a big screen on the ship's Pool Deck, my wife and I wrap ourselves in blankets to watch the second half. Judging by the temperature on deck we could have been in Iceland.

Unbelievably I find we are trailing in the game 2-1, even more unbelievably I am sat behind four Icelanders waving flags! How can that be, I thought the whole population had decamped to France. We exchange pleasantries as they fill me in on first half proceedings with an air of disbelief on their part. What can I say about the second half performance? As usual we have lots of possession but little threat, and embarrassingly exit the tournament to ICELAND! Its handshakes all round for the ecstatic Icelanders from ourselves and all the other English fans on deck, and we troop off to console ourselves in the bar.

Immediately England manager Roy Hodgson announces his resignation. After this tournament and an equally embarrassing show in the last World Cup finals what option did he have? Once again England have promised much and delivered nothing.

JULY

It is July 1st and I am having a midnight 'livener' in one of the ship's bars. I catch sight of none other than our own Sam Vokes on one of the TV screens, coming on as a substitute with Wales surprisingly leading Belgium 2-1. With only about 10 minutes to play the Welsh must have thought they'd use Sam's heading prowess to defend set pieces and aerial play, as the Belgians threw the kitchen sink at them. This was clearly not Big Sam's plan though as he magnificently rose to head home a right wing cross and seal an unlikely 3-1 victory. Our Sam a hero, and the Welsh make the last four!

July 7th - it's my birthday! Yes, I've made it to State Pension age, with still my own teeth, but alas not much hair! What's more as I check the Internet it appears that we have agreed a deal with Charlton Athletic, and personal terms with one of the Icelandic heroes of Euro 2016, Johann Berg Gudmundsson. The deal is not completed yet as the player is taking a well-earned break after featuring in all of Iceland's five Euro games.

July 10th sees the end of Euro 2016 and a disappointing final ends with Portugal beating hosts France 1-0 with an extra time goal. I can't say I was over enthused with the competition apart from the successes of the smaller nations including, Wales, Northern Ireland, Republic of Ireland and Iceland. Too many teams came to stifle the better sides and in the main these so called 'better' sides did not have the craft to break them down. This is often the case in International football and it doesn't make for a very exciting spectacle. Roll on the 'Blood and Guts' action of the Premier League.

The end of the Euro tournament also brought about the end of the BBC Predictor League. I can report a creditable result in the Goon Boys League for myself finishing fifth of seventeen, pleasingly one place above daughter Stephanie, aka Miss Chatterbox. Eduardo took the title, followed by the league creator TDob's father, aka Codger Rovers, so named as he is an old Codger who is always roving about. TDob could only manage a mid-table 9th position, a sobering experience for the lad. Apparently the League will continue as a Premier League competition, another opportunity for me to demonstrate my superior knowledge of domestic football. In the Overall League I managed to come in 19,320th out of a total of 381,115 competitors, a top 5% finish!

We are now getting well into July and there seems to be much anguish still about the lack of any incoming transfer activity. Odd rumours are still circulating but Monday 11th sees website reports of a rejected bid of £3.5m for Republic of Ireland and Derby County midfielder Jeff Hendrick. Looked a decent sort from what I saw of him in the recent Euro Finals. As usual for the fans though it's wait and see.

July 12th is the date for the annual 'bloodfest' that is officially billed as the Dotcom Walkers Annual Bowls Challenge. This is traditionally contested between Burnley and the Rest of the World! Not bad when a small town such as ourselves can take on the best of the rest. Over the years this has developed from an amiable outing of enthusiastic once a year bowlers into, at least on behalf of the Preston Mob, a win at all costs day of semi professionalism and gamesmanship.

In recent years this has manifested itself in the Rest of the World (ROW) always having home advantage, fielding 'ringers' in the team who cannot be far short of Waterloo Cup standard, and supplementing the under strength Burnley team with 'stool pigeons'. This year proved no exception. I was tipped off some weeks ahead of the tournament that many of the opposition were engaged in late night training sessions all around the Preston area. Undaunted we carried on with our own training sessions in the hostelries of Burnley and environs.

One change this year was the ceding of the venue to home soil for the Burnley contingent...Sabden! So it was on the day that a highly depleted Burnley team, ravaged by injuries, sickness and holidays, took to the immaculate green at Sabden Bowling Club. Unfortunately, only six lads and lasses who could claim Burnley residency turned up, while the ROW had a line-up of twenty to select from. To make things a bit more even six transfers were effected from ROW based on the purely arbitrary distinction of geographical proximity to Burnley. All the transferees had one thing in common with their Burnley counterparts, none had picked up a bowl in twelve months, and none new a finger peg from a thumb peg! Almost as bad as one member of the ROW team who brought his own bowls, only to be informed he had brought a pair of indoor flat green bowls with no bias, well done Dave Johnstone.

Needless to say a very enjoyable couple of hours in the Sabden sun ended in a totally predictable win for the visitors, however the organiser spared our humiliation by declaring the contest as East v West (Lancashire presumably), rather than Burnley v ROW, so the honour of our fine town stays intact. Just a final message to the Preston Mob, for God's sake guys, 'It's only a game'!

Back to the serious business and the press are reporting bids of £3.5m for Hendrick (Derby) and £4m Stephens (Brighton) both rejected by their respective clubs. Also on 13th July a final take it or leave it offer, believed to be £900K, for Charlton Keeper Nick Pope is also rejected by the London club. This was followed later the same evening with news of an increased bid of over £5m for Hendrick.

There's no doubt that all the extra money sloshing about from the new TV deal is creating havoc in the transfer market with ridiculous prices being quoted, and paid, by some of the bigger clubs. I can't see us getting involved in that but it does beg the question as to where the much needed new recruits are going to come from. Still no concrete signings before the Clarets play the first friendly game at the end of their training camp in France, and only the Icelander, still on holiday, as a likely signing. The fans website messageboards are degenerating into vitriolic slanging matches as the posters take out their transfer frustrations on each other. Time for everybody to calm down a little I feel, and have a bit of confidence in the custodians of the club to do the right thing.

Friday 15th July gets the 'friendly' season rolling with a game against Swiss opposition, FC Stade Nyonnaise in Nyon. With Sam Vokes, Stephen Ward, and Tom Heaton still not back with the squad following their participation in Euro 2016, it's very much as you were with the squad plus a few additions from the junior ranks. It's the usual first pre-season type game; a gentle run out against lower ranked opposition, and a chance to involve as many players as possible with ten changes of personnel at half time. Just a case of getting a feel of the ball again and stretching legs without risking injuries. Not surprisingly the Clarets run out 3-1 winners with all the goals coming in the first half. Burnley goals coming from

Andre Gray (20 minutes), Ashley Barnes (25), and Michael Keane (45). Young goalkeeper Conor Mitchell got nearly 30 minutes on the pitch coming on for the vastly experienced Paul Robinson just after the hour mark. Training camp over the Clarets headed back to the UK ahead of the next friendly at the Globe Arena, Morecambe on the coming Tuesday evening.

One piece of good news in all the gathering gloom was the announcement that Ben Mee had signed a new three year deal with the club. The extremely popular defender, last season's supporters clubs 'Player of the Year' who had been rumoured to be attracting attention from West Bromwich Albion, was overjoyed with the deal.

"It's brilliant and I am delighted to extend my stay here at Burnley. After such a great season last year, and getting married in the summer, things just keep getting better and hopefully it will improve even more.

"I feel comfortable and at home here and we've been chatting for a while. Obviously it's been a busy summer, so it was something we put on a back burner, but it was always going to get done.

"This club is going somewhere the minute. It's been ever-changing throughout my time here and you can see the things going on at the training ground and the way the team is going. It's exciting and we are definitely moving forwards. Now I just want to help keep the team in the Premier League. That's my short term goal and I want to be a big part of it.

"There's a togetherness and a will to do well and I am sure that will stand in us good stead."

Well said, Ben!

And would you believe it Ben's inspirational oratory clearly had an effect as our proposed goalkeeper target, for whom only a couple of days earlier it was reported the deal had fallen through, was on the 16th July, said to be about to sign. Welcome aboard Nick Pope our second 'almost' signing from Charlton Athletic.

On Tuesday 19th July we all breathe a huge sigh of relief as the signings of Gudmundsson and Pope are finally confirmed. Welcome to Turf Moor! Let's hope there's a few more to follow.

Tuesday also marks the day of a slight deviation from the usual Dotcom Walkers ramble. Today, to mark the bi-centenary of the completion of the Leeds-Liverpool canal, we are taking a barge trip through the 'mile-long' Foulridge tunnel. It's not actually a mile but as near as damn it weighing in at 1640 metres, a major engineering achievement in the history of the 127 mile long canal.

The plan for the day was to leave Foulridge Wharf at 11.00 a.m. and transit the tunnel towards Barrowford Locks. After a brief stop there the barge would retrace its steps to Foulridge where lunch would be taken followed by a short four mile walk. On the hottest day of the year with temperatures hitting 30^{0}C, unheard of in East Lancashire, this seemed a perfectly reasonable proposition.

All went well with the barge trip and as planned we arrived back at Foulridge wharf for 13.00 hours. I say all went well, there was some controversy caused by seating arrangements! The seats were arranged as four per table, two facing forward and two backwards. Not a problem as the unfortunate twosome going backwards would have the viewing advantage when the boat turned round at

Barrowford. As you can imagine there's not a lot to see in a mile-long tunnel except the ends! However, this did cause some consternation as long term adversary Jim (Skipper of the Yard) complained that the view had been brighter on the outward journey than it was on the return! This was met by much derision from my travelling companions, but it never ceases to amaze me how such a trivial thing can cause friction!

At the same time Bob Clare brought up the subject of the annual wager between Jim and myself which hinges around whether Burnley and PNE will start the next season in the same league. The score so far stands at 1-1, but with Jim the loser on the last occasion he declared he was unwilling to continue the bet for a third year. His rather tame excuse was that he didn't think Preston would be promoted and he didn't want to see Burnley relegated, at the same time claiming that money was not the issue. A quick recce of other North Enders present drew a similar blank of takers. The only option now is to put the proposal to the unfortunately named Chris McCann, currently holidaying in Turkey and hopefully dodging the bullets from the attempted coup. Will nobody uphold the honour of Proud Preston?

Most walkers opted to picnic lunch whilst a few of the more affluent members decided to take lunch at Café Cargo. Group leader Bob Clare signalled the intention to start the walk at 13.30 and we paupers sat by the canal to enjoy our meagre rations in the sun, and very pleasant it was too.

By 13.30 still no sign of the 'prawn sandwich brigade' due to heavy demand slowing the café service. Unperturbed we continued to swelter in the sun until about 13.50 the stragglers emerged from the air-conditioned luxury and approximately 30 walkers got under way. Foolishly I had it in mind that the walk would involve a gentle stroll along the canal then a loop bringing us back via Foulridge Reservoir, all at relatively low level. No such thing! With 'Sherpa' Ed Walton taking the lead we were headed for a much more serious challenge involving the ascent of Noyna Hill. With the extremely high temperatures and the fact that many of the group were already 'par-boiled' it became clear that the group was about to fragment. The wisest - including the Dotcom's youngest 'walker' Nieve, who at seven month's old the youngest by some considerable distance - headed for home. After a little more uphill climbing and with water supplies running low, the group split again some taking the 'low road', whilst other continued on the 'high route' of the original plan.

Suffice it to say that this proved a bridge too far for heat exhausted Andy L, and the day was saved by the noble Don Beal and Gwen Walton setting off to run a good distance back to pick up a car and effect a rescue. Fortunately, no harm done and everybody made it back wiser but sweatier. For the Burnley Contingent and one or two of our Preston friends a much needed rehydration stop at the excellent Hare & Hounds Foulridge, soon restored normal service. A great day out but a sobering lesson of the effects of walking in high temperatures.

The same evening saw the Clarets take on Morecambe at the Globe Arena in the second pre-season friendly. Once again a game of many personnel changes ended 1-1, an Andre Gray equaliser cancelling out Morecambe's early second half lead.

More good news on the contract front as on 20th July our captain and England goalkeeper Tom Heaton signed a new four year contract with the club until 2020.

By the evening of the same day news was coming through of the possible signing, on a season long loan, of Liverpool full back Jon Flanagan. The very promising 23 year old defender currently coming back from a serious knee injury, was left out of the Reds team playing a friendly at Huddersfield to 'mull over' the possible move.

The uncharacteristic hot spell of Burnley weather continued throughout the week and into Saturday allowing a long afternoon in the garden for weeding and tidying. A short drinks break gave me the opportunity to check progress on the state of play in the third pre-season friendly at Bradford City. How pleasing to note that on 18 minutes we are 1-0 ahead, courtesy of Andre Gray. Then the Clarets go goal crazy as two more are added within six minutes, the goals coming from Andre Gray again and Ben Mee.

Shortly before half time Ashley Barnes feels a hamstring and is replaced immediately by Lukas Jutkiewicz who himself then suffers a tight hamstring and fails to reappear for the second half. On the stroke of half time the Bantams pull a goal back but it's a comfortable half time lead. The second half gives a Burnley debut to new keeper Nick Pope and he starts his Clarets career with a 'clean sheet'. A late goal from Michael Kightly rounds off an encouraging warm up display, and it's on to Bolton Tuesday night for game four. Prolific striker Andre Gray is certainly starting the season where he left off with four goals in the opening three friendlies, however much sterner opposition lies ahead.

Still no positive news on our much awaited transfer targets, except that Derby are now believed to have rejected a Clarets bid in the region of £7m for Jeff Hendrick. It's very quiet on the other strongly rumoured midfield target,

Brighton's Dale Stephens, and again we are left hoping for further developments in the coming week. Tensions on the 'Up the Clarets' fans website messageboard are rising daily and keyboard violence is threatening to erupt if something doesn't happen soon!

Ahead of the fourth friendly at Bolton it's time for the last outing of the Summer term for the Dotcomers. Today it's another diversion from the norm as we take one of our annual trips to TOP (That Other Place) as we like to refer to Yorkshire. Today we will assemble in Settle before getting the bus to Hellifield, and an opportunity to use our bus passes! The plan is then to walk back to Settle following a stretch of the Ribble Way. Group Leader Bob Clare remarks that we are truly showing signs of old age as in the past three weeks we have played bowls, had a canal barge trip, and now used our bus passes. Aah the joys of retirement! Another splendid stroll in the countryside clocking in at nine miles, and with an end of term pint of Hawkshead Bitter at the Royal Oak Settle, we put the walking term nicely to bed.

I took the opportunity to sound out Mr McCann of the Preston mafia as to whether he would be taking up the annual wager on behalf of the Prestonians, but once again he declined. Will nobody step forward from the opposition?

The fourth friendly at Bolton saw one or two surprises in the starting line-up with youngsters Aiden O'Neill and Daniel Agyei included from the start. A first half penalty won and finished by Andre Gray saw the Clarets lead at half time. However, this was short lived in the second half as our hosts upped their game and levelled on 48 minutes. A number of personnel changes then ensued before one of our substitutes, young winger Josh Ginnelly, won the game in the dying minutes - Josh's reward for his winner being a half season loan deal at League One Walsall.

By Friday 29th July still no further signings! New names thrown into the ring are left back Charlie Taylor at Leeds and Moroccan international Hakim Ziyech currently at FC Twente in Holland. We are rumoured to be about to bid £6m for Taylor who would appear to be acceptable to most of our internet messageboard fans. Ziyech is apparently very highly rated and rumoured to be interesting Roma, no contest there then if we are serious about him. Why would he want the delights of sun kissed Rome, when we can offer the sights of the Leeds-Liverpool canal and the Stoneyholme Gasometer.

On the penultimate day in July, the Clarets round off their sequence of away friendly fixtures with a thoroughly convincing 3-1 victory over Glasgow Rangers at Ibrox Park. Once again Andre Gray goes goal crazy netting all three as we take a 3-0 lead. A Ben Mee own goal completes the scoring, in for what by all accounts is a quite impressive Burnley display.

Last season's inspirational figure Joey Barton, seems a forlorn shadow of his former self as he tries to lift his new colleagues. Oh well Joey, it might not be Burnley but I'm sure the money will make up for it.

AUGUST

By Friday 5th August the frustrations of many fans regarding the seemingly unsuccessful dealings in the transfer market are threatening to mar what should be a glorious return to the Premier League.

Understandably most fans expected, with the windfall of the extra TV cash, a number of quality recruits to be in place with the squad by now. However, for whatever reason they have still not materialised. We seem to be constantly having bids rejected. Are we pitching the bids too low? Do the selling clubs not want to sell? Are the players wage demands too high?

Unfortunately, none of us know the answers, and in the absence of any comment from the club's recruitment team, we can only speculate. Sean Dyche seems to be trying to put some pressure on the Board of Directors to 'loosen the purse strings', but he is also well aware of the dangers to the club's long term stability that could ensue. Many of the fans who regularly post on the website messageboards seem to be laying the blame, rightly or wrongly, at the door of Chairman Mike Garlick. To be honest I wouldn't want to be in his shoes at the moment.

For my own part I am prepared to remain calm and make judgement at the end of the transfer window, which still has almost a month to run. It's doubtful anyway that many, if any of the potential newcomers would be automatic starters for the team in the opening fixture, now just over a week away. One of Sean's obvious strong points is his loyalty to the guy who 'has the shirt', and I'm sure he would want to reward the players who got us here by giving them first chance.

So for now it's a case of daily monitoring the Internet for any snippets of news regarding transfers we can find, and marvelling at some of the suggested names. The long drawn out saga of whether Jon Flanagan is joining on a year-long loan from Liverpool still rumbles on. It is now over two weeks since it was 'leaked' that the player was making his mind up over the deal. All I can say is Jon must be a very indecisive fellow, how long must it take him to get dressed?

More exotic names recently linked include Belgian International Steven Defour, and Norwich City's Republic of Ireland International, Robbie Brady. Ah well, we can but dream!

Anyway, enough of all that and on with the serious business of tonight's home friendly with Spanish side Real Sociedad. I'm looking forward to an early evening kick off on a warm and pleasant day. The big decision is whether to issue my fellow Claret buddies with their newly acquired lucky charms purchased on my summer travels through Europe. Should we try them out tonight in a meaningless friendly or hold them back for the 'big one' next Saturday? Decisions, Decisions! I am beginning to know how Jon Flanagan feels.

As I arrive at the Turf in good time I learn that Mr Flanagan has indeed made his decision and signed on the dotted line. He is also alleged to have said that Burnley are a massive club with passionate fans. Steady on Jon lad, wait till you fall foul of the website warriors! Anyway, welcome aboard Jon, with his pedigree he should be a valuable addition for the battles ahead.

Same as Jon, I also make a monumental decision and decide to save the 'lucky charms' till next week when all their power will be needed in the Premier League opener.

Back at the Turf and we welcome our visitors from sunny Spain with typical Lancashire hospitality, a heavy rain shower! That'll have them racing for their poncho's and sombreros.

To be fair to our visitors, after a promising start by the Clarets, they then decide to give us a bit of a footballing lesson in the arts of ball retention and movement off it. The Senors take a first half lead courtesy of a headed goal from a well flighted free kick. Around this time a 'red mist' descends on Dean Marney and after two or three risqué challenges, he is fortunate that the leniency of the referee saves him from the early bath. Did nobody tell Deano it was a friendly.

The second half mirrors the first with the Spaniards in control but contriving to miss a couple of gifted 'sitters'. Then with time running out, we snatch a draw from the jaws of defeat with yet another fine Andre Gray goal. In the end a lucky draw in a game where we were very much second best, but we'll take that. An impressive nine goals in six friendlies for Andre, how important are his goals going to be this coming season. I head for home slightly chastened by the performance against quality opposition and apprehensive of the Premier League battles around the corner.

In the aftermath of the game I begin to ponder if Sean Dyche is beginning to weary of the challenge. Unlike last time's promotion so far we seem to be missing his rousing inspirational speeches. This time we seem to be getting more lectures on the harsh realities of life for a club with the smallest budget in the Premier League. Come on Sean now is the time to lift the lads, let's get some of the old defiance back.

Well there's a week to go before the start of the season and as usual the soccer pundits are emerging from their shells, with in our case the usual prophesies of doom. The Mail on Sunday reckon the Bookies have us as 'relegation fodder', whilst their stargazer agrees. He suggests, *"Turf Moor is proving to be a tough sell. Liverpool's Jon Flanagan will add bite but Joey Barton has left and Sean Dyche is desperately seeking a new midfielder but a thrifty outlook on transfer fees and wages is proving a hindrance.* He backs that up with:

"Doesn't look like lessons of two years ago have been applied this time"

Meanwhile our old pal Paul Merson in a Sky article predicts his Premier League table, and unsurprisingly he has us bottom. He goes on to say that he likes us! But you sure have a funny way of showing it Paul!

It would appear that we are already wasting our and everybody else's time by even bothering to show up. One of the more ridiculous comments I have seen was that should we in fact be relegated and then subsequently promoted, Sky/The Premier League would not let us back in because we don't spend enough money. Hmmmm!

A bit of Sean Dyche's bulldog spirit re-emerges in an article in the Daily Mail of Wednesday 10th August as he makes a stand for English managers. He wonders why foreign coaches are heralded as 'geniuses' whilst employing exactly the same methods as ourselves and indeed other teams managed by English bosses. In the feature he says:

"They questioned me for playing 4-4-2,' Dyche said of his last Premier League campaign, *'and then everyone played it last year and it was, "Amazing Claudio Ranieri, tactical genius".*

'Jurgen Klopp came in and played sort of a 4-4-2 and let's run really hard and press, people thought it was incredible..." Wasn't Sean Dyche doing that years ago when we got here? Oh well".

'Antonio Conte came in at Chelsea and he got commended for bringing a hard, fast, new leadership to Chelsea, which involved 800 metre runs, 400 metre runs and 200 metre runs.

'Come to my training and see Sean Dyche doing that and you'd say, "A young English dinosaur manager, hasn't got a clue".

So is it perception or is it fact? I have no problem with it. It's the reality I see.'

The pre-season noise about dieting has also tickled Dyche, keen to stress he was not denouncing the ability of individuals.

'I saw (Gael) Clichy talking about the diet that Pep Guardiola has brought in. He's stopped pizza. Last year Ranieri was adding pizza. Two geniuses, one adding pizza, one taking it away.

'I'm being flippant but serious as well. It's true, that is the misconception.

'Clichy was talking about this amazing new diet. We've been doing that since I got here. I did it at Watford, so are other English managers. But because I'm Sean Dyche you wouldn't be interested.'

About to face two foreign managers in the first two games Sean continued:

"There's no problem with me and foreign managers, but this is my view on it. A job comes up and (fans are asked) who do you want, a foreign name is mentioned, and they go, "Oh yeah I've heard he's a great tactician".

'We watch it sat on the bus wetting ourselves laughing. The fan has never heard of him. I have total respect to the man stood next to me but I don't think about schmoozing.'

Wednesday 10th August sees the completion (well almost) of the First English Football League Cup (EFL Cup) as it is now rebranded. With our elevated league status we are exempt from the opening round but come in instead at Round 2. We also enjoy the privilege of being top seeds ensuring we get a draw against lower league opposition in this round.

What a delight then to learn that we had been paired with our nearest local rivals Accrington Stanley, although it seems odd to describe them as such. I think it's fair to say that most Burnley fans wish nothing but the best for little Accy, well on all occasions bar this upcoming one that is. None of the dislike and bitterness which is reserved for the enemy a matter of a few miles further down the road! The tie is scheduled for the tiny Crown Ground, Accrington and I look forward to making my first visit there, providing I am able to get a ticket!

It's now Friday 12th August and the eve of our third assault on the Premier League. I have to confess that at the moment I am feeling strangely underwhelmed at the prospect. Whether it is the disappointment so far of failing to land any of our major transfer targets, or a sort of inner dread of what is to come, I'm not sure. I must snap out of it, tomorrow sees the start of another season in the top flight which last season's magnificent endeavours have earned us. Not a time for negativity now and I'm sure that's the message that Sean Dyche is driving home at this time.

Once again the enormity of our survival task hits home as all the pundits start wading into us as they warm up for the big kick-off. Sky's Big Five, Jamie Redknapp, Matt Le Tissier, Paul Merson, Charlie Nicholas and Phil Thompson all tip Hull and ourselves for the drop.

We fare slightly better with the Daily Mail's motley crew, six out of the eight tipping us as 'goners'. Full marks here to Ian Ladyman, and Dominic King who are 'Keeping the Faith'.

Over on the BBC Sport website Phil McNulty writes his article, **'Premier League 2016/17: Who will finish where?'** Not surprisingly I have to scroll downwards, seemingly into the bowels of the earth, to discover how he rates us. Once again unsurprisingly he has us at number 19, one off the bottom who he graciously donates to Hull City. But I have to admit I rather like Phil and I think he rather likes us as he says:

"Burnley is another exemplary club that is a pleasure to welcome back to the Premier League under the management of Sean Dyche.

This will not be the only place where their hopes of survival are written off and it is a prediction made in the hope that it will be proved spectacularly wrong.

The Claret's difficulty is competing in an increasingly fierce transfer market but they have struck a significant blow by rebuffing the interest of champions Leicester City in defender Michael Keane.

It will be a long hard season but perhaps, helped by the atmospheric surroundings of Turf Moor and the excellence of Dyche, Burnley can make this forecast go astray."

That's more like it Phil, sounds like a man who understands our predicament and wishes us well against all the odds.

Anyway at the end of the day, who cares what the pundits say? None of them predicted Leicester would be champions! Shows what they know.

By early evening of Friday 12th there is still no news on incoming transfers but there is of two going out.

Firstly 'fringe' player, striker Chris Long is off on a season long loan to League 1 Fleetwood. It has to be said that after signing last summer from Everton Chris has not really featured much and the move is without doubt in the best interests of both parties.

Also going out on loan is Development squad member George Green who leaves for Scottish Premier League club Kilmarnock. Hopefully both players will be able to continue their development by getting some regular competitive football and come back all the stronger for it.

Then, just as I'm resigning myself to another day of false transfer hopes comes news that Anderlecht midfielder Steven Defour who has been tracked for some days is rumoured to be on the brink of joining us in a four year deal. The much capped Belgian international is very much being touted as a 'stellar' signing and certainly one to get the pulse racing. Rumour has is that he is due at Burnley for a medical on Monday. The expectation levels that the deal will go through are certainmly rising as his club Anderlecht are announcing it as a done deal.

It had appeared that we had missed out on this target and that he was about to sign for Abu Dhabi club Al Jazira for a much better salary package. However, there is obviously a spanner in the works there and we look set to land our man. He is very much seen as Barton's replacement, playing as a combative central midfielder. He certainly won't be coming cheap but he has an excellent pedigree and hopefully will add some extra class in our engine room. The fee is being suggested as £7.25m

Now though it's Saturday 13th August and time for all the talking and conjecture to be put aside as we once again embark on 'the great adventure'

Game 1 - Saturday 13th August, 15.00 - Burnley v Swansea City

After my usual Saturday morning's hour of torture in the St Peter's Centre Gym it's time for a quick bite of lunch then off to the Talbot Hotel for pre-match drinks. Firstly, though some big decisions to be made regarding my 'match kit' and 'lucky charms'. My pals and I have been steadily acquiring lucky charms on our holidays around the globe and it's now becoming a full time job to lug the whole bloody kit and kaboodle around with us.

It's a brave man however who dares to challenge the Gods of Fate by leaving any charms behind though. So today I go with 'Worry Beads' from Samos, and wrist bands from Turf Moor, France, Zanzibar and my latest untried acquisition from Bodrum, Turkey. However, as the day is quite warm I decide to dispense with my Claret's scarf which is unbeaten at Turf Moor since acquired as a 2015 Christmas present. Hopefully my 'lucky' Clarets polo shirt should be able to carry the day.

After a couple of excellent pints of Moorhouse's Premiership Bitter to get us in the mood (funnily it tastes just the same as last year's Championship Bitter) we head for the Turf. Now this is where it all starts to unravel!

This year I have had the good fortune (?) of becoming a senior citizen, yes an OAP! With this badge of honour come some nice little perks, free prescriptions, free bus passes, and last but not least concessionary season ticket prices at Turf Moor. Back in the discount period I renewed as always my membership and was informed I was indeed entitled to the generous new rate. I was informed at the time that as I was changing price category I would be sent a new membership card nearer the start of the new season.

Suffice it to say that within two weeks of the opener no card had appeared. No big problem I was visiting the ticket office to pick up tickets for the Real Sociedad friendly and would sort it then. All went well with the friendly transaction and then I pointed out to a pleasant young man and lady who were attending to me my predicament with the season ticket.

No problem Sir! We can sort that for you now. Well five minutes into the sorting much head scratching and looks of bewilderment were passing between my two new young friends. No problem, a call went out to a senior member of the team for assistance. That's another thing about age, if you want something 'sorting' always go for experience. Five minutes later and I had my brand spanking new membership card.

Slightly perturbed by the confusion that I had just witnessed my parting shot was to ask my now not so 'new' friends if all would be well at the turnstiles on the big day. I believe my actual words were "I don't want any cock-ups." No Sir, everything is fine.

On approaching 'lucky turnstile 39' James Hargreaves Upper with seconds to go before kick-off I was slightly apprehensive, and as it turns out, quite rightly so! Refused admission, TICKET NOT VALID! What to do now? A baying alcohol fuelled crowd surging behind me wanting to get in and not miss any goals. Me too!

Nothing for it but to leg it to the Ticket Office on the far side of the ground, and me a Pensioner! Would you credit it, I get there and there's a queue! Minutes passing, roars from the crowd, and me stuck in a bloody queue. Eventually I am attended to and issued a paper ticket for the game and assured that all will be well next week for the Liverpool game. OH YES I've heard that one before! I won't be getting caught like that again, I'll be down that ticket office well before Saturday having my membership card thoroughly checked out.

Anyway, now some eight minutes into the game and I am legging it back in the direction of my seat. Next big error, in my haste to get in I enter by what I now know to be 'unlucky turnstile 35' instead of Championship winning turnstile 39. I won't be doing that again!

A quick glance at the team shows no new faces in the starting eleven and thankfully no goals scored. A fairly even first half with no real clear cut chances at either end sees the blank score line through to half time. It's pretty much as I expected more possession for the visitors and plenty of chasing for the Clarets. Our problem seems to be that we have to fight hard to win the ball then often give it away cheaply. I think this stems from the fact that we break too slowly, with too much sideways and backward passing, the opposition gets back into position, then we are forced to 'lump it' long.

The second half continues much along the same lines but as the game wears on we are gaining the ascendancy. Swansea make and miss some good chances, we have a valid penalty claim rejected with a blatant shirt pull on Michael Keane who should have had a point blank header. Fabianski in the visitor's goal, often a thorn in our side, makes a good save from a Sam Vokes effort turning his shot round the post. Then that fateful moment that we all dread.

On 82 minutes, Swansea substitute Jefferson Montero skips past Matt Lowton down the left, his cross is met by centre forward Fernando Llorente who heads goalwards. Tom Heaton diving at full stretch gets his hands to it but can only palm it out to the incoming Leroy Fer who nets from close range. Cue the bombardment of the Swansea goal as they drop deep to protect their lead with time running out. One last chance as Gudmundsson's free kick comes back off the wall to Marney whose wicked bouncing shot is miraculously turned away by Fabianski.

Then that's it, once again our opening fixture in the Premier League ends in defeat. First time out it was a loss at Stoke, second time at home to Chelsea, and now this. One positive though, both the others were two goal defeats, at least we are down to one.

I'm not too disappointed but it would have been nice to get some points on the board against one of the lesser fancied teams. The key I think is strength in depth. Swansea had a very experienced bench and as players tired were able to replace with substitutes of at least equal quality. We are not at that point yet but hopefully the next couple of weeks will see some serious strengthening of the squad.

Match of The Day (MOTD) showed a pretty fair reflection of the highlights. Both pundits, Alan Shearer and Ian Wright agreed that we had been denied a clear penalty for the shirt pull. 'Wrighty' also thought the Swans had a bit more quality and I can't argue with that. Gary Lineker thinks we need to spend a bit more money, and likewise I can't argue with that either.

But I still think the real problem was caused by leaving my unbeaten scarf at home, and bloody turnstile 35!

Result - Burnley 0 – 1 Swansea City (Fer 82)

Burnley Team

Heaton, Lowton, Keane, Mee, Ward, Boyd, Marney, Jones (Jutkiewicz 87), Arfield (Gudmundsson 75), Gray, Vokes

Subs Not Used - Robinson, Darikwa, Tarkowski, Ulvestad, Kightly

Swansea City Team

Fabianski, Naughton, Fernandez, Amat, Kingsley, Fer, Britton (Sigurdsson 60), Cork, Barrow (Montero 64), Llorente, Routledge (Rangel 87)

Subs Not Used – Nordfeldt, Van der Hoorn, Dyer, Fulton

Attendance – 19,126

Season To Date – Played 1, Won 0, Drawn 0, Lost 1, Goals For 0, Goals Against 1, Points 0

League Position after Game 1 – 19th

A lovely day out in Harrogate to meet up with daughter Stephanie and partner Tom, topped off with an excellent Fish and Chip Tea at Gravelly's (I understand one of the owners is a Claret) has my spirits revived by Sunday evening. Although Liverpool's 4-3 away victory at Arsenal has me somewhat concerned about the next fixture…

On Monday 15th the signing of Steven Defour is all but confirmed and a huge sigh of relief can be released. However, interestingly rumours are filtering through of further outgoings. Kevin Long is believed to be on the verge of a move to Bristol City, but even more surprisingly first choice midfielder David Jones is being linked with Sheffield Wednesday. The Jones rumour certainly comes as a shock and it is suggested that Wednesday have triggered a buy-out clause in his contract.

By Tuesday it's more than a rumour and Jonah is on his way to the Owls, for a fee being suggested as £1.5m. That's a bit of a shock, he's a player who has been very capable for us and never let us down. Best of luck with the move David. This must surely mean more centre midfielders on the way as even with the signing of Defour we are now down to three recognised players for the two positions.

Now did I mention my little difficulty with my membership card (season ticket in old money)? Yes, I believe I did. Well by Thursday 18th August I fear there may be something of a saga developing with it. Determined not to be caught out at the turnstiles this time, I took the opportunity whilst in town, of calling at the Ticket Office to re-acquaint them with my problems.

What luck who should greet me but one of my new young friends from my previous encounter. I launched straight into a report of my turnstile problems, and was re-assured to learn that it had happened to quite 'a lot'! Handing over my card (big mistake) my new friend then disappeared shortly to re-appear with the news that the card showed as active in the office, but unfortunately not at the turnstile! I would have settled for it the other way round.

My new young friend, who by the way has a lovely smile, then decided she would KEEP my card and I would be informed by phone what would happen. It's now Thursday evening, the game is Saturday afternoon, I have no phone message and crucially no membership card. What will tomorrow bring? Watch this space.

By Thursday the anticipated deluge of new signings following the capture of a Belgian had still failed to materialise. However, we had managed another outgoing loan transfer as highly promising Development striker Danny Agyei joins Coventry City until January. Oh well we are certainly leaving a few empty clothes pegs in the changing rooms for the much awaited newcomers.

Readers of my previous tome, 'With Heads Held High' will be aware that the Burnley contingent walking group have had in the past, problems with horses. The famous 'farting horse' of Musbury Tor is now a legend in the group. Well Thursday 18th threw up another incident with our equine friends which certainly amused me at least.

Fellow Claret, John W has an inbred mistrust of horses, which he puts down to the size of their teeth! I have tried to re-assure him on many occasions that they are herbivores but to no avail. On a lovely summer's walk from Great Harwood skirting Whalley Nab and returning via Mitton Fold we again encountered two of the magnificent beasts.

Good old John was some distance ahead of me as we crossed the horses' prairie, when suddenly up went the shout, *"Piss off you big bastard!"*. On looking up I could see, two young horses definitely showing a keen interest in John. Now he may not like horses, but these two certainly seemed to like him. As John quickened his pace, so did the horses, and they have four bloody long legs as well as big teeth. *"Piss off you big bastard"* once more was heard, only this time more loudly and with more of a hint of panic as John raced for the stile in the fence.

Luckily for him the horses called off the chase and let our somewhat shaken compatriot regain his composure safe behind the fence. Whether it was his red T-shirt, or they could smell his fear and dislike of them we will never know. But one thing I know is that I will never again cross a field of horses in close proximity to John W. A bigger show of cowardice in the face of the enemy I have not seen since my daughter Stephanie's retreat from the mad cows of Clapham!

By Friday midday I am beginning to have serious concerns regarding my malfunctioning membership card. Then suddenly as I am about to eat lunch, a phone call from a nice chap called Ed in the Ticket office. Ed reassures me that all is now well with my card and I can collect it at my leisure. Oh me of little faith! How could I have doubted it? Still the proof of the pudding will be whether it functions at the turnstiles tomorrow.

A quick scan of the Up the Clarets website again reveals no further progress on incoming transfers but yet another outgoing. This time it's Development squad player Luke Hendrie who is going to join up with fellow Claret George Green at Scottish Premier League club Kilmarnock.

Luke goes on loan till January 2017 and that must make about 10 young players out with other clubs to gain valuable first team experience.

Tomorrow we are back in Premier League action, once again at the Turf due to the switch of the fixture originally scheduled for Anfield. If I was apprehensive about last week then you can probably quadruple my fears about this one. Our visitors seem to have an abundance of attacking talent and come here on the back of a 4-3 victory at Arsenal last time out. If they hit peak form I'm going to be watching most of this one with my eyes closed.

Still we have our 'stellar' signing Steven Defour available to call on and he will surely feature following the departure of Dave Jones to Sheffield Wednesday. Jon Flanagan our on loan player from Liverpool will be unavailable for selection due to the game being against his parent club. At least he managed some action last night in the Third Direct Development League Cup Final (phew, that's a mouthful!). The game held over from last season for want of a suitable date resulting in a 2-1 win for the Clarets over Stoke City. Jon clearly enjoyed the occasion and quipped afterwards that he had won one trophy per game in his Burnley career.

Saturday's here and its time to dust off the 'lucky charms' and remember to give unlucky Turnstile 35 a wide berth.

Game 2 - Saturday 20th August, 15.00 - Burnley v Liverpool

The usual pre-match rituals are observed, lucky charms placed on appropriate wrists and in correct pockets, pints of Moorhouse's Premiership Bitter duly despatched, and more importantly entry via lucky turnstile 39. I must confess some feelings of apprehension approaching the ground as to whether my membership card would work this time, but my fears are groundless as I'm given the nod at the gate.

In my seat just in time for kick off on a wet and windy August day (typical Burnley summers day), I note one change from last week's line up, Steven Defour for the departed Dave Jones. A packed crowd and a lively atmosphere although the 'scousers' seem strangely subdued especially as they are starting strong favourites.

Only two minutes in and what a magnificent start! Andre Gray intercepts a poor ball from Liverpool full back Nathaniel Clyne, and feeds strike partner Sam Vokes. Sam on the edge of the penalty area, back to goal, executes an excellent turn and fires an unstoppable effort past Liverpool keeper Simon Mignolet. The first league goal against Liverpool since Ray Hankin's effort in 1975, and how joyously it is greeted by the delirious Clarets fans.

I am absolutely elated but also chastened by the fact that there are still 88 minutes to play. Following our shock opener the game settles into the predictable pattern of pressure and possession by our visitors, and resolute defending and attempts to counter attack swiftly by our heroes. Liverpool, playing in a 'high viz' lemonish kit, are enjoying a lot of the ball but seem to be at a complete loss of how to penetrate our extremely well organised rearguard. Shots aplenty are raining in on our goal but all from distance and in most cases either wide or high, or indeed both.

The Brazilian playmaker Coutinho is obviously of the belief that he can score from range as he peppers the crowd behind the goal with his efforts. The fans reply with the chant

"You're not Danny Ings", and he certainly is not. In fact our hero of old Danny is nowhere to be seen in the Reds team or on the bench. What a waste!

To me it is incredible that a team like Liverpool with such a wealth of talent to choose from can't field a recognised left back. Instead they opt to play England midfielder James Milner in a totally for him alien position. This plays completely into our hands as it soon becomes apparent that James has no confidence in his left boot. Every foray down the left flank ends with Milner having to check back onto his right foot before crossing, giving Matt Lowton a much easier afternoon than he could have hoped for.

The game rolls on in this predictable fashion until on 37 minutes Stephen Ward breaks up a Liverpool attack, and feeds Steven Defour in his own half. Defour without hesitation sets off straight towards the Reds goal and over the halfway line sees Andre Gray peeling off to his right. An accurate ball into Gray's path has Andre on the edge of the box and cutting in between the central defenders. In a flash Andre shoots left footed and the ball nestles once again in the corner of the visitors net. I can only imagine the shockwaves that scoreline must be causing in millions of homes around the UK and the rest of the football world.

Hard to believe it maybe but it is thoroughly deserved. Our illustrious visitors are visibly shaken. Can we get to half time with a two goal lead? Indeed we can as we play out the rest of the half with no scares.

As I check my phone for score updates I am intrigued to see an email from recent émigré to Australia, walking group buddy Jim Kendra. Jim has found that the game is being shown live on Aussie TV, and decides to tune in. God knows what the time is where he is but Jim is more concerned with the appearance of the crowd emailing:

"I see people with raincoats and no shadows so not sunny"

Jim has only been gone since late July, but already he has lost his memories of English summers.

This email is quickly followed by a second:

"Goal, Wow!!!!!

A quick check on the BBC Sport website report on my phone shows a first half statistic of Burnley 22%, Liverpool 78% possession. I'm slightly surprised at the scale of the disparity but also reassured that for all that control of the ball they have caused us minimal problems.

Into the second half and the game continues along the path of the first half with Liverpool possession and Burnley resolute defending. On 56 minutes new signing Steven Defour comes off, a promising Burnley debut over, and is replaced by another summer signing Johann Berg Gudmundsson. The Icelander takes up a left wing position with Scotty Arfield moving inside to partner Dean Marney. Liverpool ring the changes but the pattern of the game continues and apart from a couple of saves by Tom Heaton from long range efforts we remain comfortable.

As the game draws to a close Andre Gray is substituted earning a standing ovation and is replaced by Development squad youngster Aiden O'Neill making a first ever league appearance. Then within minutes referee Lee Mason blows the full time whistle and we have an unexpected but thoroughly deserved first Premier League victory of the campaign. A magnificent battling performance in which every player was a hero. Andre Gray was named 'Man of the Match' by the sponsors but in reality it could have gone to anyone in Claret and Blue.

A word here about the refereeing of this fixture. I expressed the belief on many occasions previously that particularly when we play the 'bigger' teams in the league that referees invariably favour our opponents. This was once again a classic illustration of this case. Throughout the entire game the referee and his assistants gave us very little, every 50/50 decision went unerringly in favour of the Reds (or in this case Lemons). This is a dangerous trend and on another day could have cost us dearly. One incident, clearly highlighted in TV replays, saw a ball obviously well over the line dragged back by a Liverpool player and play waved on. Can we please have a bit more fairness and impartiality from the officials in the forthcoming fixtures.

Result - Burnley (Vokes 2, Gray 37) 2 - 0 Liverpool

Burnley Team

Heaton, Lowton, Keane, Mee, Ward, Boyd, Marney, Defour (Gudmundsson 56), Arfield, Gray (O'Neill 90+3), Vokes (Jutkiewicz 82)

Subs Not Used - Robinson, Darikwa, Tarkowski, Kightly

Liverpool Team

Mignolet, Clyne, Lovren, Klavan, Milner (Moreno 77), Lallana (Grujic 78), Henderson, Wijnaldum, Sturridge (Origi 65), Coutinho, Firmino

Subs Not Used - Manninger, Can, Matip, Stewart

Attendance - 21.313

Season To Date - Played 2, Won 1, Drawn 0, Lost 1, Goals For 2, Goals Against 1, Points 3

League Position after Game 2 - 8th

Eager to bask in the glory of our wonderful achievement I return to the BBC Sport website. I'm a little deflated to find that our friends at the Beeb have chosen rather to focus on the match statistics rather than the important facts.

The report shows a final figure in favour of Liverpool for possession of 81%/19%, with shots as 26/3, shots on target 5/2, and corners 12/1. What they seem to have overlooked is the fact that it doesn't matter how much possession you have, it's what you do with it that counts.

Sean Dyche said much the same in his post-match interview for Match of the Day:

"I thought we made Liverpool look uncomfortable. "We think we can be a threat to teams.

"We have never been bogged down with all the stats about possession. There is something marvellous when you see someone giving everything to the cause. That's what I thought we did."

Good old Dominic King, who I previously suspected of having a soft spot for the Clarets, goes some way to redressing the balance with his article in the Mail on Sunday. Under the heading, 'ROCK ON, BURNLEY', he goes on to report that before kick-off the Burnley DJ, twice dived into his record collection to play David Bowie's, 'Heroes' at full volume.

He goes on to say;

"Should Burnley go on playing in the indefatigable manner that saw them bring Liverpool crashing back to earth, that is what Sean Dyche's squad will become.

Their third crack at trying to get established in the Premier League is up and running after a thumping afternoon at Turf Moor."

Pointing out that following Liverpool's scintillating performance at Arsenal last week they were expected to go through the gears and get an early foothold in the race for a top four place.

"Andre Gray, rose to the occasion and, inspired by the class of new record signing Steven Defour, never looked like losing once they had grabbed the advantage. Liverpool had the ball, Burnley took the points."

Commenting on the upbeat tone of Dyche's programme notes in an effort to galvanise the fans support, King went on to say;

"His words, clearly, had had some effect as this wonderful old stadium was at its atmospheric best, a tremendous noise greeting the home side as they bounced out of the tunnel, with particular adulation reserved for Defour on his home debut."

He rounded off the piece with;

"Burnley were in full control and come the final whistle there was another explosion of noise and another airing of Heroes. They just have to make sure now it is for more than one day."

On Tuesday there's news of another empty peg in the dressing room as Rouwen Hennings heads back to Germany. Rouwen will be joining Fortuna Dusseldorf of Bundesliga 2 on a season loan. That's not come as too much of a surprise as of late he has fallen down the pecking order, recently not even making the bench. It's thought highly likely that at the end of the loan the move will become permanent. A pity that, a bold move to bring him here never really worked out. With Andre Gray and Sam Vokes both having good Championship seasons his first team opportunities were very limited and he never really made his mark.

On Wednesday we learn of an unwanted diversion that has the potential to derail our plans. The FA have hit Gray with a misconduct charge surrounding homophobic comments on social media. Tweets on his Twitter account from 2012 had re-surfaced immediately after his goal against Liverpool on Saturday. Andre's raised profile has certainly not done him any favours this time. The striker had issued an apology immediately they came too light and stressed he was;

"at a very different point in my life back then."

At worst the charge could result in suspension for crucial top-flight fixtures. He has until 31st August to appeal.

With the loss of Chris Long, Rouwen Hennings and Danny Agyei, all out on loan, and Ashley Barnes currently out injured, the striking department suddenly looks a bit stretched. Surely we are in the market for an additional goal scorer but with the 'window' about to close in less than a week we had better get a move on!

Next up though is our EFL Cup match at near neighbours Accrington Stanley.

EFL Cup Round 2 – Wednesday 24th August, 19.45 – Accrington Stanley v Burnley

With another massive Premier League match coming up on Saturday at Chelsea it's no surprise that Sean Dyche makes major changes for this fixture. Out go the goalkeeper, the back four, the entire midfield, and one striker! The only starter from last Saturday is Sam Vokes, and what's the betting he doesn't get a full 90 minutes.

Well! What can I say about that? Not a lot and so I won't! In a dreary encounter played in front of a sparse crowd, mainly due to Sky TV televising the game live, we exit the competition at the first attempt. A goal for our hosts in the very last minute of extra time puts an end to the tedium for the long suffering spectators.

If the game did anything it highlighted the lack of strength in depth of the squad, which in the long run may not be a bad thing. Some squad members did little to allay some fans fears that they are not good enough for the Premier League, and indeed on this showing for League 2. Only two players seemed to emerge with any credit, James Tarkowski who I suggest had nothing to prove, and young Aiden O'Neill getting his first start in competitive action.

It was unlike Sean Dyche to make so many changes going into the game, in previous cup competitions two or three are usually the norm. This suggests that Sean either seriously underestimated the opposition or he saw it as a useful run out for the squad and wasn't too bothered about the result. I suspect the latter in this case, Mr Dyche not being a man to take any opponents lightly.

Anyway a team sitting eighth in the Premier League went out to a team seventh from bottom of League 2, that's what the stats will show. Some good ammunition for fans of other teams to fire our way but we can take it. The prize for progressing is an away tie to West Ham United at the Olympic Stadium in London. We wish our friends at Accrington all the best for what will be for them a fantastic occasion. Let's hope they put one over another team in Claret and Blue.

Oh and incidentally, Vokes didn't play the full 90 minutes and picked up a booking to boot. Says it all really.

Result - Accrington Stanley (Pearson 120) 1 – 0 Burnley

Burnley Team

Pope, Darikwa, Tarkowski, Long, Flanagan, Kightly (Arfield 81), O'Neill, Ulvestad, Gudmundsson, Vokes (Gray 67), Jutkiewicz (Boyd 105)

Subs Not Used - Robinson, Lafferty, Anderson, Massanka

Accrington Stanley Team

Parrish, Pearson, Hughes, Beckles, Conneely, Donacien, McConville, Hewitt, O'Sullivan (Davies 101), McCartan (Boco 68), Kee (Lacey 84)

Subs Not Used – Jones, Hery, Sykes, Chapman

Attendance – 3,170

The match thread on the Up the Clarets messageboard had some interesting posts;

FCBurnley thought *"Possibly one of the worst games i have seen"* (sic)

Whilst he then went on to add *"Fortunately Bein Sports are not showing the extra time. What a relief."*

I think the most telling post though came from Sidney1st

"I'm going to go and pull a tooth out, I think I'll enjoy it more."

That was the worst possible result imaginable for me as on Thursday my wife and I leave for our annual Bank Holiday weekend in Wragby, Lincolnshire. This is our opportunity to catch up with friends who a couple of years back deserted the charms of our hilly northern outpost for the flat agricultural lands that time forgot. My old pal of many years Steve C, whom some of you may remember from previous diaries, bizarrely now claims to be a Hull City Supporter. I am fully aware that this is not true as he couldn't name a single Hull player, but it suits his purpose as he acts as 'wind-up merchant' concerning anything Clarets related. What a time to be going to Lincolnshire then on the back of an embarrassing defeat at Accrington, and with Hull City, also favourites for relegation, currently sitting joint top of the league with maximum points from two fixtures. To compound matters we have an almost impossible task to come at Chelsea!

Game 3 - Saturday 27th August, 15.00 - Chelsea v Burnley

This was going to be an almost impossible game for me to follow. I had my phone set up to receive vital information alerts about the game, line-ups, Kick-off, goals etc, from the BBC Sport website as we journeyed into the lovely city of Lincoln on match day.

Any of you who may have been to Lincoln on this Bank Holiday weekend will know that it plays host to a most extraordinary annual event, the Lincoln Steampunk Festival. When anybody asks me what it is I am always at a loss to describe it. I'm not going to even attempt to do that here but would refer anybody interested to Google Steampunk and sit back to be amazed. Lincoln stages the largest and longest Steampunk festival in the World, attracting participants from around the globe. The Festival blurb states:

"For four glorious days the historic streets of Lincoln are thronged with thousands of splendidly dressed Steampunks enjoying a festival which strives to combine, art, literature, music, fashion, comedy and simple good fun."

Give it a look sometime, you'll be amazed.

Ahead of kick off time we strolled the city taking in the sights and enjoying the good weather. I was conscious that I would need to monitor the game sparingly as my wife would take a dim view of my following it too closely, and also chief antagonist Steve C would be looking for any opportunity for a 'dig'. My suspicions being that there may well be several opportunities for that.

After an interesting lunch at Brayford Marina, Fish fingers on Ciabatta (there were 4), comes the first jolt to the system. Not long into the game and the dreaded goal alert! I hesitate to look fearing the worst, yet hoping for the best. As they say, it's always the hope that kills you. A brief message on the phone, Chelsea 1-0 Burnley, Hazard 9'. That's the cue for Steve C to chirp up with, *"what did you expect?"* and *"probably be another four yet."*

I have to confess I thought he might be right but certainly wouldn't let him know that. On we walked up a steep hill, aptly named 'Steep Hill' or probably should have been 'Very Steep Hill', in the direction of the Cathedral Quarter. No further alerts as we toiled upwards but I couldn't make my mind up whether that was because there were no further goals, or my phone had lost the signal. How negative of me, I did suspect the latter.

Eventually we made the sanctuary of a pub close to the castle walls. Relaxing with a pint and knowing half time was fast approaching I was reflecting that 1-0 half time wouldn't be a bad score, and would give us a launchpad for a second half comeback. Wrong again, the dreaded alert! Could it be the half time whistle? No, same brief message on the screen, Chelsea 2-0 Burnley, Willian 41. At this point I did toy with the idea of switching the damn thing off and 'going blind' for the second half, but no, as they also say, hope springs eternal.

Back on the road to Wragby now and expecting an avalanche of goal alerts, I am relieved to hear no further beeps. That is until almost back at base and with the clock running down fast, BEEP! Could it be the final whistle, and a creditable 2-0 defeat (if such a thing is possible). No could it hell! Same message on screen, Chelsea 3-0 Burnley, Moses 89'. Oh well all I can hope for now is a resounding Manchester United victory in the tea time kick off at Hull. That will keep my antagonist quieter.

By all accounts we got exactly what we deserved at Chelsea, but no disgrace losing to a far superior outfit. The gulf in class between the likely top four sides and the likely bottom four sides in the Premier League is huge. It was unfortunately a mis-match.

To compound matters we finished the game with a centre midfield pairing of Aidan O'Neill an 18-year-old making his first league start, and James Tarkowski a centre back making his Premier League debut. This against one of the strongest teams in the league, gave more ammunition to the growing band of fans once again disillusioned by the Clarets transfer window activities. With only a few days left before the window closes till January the pressure for the Directors to sanction more cash for transfers is approaching fever pitch. Panic is setting in among the fans, let's hope it's not among the Board and management. Time will tell, but time is short.

Fortunately, Manchester United saw off Hull City, albeit with a 92nd minute goal from substitute Marcus Rashford. PHEW!

Result - Chelsea (Hazard 9, Willian 41, Moses 89) 3 - 0 Burnley

Burnley Team

Heaton, Lowton, Keane, Mee, Ward, Boyd, Marney (Tarkowski 72), Defour (O'Neill 57), Arfield (Gudmundsson 57), Gray, Vokes

Subs Not Used - Robinson, Darikwa, Kightly, Jutkiewicz

Chelsea Team

Courtois, Ivanovic, Terry, Cahill, Azpilicueta, Kante, Willian (Moses 77), Oscar, Matic, Costa (Batshuayi 80), Hazard (Pedro 81)

Subs Not Used - Begovic, Fabregas, Loftus-Cheek, Aina

Attendance - 41,607

Season To Date - Played 3, Won 1, Drawn 0, Lost 2, Goals For 2, Goals Against 4, Points 3

League Position after Game 3 - 13th

By Bank Holiday Monday, and with the window set to slam shut on Wednesday night, the disgruntled supporters are really starting to vent their spleen, and nobody seems immune. The Chairman is a favourite target but also coming in for serious flak are the mysterious Recruitment team. Even Sean Dyche who is thought to be untouchable is coming in for criticism with suggestions that his identification of potential targets is too restricted. Further flames are added to the fire with rumours circulating wildly that none other than the 'car crash' club Hull, have agreed a fee of £10m for our long term summer target Jeff Hendrick of Derby. If he is the man, as many have suggested that Dyche really wanted, then a manager who already seemed to be despairing of our dealings, could be close to tipping point.

Even Up the Clarets messageboard editor Tony Scholes, usually pretty supportive of the club's directors and management comes out swinging in an online article entitled, 'Same old targets - same old story'. Tony bemoans the fact that even before last season ended Burnley had identified Derby's Hendrick, and Brighton's Stephens as prime targets. Now four months down the line and time running out we are still believed to be pursuing the same targets! A hard hitting Tony believes that despite the many valid reasons why deals have not been done, to reach the position we are now in is negligent. If we fail to further strengthen before the window closes, he feels that will be nothing short of a disaster.

I can't help but agree with his summary of the situation. Our previous sojourns into the top flight have failed through our inability to strengthen the side sufficiently for the immense challenge that promotion brings. It would appear that nothing has been learned from that and from where I sit at this moment a long and almost hopeless rearguard action is about to unfold. When Chairman Mike Garlick stood on the Town Hall steps at the start of the Promotion Parade he assured the fans that more money was available this time for a serious challenge. As of the 29th August this money remains largely untouched.

It's even more galling when we look at the amount of 'ins' against 'outs'. Since we were crowned Champions, amongst those going out are, Barton, Gilks, Jones, Taylor, Hennings and Long (Chris) some forever, others on loan. As I write in have come, Pope, Gudmundsson, Flanagan and Defour. To myself and many others the squad currently looks weaker than the one which gained promotion. We realise that there is still time to address the situation but in the words of Tony Scholes when asked if he was hopeful;

"Hoping is the word, Hoping, not hopeful."

On Tuesday 30th August some of Tony's hopes are realised as the Clarets announce the signing of young Chelsea striker Patrick Bamford on a loan to the end of the season. Bamford was a striker we had previously pursued unsuccessfully and had gone on to have an impressive loan with Middlesbrough. That will go some way to offsetting the in/out balance and provide some competition for forward places.

Also surfacing on the same day were strong rumours that we had pipped rivals Hull City to the signing of Eire and

Derby County midfielder Jeff Hendrick. The player had seemed all set to sign for Hull until we matched the offer believed to be £10.5m! A lot of money for a Championship midfielder but certainly the target Sean Dyche had identified as key.

By transfer deadline day, the 31st it was reported that the player was undergoing a medical and the signature appeared a formality. However, things were starting to hot up with rumours of midfielder Freddie Ulvestad leaving on loan to Charlton Athletic, and striker Lukas Jutkiewicz similarly heading to Birmingham City. Sky Sports sources are also hinting at a couple of possible incoming deals also 'bubbling under'. At lunchtime it looks like we are in for a busy day on the transfer front.

News from the south coast suggests that long term target Dale Stephens has submitted a transfer request in a bid to force the issue regarding our interest. This is swiftly followed up by a further improved bid by ourselves which is once again swiftly and forcefully rebuffed. I'm still hopeful that something can be done here, Brighton surely don't want to keep a player who clearly wants to leave. The danger to his club being that after this window his transfer value is falling sharply as his contract runs down.

In mid-afternoon a new rumour appears linking us with Polish international winger Kamil Grosicki currently playing his football with Rennes in France. It's believed there is also interest from West Ham and Everton, but strangely we appear to be favourites. This guy looks just the type of winger we need to give us a bit of variety, quick and direct with a good set piece delivery, let's do it!

This deal then seems to have a little on/off interlude but by teatime seems to be firmly back on. Photos are posted of him boarding a private jet in Warsaw seemingly heading for Burnley via Manchester. He'd better get a move on the window closes at 23.00 hours and a medical will be needed before the deal can go through.

Avid but anxious Clarets fans then start tracking the flight of the jet on Flightradar and posting its progress on the Up the Clarets messageboard. Reports come in of the plane crossing the coast near Mablethorpe apparently heading for Manchester. How sad are we! Most reports have him safely down on the tarmac except for one poster who worryingly reports a lost contact with the flight at 1950 feet. Shot down by an envious rival club perhaps? The next reports indicate that the medical is swiftly passed and he is as good as a Claret.

It's now almost 22.00 hours and exhausted by tracking all the posts on various messageboards I decide it's time to turn in. A last look shows two more players going out of the club, Cameron Dummigan to Oldham Athletic, and Ntumba Massanka to Morecambe. Boy, we are shifting some players out in numbers now. Time for bed to dream of exotic new superstars and hopefully the icing on the cake a late arrival of Dale Stephens.

SEPTEMBER

Waking refreshed from a good night's sleep I head for the kitchen and breakfast ahead of hopefully a lovely day walking in the Yorkshire Dales. I decide to resist the temptation to check the internet for any late developments in the transfer window. However, I am unable to deny the urge for long as I am eager to see if we have indeed managed to add Dale Stephens to a very good last day's activity in the market.

First glance shows no big messageboard thread which there would surely have been if a deal had been done. Strangely though, the 'Grosicki' thread has grown to about 1000 posts. What the hell has happened? Disaster as I read that the deal has not gone through and has been pulled by the Clarets at the last minute! Suggestions are that Rennes have scuppered the deal by demanding more cash but details are sketchy. What a blow and what a lesson in not counting chickens before they hatch! What had the makings of an excellent last day's business has suddenly gone somewhat flat, and with the window closed we now go with what we've got until January.

There's much discussion about the Grosicki affair among the fifteen hearty Burnley souls who set off on the Thursday expedition. In the absence of any hard news on the failed transfer, most of the blame is being laid at the feet of our French cousins, with a lot of the old clichés about not being able to trust the 'Frogs' readily bandied about. Still it's a nice day and a lovely walk from Hanlith down the River Aire to Bell Busk and back soon sees spirits restored. This of course aided by the customary pub stop near the end of the walk at Kirkby Malham.

A little mention here for the excellent village pub here, the Victoria. This is an ale house we have attempted to frequent on many occasions in the past. Unfortunately, we have been thwarted due to the landlord's preference to stay closed during weekdays till five p.m. Now the pub is under new ownership and obviously attempting to build up trade with much more walker friendly opening times. A good choice of local real ales, we opted for Naylor's Brewery, Aire Valley Bitter, and plenty of lager choices for the less discerning drinker available here. We were engaged in conversation by a friendly Yorkshire chap in the bar who asked us from whence we came. On hearing that it was Burnley he proclaimed;

"Tha'sll a come for some fresh air then!"

Don't let that put you off though. Actually, on further discussion it transpired his Dad and Brother were Clarets fans, and I think I may have been able to talk him into buying the previous two Premier League diaries. A good day out and book sales as well! Seriously though, if you are in the area give the Victoria at Kirkby Malham a try, you won't be disappointed.

On returning home I learn that we may indeed have been a little hasty blaming Rennes for the collapse of the Grosicki deal. Rumours are now circulating that the player and his agent may not come out of this disaster in a particularly good light. Suggestions are that the player has substantial gambling debts that the French club were paying off for him. Quite reasonably as he would no longer be their player that situation would cease. Unfortunately, there seemed to be some assumption that Burnley FC would then take on this commitment. Highly and quite rightly unlikely!

So in the end a frantic transfer window closed with Burnley breaking their record transfer fee not once but twice - initially for the signing of Steven Defour which was then subsequently smashed by the fee for Jeff Hendrick. It's estimated the total outlay in the window was in excess of £20m with a total of five players permanently signed and Patrick Bamford brought in on loan.

A few eyebrows were also raised by the large number of players leaving the club either on loan, or in the case of Renny Smith and Cameron Dummigan on permanent deals. In total fifteen players exited Turf Moor; some till January, some till the end of the season, and some I'm sure who's contracts are expiring, never to be seen again. I suppose it was inevitable that with our elevated league status there would be a need to upgrade the quality of the squad. Many of the players going out on loan are youngsters from the Development squad. These will hopefully get valuable playing experience in a competitive atmosphere and come back stronger for that. Anyhow, barring the signing of any out of contract players, the onus is now on the current squad to get us through to January in a fit shape to push for Premier League survival in the second half of the season.

A blank weekend for Premier League action due to World Cup qualifiers and International friendlies follows the closure of the window. Seven Clarets go off on full International duty, and one joins his national Under 21 squad. Our full internationals on duty are Tom Heaton (England), Sam Vokes (Wales), Stephen Ward and Jeff Hendrick (Republic of Ireland), Johann Berg Gudmundsson (Iceland),

Steven Defour (Belgium), and Scott Arfield (Canada). Our representative at Under 21 level was young goalkeeper Conor Mitchell for Northern Ireland. All enjoyed varying degrees of success but probably the happiest were Jeff Hendrick who scored within two minutes in a 2-2 draw, and Sam Vokes who also netted in a 4-0 win.

Tuesday 6th September saw the resumption of Lancashire Dotcom walks. The opener was a gentle re-introduction of about 5.5 miles in the Hodder Valley starting from the Three Fishes at Great Mitton. It was good to restart the banter and amiable hostilities with our Preston friends who due to a poor start to the season, three points from a possible fifteen, were somewhat subdued. A pity though that Blackburn John had absented himself, allegedly on holiday, as the Rovers currently prop up the Championship with one point. Coffee and bacon butties to start the walk, then an excellent two course lunch to finish it, with a good choice of real ales. What could be better? Unfortunately for me I think I made a poor choice with the beer opting for a Thwaites brew, 1814, which is brewed specifically for the Ribble Valley Inns group. I would have gone for the Burnley brews from Moorhouse's or Reedley Hallows but unfortunately both ran out at the time of purchase. One or two notable members of the Burnley Contingent found the cost of £15 a bit expensive for their taste and opted to duck out. Geoff Ashworth, you know who I am referring to!

Tuesday's walk was followed by another favourite Burnley contingent outing on Thursday to Austwick and the Norber Erratics. An almighty downpour greeted our arrival but within fifteen minutes it stopped and the rest of the day was in pleasant sunny but breezy conditions. A great walk taking in the Erratics, Crummack, then back to Clapham via

Long Lane and through the fields to Austwick. All topped off with an excellent pint of Thwaites's Wainwright at the Game Cock Inn Austwick, a Dales day at its best!

It has been a quiet few days on the football front but by Friday 9th I am expecting things to hot up. Not least as next up is Hull City at the Turf, the team that Lincolnshire émigré Steve C purports to follow. I'm expecting a lively interchange of texts between here and the 'flatlands' in the next twenty-four hours. Although our recent record against them is very good, barring a 3-0 defeat at Hull on Boxing Day 2015, I'm taking nothing for granted. Even at this early stage of the season, week four, this is clearly an important game to win as Hull are likely relegation candidates as are we. Seems a bit early to call fixtures 'six-pointers' but this surely feels like one.

Will there be debuts for new recruits Jeff Hendrick and Patrick Bamford? We'll know soon enough.

Game 4 – Saturday 10th September, 15.00 – Burnley v Hull City

The answer to the above was no. Both Hendrick and Bamford unsurprisingly have to settle for a seat on the bench as they continue their integration programme. Johann Berg Gudmundsson however does get a start at the expense of Scott Arfield. Scotty has had a long, and late in the week return flight from his transatlantic adventures with the Canada national team.

Not a bad day weather-wise, a bit cloudy to start but turning into glorious sunshine late in the game. Unfortunately, that was the only thing glorious about the end of the game! What a sickener as the Clarets manage to turn a much needed three points into a measly one as they concede with what must have been the penultimate kick in the match.

A fairly slow start from the Clarets against a Hull side who certainly don't seem to be lacking in confidence. It's a fairly familiar pattern as the opposition enjoy more possession of the ball and we maintain a solid defensive shape. New recruit Steven Defour seems to be settling in with the team nicely and is certainly showing promising signs. His confidence and fitness certainly seem to be improving with every game, and we may have unearthed a gem here.

As an attacking unit however we are a less than potent force, a lack of width and ability to get to the by-line means the strikers are starved of any meaningful service. Indeed, I stand to be corrected, but I believe Andre Gray must have gone 30 minutes without a touch of the ball. At the other end Hull are also fairly impotent, although Meyler does brush the post with a cross shot. The best we can muster is a goalmouth scramble which eventually comes to nought. Half time and all square, it looks like one goal will settle this one.

The second half continues much along the same lines until… on 72 minutes, Defour continuing his fine form of the first half goes one better. Bringing the ball under control brilliantly just inside his own half he sets off on a driving run. Taking full advantage of the space afforded by a retreating rearguard he advances almost to the Hull penalty box and pulls the trigger. A magnificent powerful right foot drive gives the keeper no chance and nestles right in the corner of the net. A superb solo goal and already he is establishing himself as a crowd favourite.

Unfortunately, that's almost the last of the action for our new hero as he feels his calf muscles tightening and is replaced by new record signing Jeff Hendrick. As we look to see the game out Arfield replaces Gudmundsson, and with 10 minutes to go Bamford gets his first taste of Clarets action replacing Gray. As the clock winds down we begin to live dangerously and survive one or two scares. I can't help thinking that we are conceding too much ground to our opponents as we defend deeper, encouraging Hull to come at us. Still as the fourth official signals four minutes of added time surely the points are ours. The four minutes gone and the last act appears to be a corner for our visitors. This is partially cleared to just outside the box. As a Hull player tries to get a shot away Ben Mee attempts to block but only succeeds in conceding a free kick.

It's a dangerous position just outside the box and fairly central, tailor made for a dead-ball specialist. Unfortunately for us that is just what our opponents have in Robert Snodgrass. Cool as a cucumber and with unerring accuracy he gets the ball up and over the wall and into the corner of the net past Tom Heaton's despairing dive. Euphoria turns to instant despair for all of a Claret persuasion and I must confess to an outburst of profane language. It was one of those games where ultimately a draw felt like a defeat.

To be fair, Steven Defour, apart there was not much in our performance to enthuse about. It is difficult to see how in the way we are currently set up we will score enough goals to stay up. There was little or no creativity and as a consequence little or no goal threat. A point each was probably the right result.

Home then to await the inevitable texts from Steve C in his Lincolnshire bunker, I'll just have to ignore them as best I can. On arriving home though I am somewhat cheered as a little research restores some of my faith. A quick delve in my archives reveals that in our last Premier League season it took seven games to reach four points, this time we are there in four. Progress!

Result - Burnley (Defour 72) 1 - 1 Hull City (Snodgrass 90+5)

Burnley Team

Heaton, Lowton, Keane, Mee, Ward, Boyd, Marney, Defour (Hendrick 75), Gudmundsson (Arfield 76), Gray(Bamford 80) , Vokes

Subs Not Used - Robinson, Flanagan, Kightly, Tarkowski

Hull City Team

Jakupovic, Elmohamady, Davies, Livermore, Robertson, Clucas (Maloney 83), Huddlestone, Meyler (Mason 73), Snodgrass, Hernandez, Diomande (Keane 70)

Subs Not Used - Marshall, Maguire, Weir, Markus

Attendance - 18,803

Season To Date - Played 4, Won 1, Drawn 1, Lost 2, Goals For 3, Goals Against 5, Points 4

League Position after Game 4 - 15th

After game week four our official position in the table is 15th. We could argue that we are actually joint 10th on the same points as Watford who actually occupy that lofty spot. However, on goal difference we are one goal worse off than them but equal with Swansea and Bournemouth. Premier League champions Leicester City sit one place below us on the same points but with a one goal negative goal difference. They will be next up on Saturday 17th at the King Power stadium.

Tuesday's walk this week was definitely on 'home turf' as we visited Towneley Hall as part of the Heritage Open Days project. In the morning we had a guided tour of the Hall, followed by lunch and then a short walk through Thanet Lee Wood, the park grounds and environs. On a magnificent sunny September day, Towneley was certainly looking at its best and undoubtedly an attraction worthy of being Burnley's 'Jewel in the Crown'.

It was an excellent guided tour by volunteer museum assistant Derek Hartley, a guy who certainly knows his stuff. His input was much appreciated not only by our friends from the west of the county but also by a good sprinkling of Burnley residents among the group. His encyclopaedic knowledge of the Towneley family and Hall enhanced a brilliant outing.

The short walk, not necessarily a bad thing in the unseasonal high temperatures, rounded of our adventure nicely. It also served as a warm up for Thursday's planned Burnley contingent trip to Ribblehead and a more challenging walk.

Writing the report for Game 5 I have to say has required a few days of restorative therapies. Firstly, a day out to the National Railway Museum at York, an excellent trip and best of all, free entry! Next, a Tuesday outing from West Bradford with the Dotcomers - another lovely sunny day and a circuit taking in the picturesque village of Waddington. This was all topped off with a pint of the splendidly named 'No Eyed Deer' at the Higher Buck. My mood suitably revived I have now summoned the strength of will to report the following proceedings.

Game 5 – Saturday 17th September, 15.00 – Leicester City v Burnley

At 14.55, five minutes to kick off, I don't know what the weather is like in Leicester but in Harle Syke, Burnley it's glorious, as our Indian summer continues. To relieve the tension, I make the decision to mow the lawn and attach and dangle myself to the radio on my iPod. Before I do that though my phone signals an 'alert' on my BBC Sport app revealing the team line-ups.

What is more there's some shock news! Sean has decided to change the formation which is about as rare as a sunhat on an eskimo. Yes, it looks like we are going 4-5-1 as record signing Jeff Hendrick comes in and Sam Vokes drops to the bench. It's not like Sean to ditch his trusted 4-4-2. The last time we did in a Premier League game resulted in a 4-1 drubbing at West Bromwich. The new signings though have added a bit more flexibility to the squad, let's hope it works.

After an uneventful first twenty minutes the system seems to be working well against the Premier League Champions. Leicester after an inauspicious start to the season are coming into the game after a confidence boosting 3-0 Champions League away victory midweek in Bruges. After the first 30 minutes there's only been one shot registered on target, that being saved by Tom Heaton's shins.

Suddenly the game springs to live with two great opportunities around the 36th minute. Firstly, Steven Defour sends a tame header straight at the Foxes keeper from close range, followed by a similar effort by Mahrez which misses the target. We seem to be going in level at half time then all the hard work is undone as we concede from a free kick, disappointingly nodded in from close range in first half added time. A needlessly conceded free kick, as Matt Lowton flattens Marc Albrighton, gives £29m new signing Islam Slimani an easy close range header for his first Premier League goal.

Worse is to follow shortly after the restart as a fortunate flick off the heels of Jamie Vardy lands fortuitously on the head of Slimani again and in front of goal he makes no mistake. Four minutes of madness is Sean Dyche's description of events and without doubt we are well and truly sunk.

The experiment with the formation is abandoned around the hour mark. We revert to 4-4-2 as Vokes comes on for Defour who currently is incapable of getting a full 90 minutes in a game. A rampant Leicester now start to pile on the pressure and the margin stretches to three on 78 minutes courtesy of a Ben Mee own goal. Attempting to stop a pass going across the face of goal Ben's outstretched boot can only deflect the ball into his own net.

After a promising first half marred by the late goal, we failed to turn up for the second period. It's 80 minutes before we manage a shot on target, a deflected free kick from long range by Johann Berg Gudmundsson bringing a good save from the keeper. Sadly, once again it's nowhere near enough.

For yet another game there's no creativity, no threat, and seemingly precious little hope. I think for myself there is a growing realisation that although it's early doors, this squad does not have the quality to survive a very unforgiving Premier League. Clearly the new signings will take time to integrate and gel, but for me we are still short of players with creative ability. A telling statistic is that after five games we are the only team not to have scored from inside the penalty box. This is unsurprising as we are failing dismally to deliver any meaningful balls into the box.

Many fans feel the squad is stronger than the last one that failed in the Premier League. I believe that may be the case in terms of squad depth, but in key areas we are weaker. We have no player who can create his own chances this time around, whereas Danny Ings's excellent control and pace last time gave us another dimension. Up front Sam Vokes and Andre Gray look well short of the required standard, but with the paucity of the service they receive so would Lionel Messi!

Result - Leicester City (Slimani 45+1,48, Mee o.g.78) 3 - 0 Burnley

Burnley Team

Heaton, Lowton, Keane, Mee, Ward, Boyd, Marney, Defour (Vokes 64), Hendrick, Arfield (Gudmundsson 57), Gray (Bamford 79)

Subs Not Used - Robinson, Flanagan, Kightly, Tarkowski

Leicester City Team

Zieler, Simpson, Huth, Morgan, Fuchs, Mahrez (Gray 85), Drinkwater (King 79), Amartey, Albrighton, Vardy, Slimani

Subs Not Used - Hamer, Hernandez, Musa, Okazaki, Ulloa

Attendance - 31,916

Season To Date - Played 5, Won 1, Drawn 1, Lost 3, Goals For 3, Goals Against 8, Points 4

League Position after Game 5 - 16th

Another trip to Yorkshire for the Burnley Contingent's Thursday outing for those of you who like to keep tabs on the walks, pubs and beers news. This time we took a circular route from Long Preston to Otterburn and back. The walk information gave a distance of 8.5 miles but my recently acquired Garmin GPSMAP 64s actually recorded 9.98. Who is kidding who? A splendid stroll with wonderful views in all directions. We had the customary run-ins with our hoofed friends this time including Highland cattle (bloody big horns), short horned cattle (short but nasty horns) and of course John W's favourites - horses!

Most of the horses were safely at a distance and across a stream as we approached Otterburn except for one inquisitive type that decided to block our path. Undeterred we pressed relentlessly forward, John W taking up a precautionary position by interposing his wife between himself and the nag. How gallant! Fortunately, the beast soon lost interest and moseyed on back across the stream. Eventually we made the sanctuary of the Boars Head at Long Preston. On the recommendation of a very accommodating landlord, a pint of Naylors (Crosshills Brewery) Brews Brothers, soon had tired limbs revived and rounded off another great day in once again excellent weather.

This coming weekend sees us without a game until the rest of the Premier League programme has been played. Coming up for us now is a run of three consecutive live televised games, the first of which is Watford at the Turf on Monday 26th. This mini break has me reflecting on our start to the season, which so far I have found rather worrying. Five games played (six if we include the EPL Cup tie), one won, one drawn, and three lost (four with the EPL game). Not the best of starts.

My take on the individual games is that in the opener against Swansea we gave almost as good as we got until late in the game and probably unlucky not to get a point. Liverpool was a magnificent performance, two fine goals and a faultless defensive display. However, looking at the Reds impressive form in their other fixtures I wonder if we just caught them on a bad day.

At Chelsea we were, not unexpectedly, outclassed. Hull City felt like we had been robbed at the end, but realistically a draw was probably the right result on the balance of play. Finally, Leicester City, a game in which we started brightly enough but once behind we were never coming back.

Anyhow, going into the weekend we sit 16th and at the moment clear of the relegation spots, just! However, right now I am unable in my mind to identify three teams that look like finishing below us. Is it pessimism or realism? One thing's for sure we need to find some more goal power and soon. Monday night would be as good a time as any.

Just as I'm about to sit down and consume my hard earned Friday night bottle of vino, the Clarets and I are hit by a low blow. News comes through of a four match ban for Andre Gray following his personal hearing with the FA regarding his infamous 'twitterings'.

Andre had been charged with six breaches of FA Rule E3(1) and, because of the aggravated nature of the offences, also of FA Rule E3(2). The player admitted three of the charges but contested the other three, however he was found guilty on all six charges. In addition to the four game suspension he was also fined £25,000, warned as to his future conduct and ordered to attend a one-to-one FA education course.

The ban rules him out of the upcoming home games with Watford and Arsenal, Southampton away and finally Everton at the Turf. That's effectively a loss of the player to Burnley of 10.5% of the Premier Leagues season. Arguably the ruling unfairly punishes Burnley when the offences were committed with the player at another club. However, 'rules are rules' and I think the best thing now is to draw a line under the whole affair and move on. Andre will no doubt have plenty of time to reflect on his rather unfortunate conduct in the weeks ahead.

The ban could probably not have been timed worse for the Clarets as striking options are severely limited with Jutkiewicz, Long and Hennings all out on loan, and Barnes still sidelined with injury. Still I'm sure Sean Dyche will be saying that this is now an opportunity for somebody else to make their mark. Cometh the hour, cometh the man? Will it be Patrick Bamford's chance to step up to the plate and make his mark?

Game 6 – Monday 26th September, 20.00 – Burnley v Watford

The weekend's Premier League results turn out to have been not too unkind on us and we enter this game still outside the relegation places, and now with this game in hand. Defeats at home for Sunderland and West Ham, and a draw for Stoke leave those three clubs still in the drop zone. We sit just above them with one point more than the Hammers, two above Stoke, and three over Sunderland. Level on points with us are Swansea and we lay one behind Middlesbrough. How nice would a win be in this one which would lift us to effectively joint 11th. Will it be….?

By 10pm the answer to that question was a resounding 'yes' as the Clarets, in determined and confident mood, record a morale boosting second home win of the season.

Arriving at the ground I am surprised to learn that there is no place in the starting line-up for Patrick Bamford. Instead we opt to go with the 4-5-1 system tried in the last game at Leicester, but this time with Sam Vokes upfront in place of the suspended Andre Gray. A start also for Johan Berg Gudmundsson - preferred this time to Scott Arfield.

Vokes is playing as a lone striker but it is very evident in the first period that Jeff Hendrick is detailed to get up in support and he is proving very effective at that. It's a good start for us with both Boyd and Gudmundsson, ably assisted by Ward and Lowton, getting the ball out wide and getting in some decent crosses.

Watford in contrast appear strangely subdued, particularly following their recent good form recording victories away at West Ham United and at home to Manchester United. They are certainly a very physical side with pace and power but little subtlety. Their game plan seems to be to sit deep and catch us with quick breaks.

At this point I must mention the Watford shorts. Playing in an all white strip, they to a man, sported the longest shorts I have ever seen in a first class game. Shorts that reached to the knees and in some cases below made our visitors look like Pathe Newsreel footage of Barnestoneworth

United of Ripping Yarns fame. How the hell they could run in those, God alone knows.

Playing with assurance and creating a few chances our approach play needed a goal now to round things off. This duly arrived on 38 minutes as new signing Hendrick met a Defour corner from the right to head down and in. The rest of the half was played out in relative comfort and we had a deserved half time lead.

As expected we experienced a bit of a reaction at the start of the second half from our visitors. In an attempt to up their tempo they switched from a starting 3-5-2 formation to a 4-4-2. However, their plans were rocked again as on 50 minutes Defour breaking quickly fed Boyd whose goal bound shot was prodded wide by a defender's outstretched foot. The initial delivery from Defour, this time from the left was cleared but then accurately recycled by himself onto the head of Keane who made no mistake from close range.

What luxury, a two goal lead. Predictably Watford ring the changes, but our heroes are defending comfortably and our threat on the break makes them reluctant to over commit men forward. There's one close shave as Watford substitute Isaac Success weaves his way along the by-line but his effort goes along the goal-line and out for a corner, which comes to nought. So there's no success for Success, who incidentally looks a more than useful player, perhaps he should have been on from the start.

At an unearthly hour as a result of the 8pm kick off, and many interruptions during the game, the game ends and a very happy bunch of Clarets fans wend their way homeward. It was an excellent team performance with Steven Defour, rapidly becoming a fans favourite picking up the Man of the Match award. In truth it could have gone to anyone in what was a very effective team effort. A victory that now lifts us to 13th in the table after a highly satisfactory night's work!

Result - Burnley (Hendrick 38, Keane 50) 2 - 0 Watford

Burnley Team

Heaton, Lowton, Keane, Mee, Ward, Boyd, Marney, Defour (Arfield 83), Hendrick, Gudmundsson (Kightly 90+3), Vokes

Subs Not Used - Robinson, Flanagan, O'Neill, Tarkowski, Bamford

Watford Team

Gomes, Cathcart (Zuniga HT), Prodl, Britos, Amrabat (Success 58), Capoue, Behrami, Pereyra (Kennedy 75), Holebas, Deeney, Ighalo

Subs Not Used - Pantilimon, Kaboul, Watsom, Guedioura

Attendance – 18,519

Season To Date - Played 6, Won 2, Drawn 1, Lost 3, Goals For 5, Goals Against 8, Points 7

League Position after Game 6 – 13th

Skulduggery is afoot! On a brief foray into town ahead of my late summer break in Madeira I spot a guy has nicked my planned Christmas busking spot outside M&S. Not only is he blowing a tune (of sorts) on his flute but he has also purloined my idea of having a sad faced dog. To add insult to injury he has also furnished it with a basket to appease the animal rights supporters.

I'm going to have to rethink my money generation schemes. At this point I have almost abandoned the idea of being Burnley's answer to George Formby as the ukulele and myself seem to be having issues. Firstly, I can't get the damn thing to stay in tune, then I don't seem to be able to strum upwards. Couple that with having no ear for music or sense of rhythm and the venture is beginning to look ill-fated. I guess I'll just have to join a boy band.

On Wednesday 27th September Sam Allardyce's short reign as England manager comes to an abrupt end. Hapless Sam couldn't keep his nose clean and his 'entrapment' by Daily Telegraph reporters ends his 'dream job' as national manager almost before it begins. Still, he leaves with a £1m pay-off after 67 days in the job. All but a few of the nation work a lifetime and don't earn that!

On the 30th September, my wife and I enjoy a most unlikely coincidence. In the queue for Jet2's baggage drop at Manchester airport, we are amazed to see almost directly behind us, Jim and Noreen, my Everton supporting pal from our Mediterranean cruise this summer. What a small world to once again, amongst the milling throng, meet our friends from the Wirral who sat with us on the flight to Rome. However, on this occasion as we head for Madeira, they are heading for the sun of Tenerife.

OCTOBER

The only downside of a late summer break in the sun is the fact that it inevitably means at least one mixed fixture. Now some of you will say that this is bad planning on my part having not properly consulted the fixture list. In defence I can only claim that the holiday was booked in January 2016, at which point we didn't even know we would once again be Premier League let alone who we would be playing. Sod's Law being what it is the fixture I have to miss is a particularly attractive one, Arsenal at the Turf.

A daunting prospect to face the very much in-form Gunners but coming quickly after the splendid victory over Watford perhaps there is some cause for optimism.

Game 7 – Sunday 2nd October, 16.30 – Burnley v Arsenal

So it is I am again following the game at long distance in a very pleasant and sunny Funchal, Madeira. I have established a good Wi-Fi contact in the excellent Porto Mare hotel complex and hopefully the BBC Sports App will give me good coverage. As an insurance policy I ask fellow Claret John W to send me text updates of the score in case I roam out of Wi-Fi range.

Out for a lengthy walk on the Funchal coastal promenade I realise that the game is underway and am heartened to see no early 'texts of doom'. On the way back to the hotel I catch a glimpse on a TV screen sufficient to confirm, 13 minutes gone, 0-0. Back in the hotel and with the

Wi-Fi connection restored I am relieved to see us reach the half time break still level.

Of course predictably at this point I receive a text from John W

"HT 0-47 Wot a shocker" (sic)

That's the reason I don't rely on 'friends' texts for information.

The pundits on the BBC reckon we are doing a good job of frustrating the Gunners and at the same time making an odd chance, the best of which is missed by Sam Vokes. Following the live text I note that once again Steven Defour doesn't make it past the hour mark. Is he injured or has he 'run out of steam' again?

As the game starts drawing to its conclusion we appear to be under heavy pressure but at 77 minutes the statistics show still only one more shot on target by Arsenal than ourselves. Next I note that Ozil has hit the post for the visitors but Michael Keane has likewise hit the bar. In sympathy with Michael I have also hit the bar, it is Happy Hour, or will it be…

The BBC App seems to be getting slower to update so I decide to follow the game via both BBC and the Up The Clarets messageboard. There's now only 10 minutes to go, can we hang on for an invaluable point? 89 minutes now are we going to make it? 90 minutes up, still 0-0, is the dreaded curse of 'added time' about to strike? Apparently though there are only two minutes to add, the statistics show only two fouls in the game by us, and three by Arsenal.

Then the lowest blow of all! Arsenal score a goal from a 93rd minute corner which the messageboard posters are claiming is both offside and handball!!! Even at a distance I am absolutely gutted and fuming. Thanks referee for ruining what was turning into an idyllic day.

Result - Burnley 0 – 1 (Koscielny 90 +3) Arsenal

Burnley Team

Heaton, Lowton, Keane, Mee, Ward, Boyd, Marney, Defour (Arfield 62), Hendrick, Gudmundsson, Vokes

Subs Not Used - Robinson, Flanagan, O'Neill, Tarkowski, Bamford, Kightly

Arsenal Team

Cech, Bellerin, Koscielny, Mustapha, Monreal, Cazorla, Xhaka (Elneny 71), Walcott, Ozil, Iwobi (Oxlade-Chamberlain 71) Sanchez

Subs Not Used - Ospina, Holding, Gibbs, Gabriel, Reine-Adelaide

Attendance - 20,982

Season To Date - Played 7, Won 2, Drawn 1, Lost 4, Goals For 5, Goals Against 9, Points 7

League Position after Game 7 - 14th

How costly has been the late goal curse. An even later goal against Hull lost us two points, this game one point, and arguably Swansea whilst not in added time another one. How valuable would four more points be at this time. However, in the time honoured Burnley fashion and in the words of the song, we will pick ourselves up, dust ourselves down, and start all over again.

On reflection it seems I missed a mightily encouraging performance which again suggested we may not be quite the 'push-over' that most pundits suggested. Once again we got very complimentary comments from Arsene Wenger who admitted himself that he believed Arsenal had maybe got lucky.

Next weekend sees a blank Premier League fixture list as World Cup qualifying games get underway. Once again we are well represented with Clarets in the England, Wales, Republic of Ireland, Belgian and Icelandic squads. Then on the 4th October comes the great news that caretaker England manager Gareth Southgate has called up Michael Keane to the full England squad following an injury to Stoke's Glen Johnson.

Keane is a player well known to Southgate through his work with England squads below senior level. His call-up is a deserved reward for his tremendous form so far this season. The Clarets having had to fight off unwanted attention for the player in the summer, seem destined to have another battle to hold on to him in January with Chelsea now being mooted as possible suitors. However, this England call-up whilst raising the players profile will also have the beneficial effect to us of raising his transfer value.

Some people have the Midas touch. You know the sort, they can fall in the proverbial pig **** and come up smelling of roses. A further indication, not that one was needed, confirmed that I am not one of those individuals.

In his absence Bob Clare, Dotcom walkers group leader, arranged a lovely walk for Tuesday 11th October. In keeping with his recent penchant for various modes of travel related walks, this one was to be a rarity, a linear walk involving a train journey. The plan was to drive to Arnside, a not inconsiderable trek for the Burnley contingent, then to get the 10.50 train from Arnside to Silverdale. The walk would then consist of a circuitous route of Silverdale and then a beach walk back to Arnside, billed as eight miles.

Bob helpfully suggested that as it would not be possible to buy tickets at Arnside station which is unmanned, we may wish to purchase them online in advance. Seemed like a good idea at the time so I dutifully set about purchasing mine from the Trainline website. The fare was £1.80 but I had the trick of my senior railcard discount up my sleeve, thereby reducing the cost by one third to £1.20. Smart move thought I till I got to the part of the transaction whereby I could obtain my ticket. Various options were presented mostly involving further expenditure for delivery, till I hit upon collection from a local station, free of charge. Brilliant so I nominated Burnley Manchester Road, marvellous. Then the catch, the purchase online carried a £0.75 Transaction fee. So my railcard saved me £0.60 but I still ended up £0.15 worse off! Not a major sum I hear you say but it's the principle of the thing that galled me.

To add insult to injury, walk leader Steve Glover subsequently confirmed that it would be possible to purchase tickets on the train from the guard. Well you can guess what happened next, 16 of us assembled at Arnside station, most without tickets. We mounted the train and it made the short five-minute journey to Silverdale giving the poor overworked guard insufficient time to collect only a small number of the fares. Yes, many Dotcomers enjoyed a freebie, whilst yours truly paid over the odds!

Still, the walk was magnificent through woods, over fields and back along the beach, all in glorious autumnal sunshine. Topped off with a pint of Thwaites's Heritage at Ye Olde Fighting Cocks on Arnside Promenade. Special mention also for Steve's magnificent estimation of the walk length, estimated at 8 miles and recorded at 7.98. What a fluke!

It's Thursday 13th October and a Burnley Contingent outing to Simon's Seat in Wharfedale, gave the opportunity for our merry band to revel in a bit of local pride. Burnley had been declared the 'friendliest place to live' in a report by Rosemary Bennett, Social Affairs correspondent of the posh people's newspaper, The Times.

In an article entitled *"A proper oasis of warmth in a gloomy north? That's Burnley"* it declared.

"It may not be the fanciest place to live and it certainly isn't the richest. But Burnley has been named the friendliest place in the UK, with friends and neighbours judged more likely to help out in a crisis than anywhere else.

"The finding comes in the Legatum Institute's UK prosperity index, drawn up because the foundation believes that existing measures of prosperity are too narrowly focused on wealth.

"Although it uses income as one of its criteria, it adds a mix of other factors including how well people get on with their neighbours, quality of schools, the natural environment..."

What a refreshing change to read something positive about the old town, instead of the usual focus on social security scroungers, drug addiction and deprivation. It's a pity that the media don't focus more often on the many positive aspects of Burnley residence. Then again we don't really want everyone to know about our little piece of paradise or we might be swamped with incomers!

A bit of a challenging day up to Simon's Seat in less than hospitable weather and with a prolonged upward climb. A missed turn added about a further half mile taking the walk distance over the nine-mile mark and prompted the comment from Lesley McDevitt, never short of a helpful suggestion;

*"I wish Simon would find somewhere else to park his **** in future".*

However, Lesley fortified by a refreshing pint of Tiffin Gold (Kirkby Lonsdale Brewery) in the impressive Punch Bowl at Earby, was soon restored to her normal jovial self. I must confess that this is a pub that we have not frequented in recent years. Following a very hospitable welcome in the excellently refurbished establishment I am sure the venue will be back on the agenda.

It seems ages since the last Premier League action, disrupted by another dismal International break, but it's almost time to go again, and thoughts start to turn to another very tough upcoming challenge. Once again for the third game in succession it's a live televised fixture on Sunday 16th at Southampton. A chance once again to meet up with ex Clarets Charlie Austin, and our own home town hero Jay Rodriguez. We wish them both all the best but obviously not this week!

Game 8 - Sunday 16th October, 16.00 - Southampton v Burnley

Not the best of kick off times for supporters especially for the long trip to the south coast, but here we go again for another Sunday treat. The game is once again being shown live on Sky TV, but not having that luxury I opt for Radio Lancashire's full match coverage with Scott Read and ex Claret keeper Marlon Beresford.

Team news reveals as expected an unchanged Clarets line-up whilst for our hosts Charlie Austin starts and Jay Rodriguez is on the bench. It's not long into the game and perhaps a portent of what is to come before Tom Heaton makes a fantastic save to keep out an Austin header.

As the game progresses it's predictably fairly one-way traffic towards our goal. Not long in and a blow for the Saints as they lose a full back to a hamstring injury and replace him with an academy youngster. On 25 minutes my phone rings and it is none other than my daughter Stephanie on her way back to Darlington from being honoured as Godmother at a christening in Chipping. Now this presents something of a problem. Not that I'm not glad to hear from Stephanie, however her phone calls can be quite protracted. She does like to give a blow-by-blow account of all that has transpired in the last 24 hours! Fortunately, she gets the message and we terminate the conversation and get back to the game after about seven minutes.

Our friends from Radio Lancashire are now sounding more reassuring as they report that we are now growing in confidence and getting into the game. The next notable action sees Steven Defour booked on 30 minutes. On 33 minutes once again we seem to be on the wrong end of a poor refereeing decision as Johann Berg Gudmundsson is downed in the box. The commentators reckon it's a stonewall penalty, but 'quelle surprise' referee Mike Dean doesn't! Worse is to follow on 38 minutes as Defour clears the ball, he goes down injured, apparently another hamstring, and is immediately subbed. His replacement somewhat surprisingly is not Scott Arfield but young Australian midfielder, Aidan O'Neill. As we approach half time the fourth official signals four minutes added time owing to the lengthy injuries sustained. The extra time successfully negotiated we make half time with the scores level.

There's heavy rain in Southampton but it's sunshine here in the friendliest town in Britain. Will that sun last long? Not for the Clarets it won't. Within seven minutes of the restart we find ourselves in a familiar position of a goal down. A scrappy affair scrambled home by you guessed it, Charlie Austin. A big ask now as to level things up we need to manage what we haven't done so far this season, an away goal!

Shortly afterwards we are again undone from a corner, this time a good finish from Nathan Redmond - and that would appear to be game up. From the growing confidence of the first half the game has changed totally and I get the sinking feeling that a goal deluge is coming. The Saints with their tails up are now exerting heavy pressure. Our Radio Lancashire friends feel the same as me, and have now completely changed their tune. Fickle buggers!

They might be right as on 66 minutes it's 3-0 as a soft penalty is awarded for a foul by Gudmundsson and Austin once again does the honours. Help! Can we finish now? We have once again collapsed and now our own Jay Rodriguez is coming on for the Saints. Thankfully he is replacing Austin, hooray. I don't think I could have stomached an Austin hat-trick, although I do have him in my Fantasy Football league outfit.

No need to worry as Michael Kightly is now coming on for us replacing Gudmundsson. An inspired substitution as Kightly's cross from a corner results in a push in the box giving Mike Dean the opportunity to award us a rather soft penalty. Southampton boy Sam Vokes duly dispatches it to give himself a bit of homecoming joy. Still 18 minutes' left - is the comeback on?

Unfortunately not. Southampton just slip back into gear and continue to force us back. Only the magnificence of keeper Tom Heaton prevents a rout.

Result - Southampton (Austin 52, 66 pen, Redmond 60) 3 - 1 (Vokes 72 pen) Burnley

Burnley Team

Heaton, Lowton, Keane, Mee, Ward, Boyd (Bamford 81), Marney, Defour (O'Neill 41), Hendrick, Gudmundsson (Kightly 70), Vokes

Subs Not Used - Robinson, Flanagan, Arfield, Tarkowski,

Southampton Team

Forster, Martina, Fonte, van Dijk, Targett (McQueen 14), Romeu, Clasie, Davis, Tadic, Austin (Rodriguez 71), Redmond (Ward-Prowse 88)

Subs Not Used - Hojberg, Yoshida, Long, McCarthy

Attendance - 29,040

Season To Date - Played 8, Won 2, Drawn 1, Lost 5, Goals For 6, Goals Against 12, Points 7

League Position after Game 8 - 14th

After the game I have to say I felt rather depressed and pessimistic which is a trait I always try hard not to succumb to. A look at the match statistics showed Southampton having 34 attempts on goal to our six. Of those 14 were on target as opposed to our one. It begs the question how on earth are we ever going to pick up an away point when we are conceding so much possession and territory to the opposition.

Three away games so far have resulted in three defeats with three goals conceded in each game. I fear we need a drastic rethink of our tactics away from home. Once we concede we are sunk, there is no plan B, and no different options from the bench. Whilst trying hard not to be negative I can't help feeling that we have learnt precious little from our previous Premier League experiences.

With main hope Steven Defour looking increasingly fragile, presumably now injured and still to complete a full 90 minutes, where is the creativity going to come from? The only positive I can grasp is that Ashley Barnes is apparently on his way back to full fitness. 'Basher' may just give us a bit of extra bite and muscularity that we are currently sadly lacking.

Game 9 - Saturday 22nd October, 15.00 - Burnley v Everton

It seems an age since I last saw a game. Indeed, it is, Monday 26th September was my last outing for a home win against Watford. It looks like it may be me that is the lucky charm not all the assorted paraphernalia that I am lugging around to every game. Let's hope so because after last week's mauling morale among the fans seems to be at a pretty low ebb.

Ahead of the game, over pre-match pints of Moorhouse's Premiership Bitter, my pals and I discuss the season so far. The consensus seems to be that we are very much facing an uphill battle. However, we all knew this would be the case and are doing our utmost to try and remain positive. We are such a small club amidst the company that we now find ourselves in but we have earned the right to be there and we won't be giving in without a fight. Our away form leaves much to be desired but at home we have proved to be a match for anybody. Today will require another exceptional performance if we are to take anything from an Everton team currently riding high in sixth place.

As expected Steven Defour misses out through the hamstring injury sustained last week, but a big surprise is the absence of George Boyd from both the team and the substitutes bench. George has his many critics but I am not one and can't help but think his impressive work rate will be sorely missed. The spare places in the side are taken by Scott Arfield and Michael Kightly.

Owing to turnstile congestion (and the fact that I can't get the gang to leave the pub) we manage to miss the kick off. I arrive at my seat just in time to see an Everton corner thankfully cleared, and am informed that but for a Tom Heaton save we would already be one down. The ground looks pretty much full to capacity on what is a lovely autumnal day in Burnley.

An impressive looking Everton line-up are dominating the early exchanges with the recalled England youngster Ross Barkley, pulling the strings. Up front is the man-mountain

Romelu Lukaku, and he is ably assisted by recent signing Yannick Bolassie. It's a slow start for the Clarets with the familiar pattern of not much possession and much chasing and harrying by our boys. Gradually though the pendulum starts to swing in our favour and on 39 minutes we are ahead albeit against the run of play. Scott Arfield playing as the furthest forward central midfielder is suddenly through on goal in a Burnley break. His rather tame shot presumably befuddles the Everton keeper who can only parry it into the path of Sam Vokes who rolls it home from close range.

The goal has given us a bit of confidence and certainly lifted the crowd. A welcome half time break comes without further concerns and we have a precious lead.

Not surprisingly the Toffees, no doubt on the end of a half time Ronald Koeman ear bashing, start the second half in determined fashion. Wave after wave of attacks are coming our way but the defence is remaining in good shape and resolute. I remark to John W that I hope we are not going to have to witness this for a further 45 minutes. Tragedy strikes on 58 minutes as on a rare foray upfield we carelessly lose the ball in the middle of the park. Quick as a flash Lukaku and Bolassie who I hope are getting in each other's way are bearing down on Tom Heaton's goal. Surprisingly Bolassie shrugs off his more muscular pal, perhaps unfortunately for us. In full stride he takes a quick sight of the target and unleashes an Exocet straight into the far corner of the net. No chance for Tom and the game all square.

Now the torture really starts, our guests sensing victory go for the jugular and its edge of the seat stuff for the home fans. Substitutes come and go for both sides as Everton try to grab their victory and we stoutly try to defend our point. The clock ticks slowly but minute by minute we are edging closer to our goal. Or should I say their goal! On 90 minutes, the unthinkable happens. Johann Berg Gudmundsson lets fly from distance with a terrific left footer. Stekelenburg in the Everton goal is at full stretch but is beaten, but cruelly the shot crashes back flush from the crossbar. We are thwarted, but no we're NOT. Who should the ball be coming straight out to, none other than Scotty Arfield now operating in his more usual left wing role. Unerringly Scott dispatches his shot straight and true into the corner of the Everton net and we are against all the odds AHEAD! Pandemonium in the stands as to a man the crowd rise to acclaim a super strike and what must be now a magnificent victory. The noise levels are incredible as all the frustration from the 'robbery' of the last home game against Arsenal is now relieved. Four minutes added time are successfully negotiated and we have a third precious Premier League victory and the priceless three points in the bag.

A delirious crowd leaves Turf Moor in buoyant mood and the ale houses of Burnley will be doing a roaring trade tonight.

Result - Burnley (Vokes 39, Arfield 90) 2 - 1 (Bolassie 58) Everton

Burnley Team

Heaton, Lowton, Keane, Mee, Ward (Flanagan 81), Kightly (Tarkowski 72), Marney, Arfield, Hendrick, Gudmundsson, Vokes (Bamford 86)

Subs Not Used - Robinson, Darikwa, Long, O'Neill

Everton Team

Stekelenburg, Coleman, Jagielka (Valencia 90), Williams, Oviedo, Barry, Gueye (Cleverley 81), Bolassie, Barkley, Mirallas (Deulofeu 75), Lukaku,

Subs Not Used - Holgate, Robles, Lennon, Funes-Mori

Attendance - 21,416

Season To Date - Played 9, Won 3, Drawn 1, Lost 5, Goals For 8, Goals Against 13, Points 10

League Position after Game 9 - 14th

Coincidentally, as I was checking some old statistics I noticed that Game 9 in our last Premier League adventure was also a home game against Everton. On that occasion, we were on the wrong end of a 3-1 scoreline, and after nine fixtures were bottom of the table with only four points on the board. In fact, it took twelve games to get to ten points so we are someway ahead of schedule this time. However, we'd better not get carried away, this time we have played six of the first nine at home, and still haven't collected a solitary away point. What better time to start rectifying that than this coming weekend.

We are now almost one quarter of the way through the programme and in fact half time on Saturday will mark the exact point. Another real David v Goliath clash in prospect, this time against none other than arch villain Jose Mourinho's Manchester United. There's certainly some 'bad blood' in the air between the Clarets fans and Mourinho following the last meeting with him, a 1-1 draw at Chelsea. I'm sure most readers will recall his character assassination attempt on Ashley Barnes following the red card for Chelsea's Matic in the fixture.

How fitting would a victory be at Old Trafford! Let's settle an old score against the 'chosen one', 'gloating one', 'smug one', 'contemptible one', 'sour-faced one' or downright 'nasty one'. Select as you find appropriate. Poor old Jose seems to be starting to have a bit of a difficult time in Manchester, not helped by a 4-0 thrashing at Chelsea last week. (..puts our 3-0 reverse there earlier into perspective doesn't it)? An unlikely victory for us at the 'Theatre of Dreams' would surely be his worst nightmare.

I note that in the week leading up to the game Ashley Barnes scores his first goal of the season in a Development squad outing against Bury. I wonder, would Sean be tempted to put him on the bench Saturday....

A memorable walking week ahead of the United clash with two of our classic rambles. First up was the now annual Dotcom Pendle walk on Tuesday. This is a walk traditionally led by Burnley contingent's stalwarts, the Preedys. Until last year this walk had been previously dogged by bad weather, involving on one famous occasion a very wet crossing of Ogden Clough masterminded by Teresa Preedy. Last time out however a more forgiving circular route from the Nick of Pendle saw all Dotcomers safely to the iconic summit and back.

The plan this year was to attempt to repeat the feat and on a lovely day a large turnout of Dotcomers, I believe 25, were ready and chomping at the bit. At this point one Preedy arrived minus his co-leader. On cross examination it transpired that Teresa had suffered a heavy and persistent nose bleed on awaking and by 9.15 there was no sign of it abating. Dave Preedy being the sensitive soul that he is immediately took her to Burnley General Hospital Urgent

Care Centre and deposited her there. Not wanting to disappoint his fellow walkers Dave bade Teresa his farewells and left her with her bus pass, but no lunch which he decided to take on the walk along with his own!

Suffice it to say that in good weather once again everybody made the Beacon where flags of St George were hoisted and the hill claimed for England as is our want. Interestingly also found at the beacon was a replica Burnley FC shirt belonging to a recently deceased fan, a fitting resting place on Burnley's Hill. Over lunch Dave informed us that though he had not left Teresa's lunch he had been kind enough to leave her some cash (I believe a small sum) to purchase some 'vittles'.

We later learned that Burnley General Urgent Care were unable to staunch the blood flow and Teresa was transferred to Blackburn A&E. After many enjoyable hours in the company of our East Lancashire amigos she was finally released at 14.45! We didn't ask what she had for lunch!

Thursday was another ramble which has become an annual standard much loved by the Burnley Contingent. This time it was a start from Stackhouse Lane, Settle (Giggleswick?), over the tops to the famous Elaine's Tearooms at Feizor, an absolute must stop for anybody walking this route. Fifteen excited Burnley souls turned out for this one no doubt many inspired by the thought of Elaine's Bacon Baps! After about four miles the refuelling stop was reached and although packed to the gunwales excellent service ensured a most pleasant refreshment halt.

From here the route takes us up and with great views of Pen-y-ghent on to Little Stainforth, and a lunch stop by the River Ribble at Stainforth Force. At this time of year it's an opportunity to see the salmon attempting to leap the falls. Once again they didn't let us down and a memorable half hour was spent watching them try and usually failing to make the jump. But, in the immortal words of Chumbawumba, they are a bit like Burnley FC, they get knocked down but they get up again. From here a lovely river walk down the Ribble towards Langcliffe and back via Stackhouse Lane to the cars. A recorded walk distance of 9.6 miles had our merry throng fair parched. The only possible solution, adjourn to the Boar's Head, Long Preston where an excellent pint of Kirkby Lonsdale Brewery's, Monumental, certainly hit the spot.

Game 10 - Saturday 29th October, 15.00 - Manchester United v Burnley

Once again this was always going to be a difficult game for me to follow the live action. Today my wife and I were travelling by car to Darlington to meet up with friends travelling by rail from Lincolnshire, for a two-night visit to daughter Stephanie and her partner Tom.

Before leaving home on the Saturday morning I note the Daily Mail devoting a two page spread to our friend Mr Mourinho's Manchester woes. A special report entitled 'Why Jose's life in Manchester is a DISASTER' tells how lonely he is and virtually a prisoner in his own hotel room. What a crying shame! Never mind Jose I'm sure the salary will more than compensate for it. A much more interesting article can be found a page or two further in. This is an interview by Dominic King with the Clarets in-form goalkeeper Tom Heaton. Tom spent from 2002 to 2010 with Manchester United without making a single first team appearance. In the article he goes on to tell his story of life after United and his subsequent rise to the top and a place in the England squad. I bet he is looking forward to a return to Old Trafford.

Also in the same 'daily rag' is a column entitled 'What's Hot, What's not' and in the What's Hot section we find a paragraph on Michael Keane. Ian Ladyman writes:

"The Burnley defender seems bound for Chelsea next summer but he has admirers in other places, too. Arsenal manager Arsene Wenger was full of compliments when he spoke to Sean Dyche after their teams' recent meeting at Turf Moor. Chelsea had better get a move on."

I smell a bidding war brewing.

An uneventful journey north east sees Julie and myself arriving at daughter Stephanie's place of employment, Mainsgill Farm shop on the A66, about 15.15. A quick coffee and scone in the café gives me the opportunity to login to the free Wi-Fi and I am delighted to see it is still goal less. As expected we are under heavy pressure and good old Tom is performing his customary heroics in goal. Much chattering between wife and daughter and much nervous following of the live text on the BBC Sports App gets us to half time level. Apparently United are claiming penalties with reckless abandon but fortunately referee Mark Clattenburg is sufficiently strong enough to be unswayed by the huge home crowd.

Clearly the referee's decisions are making the unhappy Jose even more miserable, and following a verbal altercation with the officials he is banished to the stands for the second half.

Half time signals the start of my short drive from Mainsgill to the Premier Inn Darlington, destination for the overnight stays. Once in the room I can get into their Wi-Fi and again am delighted the score is still 0-0. Furthermore our secret weapon Ashley 'Basher' Barnes is entering the fray as he replaces the recalled Andre Gray around the hour mark. A masterstroke by Mr Dyche I think, Ashley the scourge of Jose!

My nerves are jangling now as the room TV gets BBC Final Score updates. Next news is that United, still well on top but unable to breach our magnificent defence and keeper, are down to 10 men as Anders Herrera is dismissed for a second booking on 68 minutes. About 20 minutes to go with a man advantage, can we earn the unexpected point or even nick all three?

Time for another move now to the bar of the Hungry Horse to meet up with the friends from Lincolnshire. You may recall that Steve has decided he is now a Hull City fan, although he is currently very quiet about that. Pint in hand, Jeff Stelling on the big screen with Sky Soccer Saturday, time ticking on and still level. More good news before Steve's arrival in the bar Watford go a goal up against Hull, perfect timing. Palms are sweaty now, and the clock is showing 80 minutes gone. I can't hear the updates but I can see the screen with clock slowly ticking down.

89 minutes now, surely not another late goal decider. Into added time but how long? It is Old Trafford so if it was Fergie time it would be as much as required for United to score. However, it's not Fergie time it's Jose time and hopefully he has infuriated the officials sufficiently for them to be not so generous. 94 minutes now and still playing! Then suddenly a TV shot of Sean Dyche congratulating his team and it's all over. The relief is immense. A poor deluded young lad in the bar, resplendent in his United shirt, can hardly believe what he is seeing. And what is more, neither can I!

Another fantastic battling performance, this time a contest where the Clarets defence and surely currently the best keeper in England were impregnable. The pundits will say it was one way traffic but we don't care, we have another extremely unexpected point from a fixture where few visiting teams will get anything. Points from top sides such as Liverpool, Everton and now Manchester United are suddenly fuelling a self-belief and even I am beginning to wonder if the impossible can this time be achieved.

Result - Manchester United 0 – 0 Burnley

Burnley Team

Heaton, Lowton, Keane, Mee, Ward (Flanagan 44), Marney, Arfield, Hendrick, Gudmundsson (Boyd 85), Vokes, Gray (Barnes 60)

Subs Not Used - Robinson, Tarkowski, Kightly, Bamford

Manchester United Team

De Gea, Darmian, Rojo, Blind, Shaw, Herrera, Pogba, Lingard (Rooney 73), Mata (Fellaini 73), Rashford (Depay 82), Ibrahimovic

Subs Not Used – Romero, Schneiderlin, Carrick, Young

Attendance – 75,325

Season To Date – Played 10, Won 3, Drawn 2, Lost 5, Goals For 8, Goals Against 13, Points 11

League Position after Game 10 – 14th

That result certainly set the scene for a great weekend with daughter and friends in Darlington and Richmond. A quick mention here for two excellent real ale pubs in Darlington, Number Twenty 2, Coniscliffe Rd. and The Quakerhouse, 2 Mechanics Yard. Both pubs serving a good choice of real ales with friendly service. The Quakerhouse also features live music and though perhaps not the easiest place to find, is centrally located and well worth a visit.

Needless to say, Mourinho's antics captured all the headlines in the Sunday Papers and our magnificent achievement in getting the draw barely featured. Both TV and the Press made great play of United's dominance and waywardness, but little of our battling never-say-die performance. What does it matter? We don't care, our heroes assembled at a cost probably approaching one of Paul Pogba's bootlaces, shared the spoils at the 'Theatre of Dreams'. At the end of the day that may prove to be a very valuable point.

Rumour has it that despite his bad mood Mourinho did visit the Burnley dressing room and shake hands with the players. I wonder what sort of reception he got from Ashley Barnes! His little exchange of words with referee Clattenburg later earned him a £50,000 fine and one match touchline ban. I doubt the fine will unduly worry him but I wonder if the Boardroom moguls at Old Trafford are beginning to question their choice?

Sign at the corner of Belvedere Rd and Harry Potts Way announces the next game – IN THE PREMIER LEAGUE

Alastair Campbell tries his chat up line on Sean Dyche, who is singularly unimpressed!

"Well Alastair, I'm looking to get away from here as soon as possible. I don't want to end up like Mickey Duff."

"Who's for a beer?" A smiling Ashley Barnes indicates he's in.

Sam Vokes, could he be the next James Bond? Andre Gray certainly believes so.

Jim (Skipper of the Yard) graciously concedes 'the bet' to the author at a less than packed Turf Moor.

Who said we were rubbish. I hope the stone on top is not to keep somebody in! Spotted at a farm at Dean in Rossendale.

The BDF (Bacup Defence Force) prepare to repel the Lincoln 'Yellowbellies' ahead of the 5th Round Cup tie.

Burnley's iconic panopticon 'The Singing Ringing Tree'

The author (left) with Keith Holt - Two Burnley Wood lads at the base of Boulsworth Hill.

Dave Preedy exits the facilities at Newchurch in Pendle. We knew he'd had an operation but didn't know it was so serious!

The author (right) congratulates Dotcomer 'Blackburn John' on Rovers catastrophic campaign ending in relegation to League 1. Why is he smiling?

The author forced to pose by an inappropriate sign in Croston. He still managed a smile.

Burnley has the Singing Ringing Tree, Penwortham - an electricity substation. Say no more. Usain Bolt (Dotcom Romano) seems impressed though.

Burnley Contingent enjoy lunch salmon spotting at Stainforth.

A leaping salmon hangs in mid-air, just like the Clarets' strikers.

Burnley Contingent walkers debrief at The Rifle Volunteer.

Burnley Contingent – on Ilkla Moor Baht 'ats!

NOVEMBER

After last week's momentous outing at Old Trafford the first game in November sees us back at the Turf for the visit of Crystal Palace. The Eagles are landing here on the back of three consecutive defeats to West Ham, Leicester City and Liverpool. No doubt they'll be sharpening their talons for us. It was a rather unhappy affair last time they were here in the Premier League as we let slip a 2-0 lead to eventually lose the game 3-2 in the last minute. We can certainly do without that scenario this time. It is bonfire night so I think we can expect fireworks.

Game 11 - Saturday 5th November, 15.00 - Burnley v Crystal Palace

It's that time of year again where you may catch sight of a small group of Claret bedecked pensioners sitting in the freezing cold outside the Talbot Hotel quaffing beer with their thermals and mitts on. Now you might ask why don't you go inside the lovely warm pub and drink it? Well the answer is that the pub is packed to bursting with thirsty Clarets and the noise level is not conducive to our attempts at convivial conversation.

It's an interesting logistical exercise getting the beer. Obviously, we are dressed for the usual bitterly cold November day in multiple layers of thermal clothing. However, to purchase the beer we have to enter the aforementioned pub, which due to the presence of myriads of fans, is by now red hot! The bar is usually about three or four deep in customers so there is often a few minutes' wait to be served by the extremely efficient bar staff. The first thing that hits is a temporary blindness, this is not a medical condition but due to condensation caused by the warm air hitting my frozen spectacles. Next comes the rising body temperature fuelled by the many layers of clothing making the whole exercise something of an ordeal.

After many years of enduring these extreme fluctuations in temperature we have now hit on the answer. Before entering the pub the nominated beer purchaser, sadly usually me, removes as many layers of outer clothing as he deems fit. The foaming pints are then procured and the pub exited to the delightful 'beer garden' that is Ormerod Road, Burnley. At this point the discarded outer garments are rapidly re-donned. What a performance, and all for a couple of pints!

Once again a combination of being unable to get our small group to leave the pub, and traffic congestion at the Turf Moor turnstiles, means for the second consecutive game we miss the kick off. As I get to my seat I remark to my neighbour that once again I am arriving to the sight of an opposition corner kick. Not something I want to see so early in the game. However, on this occasion it is! The corner is cleared and Matt Lowton quickly spots Johan Berg Gudmundsson (JBG) free on the left. Matt's pass sees JBG go a bit wide but as his cross comes in Matt has made ground into the box. The ball lands at his feet and he shoots first time, then follows a little contretemps between centre back and goalkeeper which sees the ball land with Sam Vokes who gleefully pokes home from close range. What a start, ahead in two minutes a similar opening to the Liverpool home game.

I think here I can take a little credit for identifying the Palace keeper Mandanda as being 'dodgy' in our pre-match beer rambles. He certainly didn't cover himself in glory with that one. Following the shock early goal Palace settle and not unusually for a Burnley game begin to dominate possession. We, as is our style, absorb the pressure and look to break quickly. This we do with devastating effect as on 14 minutes, with Palace committing men forward, JBG is put clear on goal. His powerful left footer is blocked by the keeper but insufficiently to prevent it bouncing into the net. Once again 'dodgy keeper' costs them dearly.

No such dodgy keeper at the other end as Tom Heaton and the magnificent defence contain an expensive, and on paper, lethal attack force of Wilfried Zaha, Christian Benteke and Andros Townsend. With Steven Defour returned from injury, pulling the strings half time is reached with a comfortable two goal advantage.

I must admit that I expected something of an early onslaught at the start of the second half as the Eagles looked for a way back into the game. Initially this didn't materialise and a chance to go three up and kill the game went as Sam Vokes's effort is saved when perhaps a pass to unmarked Jeff Hendrick would have done the trick. The third goal in a 2-0 game is always a vital one; usually it signals game over, whereas a goal back means it's game on.

Palace boss Pardew decided to change formation around the hour mark, introducing another striker in Connor Wickham. His impact was almost immediate as he fired home from close range a perfect cross from the now increasingly dangerous Zaha. Suddenly the visitors were scenting blood and in the ascendancy. Increasing pressure had us fearing the worst and memories of a frittered 2-0 lead in this fixture last time were re-surfacing.

These were substantially greater on 81 minutes as ironically from a Burnley attack Palace broke quickly. Townsend's run down the left saw his cross handled by Lowton and the inevitable penalty stroked home by Benteke. Disaster! What had looked at half time a comfortable home victory now looked like a struggle to keep a point.

But, cometh the hour, cometh the man. Step forward Ashley Barnes, well step forward after being left waiting, stripped to come on for in excess of five minutes. With 85 minutes on the clock could Ash, who had been dogged by serious injury, conjure something?

On 90 minutes the fourth official signalled five minutes added time, and unbelievably on 94 minutes another last gasp goal won the match. Dean Marney's determination won the ball in a Palace attack. He fed Ashley on the half way line and with the visitors heavily committed forward the break was on. Ashley advanced and spotting JBG to his right pushed the ball out to him, unfortunately the pass took JBG a little wide. Undaunted our Icelander, cool as a cucumber, returned it right footed into the box into the path of the onrushing Barnes. Without hesitation 'Basher' smashed it home left footed and surely that was that! Not quite as from the re-start the dangerous Andros Townsend thumped a left footer against the base of Heaton's left post which thankfully rebounded to safety.

What a fantastic finish to a very exciting game and a great ending for the popular Ashley Barnes. Let the fireworks begin! A fourth home victory and the points total on to 14, Europe here we come.

Result - Burnley (Vokes 2, Gudmundsson 14, Barnes 90+4) 3 - 2 Crystal Palace (Wickham 60, Benteke 81 pen)

Burnley Team

Heaton, Lowton, Keane, Mee, Flanagan, Marney, Defour (Tarkowski 74), Hendrick (Barnes 85), Gudmundsson, Vokes, Arfield (Boyd 65)

Subs Not Used - Robinson, Kightly, Gray, Bamford

Crystal Palace Team

Mandanda, Ward, Dann. Delaney, Kelly (Fryers 59), Cabaye, McArthur (Ledley 87), Puncheon (Wickham 59), Townsend, Zaha, Benteke

Subs Not Used - Hennessy, Tomkins, Flamini, Lee

Attendance - 19,196

Season To Date - Played 11, Won 4, Drawn 2, Lost 5, Goals For 11, Goals Against 15, Points 14

League Position after Game 11 - 9th

The result took us up into the top half of the table reaching the dizzy heights of ninth. Who would have predicted that at the season's start? We must remember though that the position maybe skewed by the fact that we have played seven of our eleven games on home soil. In the second half of the season we will have to face four consecutive away fixtures so we need to try and build as big a buffer as possible ahead of this.

How great was that to see Barnes get the winning goal. Underrated when he first arrived here, and struggling to make an impact when the Ings/Vokes partnership was going strong, he patiently waited his chance. When it came in the last Premier League season he took it with both hands, or should that be feet, and quickly established himself as a key player. His very effective contribution was halted by a bad cruciate knee ligament injury in the last Premier League fixture at Aston Villa which side-lined him for almost the whole of last season. This was then followed by a niggling hamstring injury which meant he missed almost all the first ten games in this campaign. Saturday's winning goal therefore must have brought him, the fans and teammates, immense pleasure and tremendous relief. Let's hope that the goal will kick-start a successful season for a real genuine fans favourite.

How fitting too that following two home fixtures where we have been denied favourable results by added time goals, the last two fixtures have reversed that trend and seen us claim maximum points at the death. Certainly, for the moment at least, fortune - good and bad - appears to be balanced.

There's no Premier League action on the coming weekend as once again we are into World Cup Qualifying fixtures. Our players depart to their respective International gatherings whilst my wife and I depart to Harrogate for a night at the International Centre with Jools Holland and his Rhythm and Blues Orchestra. Always a good night with Jools and his guest singers and this one proves to be no exception. We can only marvel at our piano maestro's dexterity with the keys and the evergreen Ruby Turner steals the show with her usual heartfelt performance.

Harrogate is a fine place for an overnight stay with lots of good eating places and no shortage of bars. A mention here for Christie's Bar, close to the International Centre, and with a good atmosphere and choice of real ales. On this occasion, I opted for a few pints of Daleside Blonde, produced by Daleside Brewery in Harrogate - an excellent choice.

We had a great weekend and will return in February for an evening at the Harrogate Theatre with showbiz legend and raconteur, Count Arthur Strong. A funny man is the Count, the creation of Yorkshire comic Steve Delaney. In his forthcoming show he will attempt, in his own inimitable manner, with his frequent use of malapropisms, pomposity and absent mindedness, to remember and recreate his favourite musical, 'The Sound of Mucus'. I can't wait!

An interesting article in the Mail on Sunday Sports section of 13th November reports on a global survey of the pay of almost 10,000 sportsmen, at 333 teams, in seven sports across 17 of the world's richest leagues. Whilst the top three in the rich list come from NBA Basketball teams and the New York Yankees Baseball team, the figures show that the Premier League remains by far the best paid football league on the planet.

The average basic first team pay in the Premier League is apparently £2,438,275, or £48,766 a week. This figure is almost double that in La Liga (Spain) which is just more than £1.2m per player per year, or £24,786 a week.

Unsurprisingly Manchester United emerge as the best paid football team in the world, man for man. The average basic first team wage at Old Trafford equates to a staggering £110,962 a week! Barcelona come in second at £108k/pw, followed by Manchester City, Real Madrid, and Chelsea. Premier League teams dominate the top 20 earners places with no less than 11 clubs. All the 20 Premier League outfits feature in the top 50 best paid teams in world football.

Equally unsurprisingly, Burnley occupy 50th position being the lowest earners in the Premier League. According to these figures, though who knows if they are true, our players earn £954k per year, or £18,000 per week. This figure dwarfs that of Glasgow giants Rangers £316k (£6k/pw) and even tops that of Celtic £717k (£13k/pw). The nearest Premier League clubs to us are Bournemouth £1.1m (£21k/pw), Hull City and Middlesbrough £1.22m (£23k/pw). Some interesting figures there, mind boggling even, and don't forget these are basic pay figures presumably excluding bonuses.

Topically, Crystal Palace players are well paid ranking 20th position with £1.96m/pa (£37k/pw). I think in view of their recent defeat to a team earning half their basic pay they should be heartily ashamed of themselves!

Tuesday 15th October signals another important date in the Dotcom walkers calendar, the annual quiz. This time the venue was The Highwayman, at Nether Burrow near Kirkby Lonsdale. A bit of a run for the Burnley Contingent meaning an early start, perhaps a ploy to tire us out. Once again its billed as Burnley versus the Rest of the World and unfortunately our current losing streak in the 'challenges' shows no sign of abating. This time we trail in a creditable fourth of four teams. The less said the better!

John W did have his own answers to some of the questions to which the correct ones eluded us. Most of these answers were unprintable and I leave you to surmise what his answer to the question, 'What would a German do with a Handy?' might be…

In fairness our cause was not helped by the loss of the full round of music questions at which I'm sure we would have shone. Question master Chris 'Bamber' McCann for some reason best known to himself, tipped a pint of Thwaites's Wainwright Ale into his own laptop computer on which the music round was set. This action did not go down well with the said laptop which then steadfastly refused to 'play ball', or for that matter music. You could say, in the words of singer songwriter Don McLean, 'it was the day the music died'.

One saving grace was a FREE lunch of Lamb Hotpot followed by Lemon Cheesecake, made possible thanks to the generosity of Leader Bob Clare and 'Satnav' Dave Johnstone. A great day out again enjoyed by the swelled ranks of Dotcomers, 29 in total this time. That is certainly testimony to the pulling power of a free lunch! Incidentally, a German would make telephone calls with a Handy, it's what they call a mobile phone.

The evening of the 15th also is a memorable one for goalkeeper Tom Heaton who wins his second full England cap getting a second half substitute appearance in the International friendly versus Spain at Wembley. Leading 1-0 at half time Tom is handed the gloves replacing Joe Hart. Shortly after the restart the lead is extended to two. That marks the start of something of a fightback by the Spanish but entering the last minute Tom remains unbeaten. Is he going to keep a clean sheet and maintain his 100% record of not conceding a goal for England? Unfortunately not as he is beaten by an unstoppable shot and worse to follow on 96 minutes as the visitors equalise. Still it's a good result against one of the world's top teams and just reward for Tom's fine performances this season in the Premier League.

Just straying a little 'off piste' here, I saw something on TV the other night that made me sit up and think. It was a programme about a zoo where two lions, male and female, were having difficulties of a sexual nature. It seems that the two had become more like best buddies than rampant young lovers. The problem seemed to be that the lioness had lost interest in the male, seeing him as a bit of on old fart. In an effort to rekindle some fire in the relationship the zoo keepers hit on an idea.

The plan was to hang carcasses of meat in the lion's enclosure the notion being that the male lion would then attack the offering tearing it from the tree. The female lion would be so impressed by the male's macho performance that she would regain her lost interest in him. Larger carcasses were introduced daily and Leo's performance was so impressive that normal sexual service was soon resumed.

Now that gave me an idea that may benefit the NHS service substantially. Why not try something along the same lines in Burnley. Instead of doling out prescriptions for Testosterone and Viagra, why not suspend pork pies from the bedroom ceiling in houses where the action is perhaps a little slow. The sight of a naked chap tearing his prey from the roof and decrusting it with vigour would surely be irresistible to any self-respecting Burnley lass. For non pork pie aficionados, perhaps black puddings might do the trick and perhaps a quorn substitute for our vegetarian friends. Just a thought!

Anyway, enough of that, it's time to get back to the serious business, football. International break over and done with, the weekend of 19th November sees a return to Premier League action, but not for the Clarets. We will bring up the rear of the weekend's action with a televised Monday evening fixture at West Bromwich Albion. Not a happy hunting ground of late for us, our last win there being in December 1969; time to nail that hoodoo. Ahead of the game the weekend's results leave us in eleventh place, one point and one place above our opponents, so a point or three would greatly help the cause.

Game 12 - Monday 21st November, 20.00 - West Bromwich Albion v Burnley

A foul day in both Burnley and the West Midlands precedes the clash at the Hawthorns. Cold, windy and extremely wet, in fact a typical November day.

The Clarets make one change in the line-up with fit again Stephen Ward replacing Jon Flanagan who drops to the bench. It's a typical line up for the Albion, stuffed full of guys from the land of the giants, and the usual physical encounter looks to be on the cards.

Whatever the game plan was it was quickly derailed as we go a goal down in four minutes. A cut back from the right wing into the box meets the stretching Dean Marney who simply pokes the ball to the lurking Matt Phillips in the six-yard box. He can't believe his luck and promptly swivels and fires home.

A most un-Burnley like performance sees us having the early lion's share of possession, something which never happens. The first 15 minutes possession statistics show West Bromwich Albion (WBA) on 32%, and Burnley 68%. A chance falls on 14 minutes to Jeff Hendrick but it comes to nought.

Costly that, as this is quickly followed on 16 minutes by a second Albion goal, again on the break. If the first derailed the game plan, this one just about destroyed it. Two goals down is not a good position to be in for a team that has managed only one away goal all season.

The game continues in the same vein, Albion playing like Burnley at home, soaking up pressure and playing on the break. We are enjoying lots of possession but making no impact.

On 37 minutes it's game over, if it wasn't already, as Darren Fletcher nets from close range from another WBA counter. Help, stop the game now this is getting embarrassing!

I've said on many occasions that possession statistics are nonsense and this is a classic example. We have had 61% of the ball, but Albion have three goals from eight attempts compared to our two efforts on goal.

Half time is reached fortunately without further disaster. My summation of our first half would be, defence fragile, attack punchless, prognosis hopeless!

The start of the second half unsurprisingly sees a change as Ashley Barnes is introduced at the expense of Steven Defour. We now revert to our previously favoured 4-4-2 in the hope of creating a bit more bite up front. Ashley is soon making his presence felt with his physical style and at least the Albion defenders now know someone is there.

It's all to no avail as on 64 minutes Man of the Match Salomon Rondon makes it 4-0. Andre Gray replaces Sam Vokes on 70 minutes and George Boyd is on for Johan Berg Gudmundsson with 11 to play. It's a bit late for a comeback I fear! The game rolls on to its inevitable conclusion as Albion are happy with their four-goal haul and we are incapable of troubling them.

Thankfully the final whistle goes and brings down the curtain on another horror show at the Hawthorns. A massive rethink is now needed on tactics away from home. Once again its goals against - plenty, goals for - bugger all! After three magnificent results ahead of the International break, we are now back to earth with a bang! Manchester City at the Turf Saturday, what next!

Result – West Bromwich Albion (Phillips 4, Morrison 16, Fletcher 37, Rondon 64) 4 – 0 Burnley

Burnley Team

Heaton, Lowton, Keane, Mee, Ward, Marney, Defour (Barnes 45), Hendrick, Gudmundsson (Boyd 79), Vokes (Gray 70), Arfield

Subs Not Used – Robinson, Kightly, Flanagan, Tarkowski

West Bromwich Albion Team

Foster, Dawson, McAuley, Evans, Nyom, Fletcher, Yacob, Brunt, Morrison (Gardner 83), Phillips (McClean 75), Rondon (Robson-Kanu 79)

Subs Not Used – Leko, Olsson, Palmer, Galloway

Attendance – 23,016

Season To Date – Played 12, Won 4, Drawn 2, Lost 6, Goals For 11, Goals Against 19, Points 14

League Position after Game 12 – 12th

On Thursday 24th November, it comes as no real surprise to learn that last season's hero Joey Barton is once again training with the Clarets. Joey's short lived reign at Glasgow Rangers has ended predictably in tears. He is now out of contract and attempting to maintain a good level of fitness in order to secure a new contract with a new club in

January. Who that will be remains to be seen but Sean Dyche is keen to repay Joey for last season's efforts by affording him use of our facilities and staff.

These days I find that after a crushing defeat such as the one at WBA I am losing a little of my love for the beautiful game. Or I believe more with Premier League football, where it is an almost impossible challenge for us, the 'have-nots', to compete with the all-powerful city teams. Even newly established Premier League clubs the size of Albion have transfer and wage budgets that dwarf ours.

Going into games like today makes me feel a little like the condemned man, with almost a feeling of dread. This can't be right surely, it's supposed to be enjoyable. I think the problem is that now the result is all that matters and the enjoyment of the spectacle has been lost.

However, after reading an article about George Boyd in the Daily Mail on the morning of this game I think my attitude is changing. In it George says, 'After West Brom, the manager (Sean Dyche) said, "Forget about it, nobody has died". He was fuming about the performance but there is no point sitting here thinking about the disappointment. We've got something to be excited about - Man City on TV. We've got a great chance to come back'!

Bring it on!

Game 13 - Saturday 26th November, 12.30 - Burnley v Manchester City

After a bitterly cold night it's a glorious sunny day in Burnley. A shortened morning Gym session and a quick bite of lunch then off to Turf Moor for the 12.30 kick off. I'm wearing so many layers topped off with thermal hat and mittens that I could be kitted out for a Polar expedition. But then again so is everybody else. On arrival the ground is full to capacity and the crowd not a bit cowed by the drubbing at WBA.

Devastating news as I learn Tom Heaton misses the game with a calf injury and his place goes to Paul Robinson. Our back-up keeper, a former England International, is now 37 years of age and without a senior game in over two years. Let's hope he hasn't lost his agility and confidence. There's one more change as George Boyd comes back replacing Scott Arfield who drops to the bench.

Where normally in these fixtures I would be fearing the worst, strangely today perhaps because of the lovely weather, I'm not.

It's a fairly slow start to the game and there are no early signs that City are going to overwhelm us. Indeed we are extremely unfortunate not to be awarded a penalty for a blatant push in the box by Otamendi on Hendrick as he cushions a Defour free kick on his chest. TV replays suggest the assistant referee could not see the challenge because the sun was in his eyes. It could only happen in Burnley in late November! Perhaps our visitors are feeling the strain of their midweek Champions League exertions against Borussia Moenchengladbach.

Then what a turn up on 14 minutes. A free kick to the Clarets is only partially cleared to just outside the 18-yard box. There lying in wait is Dean Marney who promptly smashes it back on the volley through a crowd of players and into the bottom corner of the net. Unbelievably we are one up! Great, only 76 minutes to hang on.

Deano is certainly having an eventful day, almost his next action is to get himself a booking and in the process, injure himself. Unable to shake it off he is replaced before half time by Scott Arfield.

Our goal has certainly stung City out of their earlier lethargy and on 37 minutes they level with a scrappy, scrambled goal from a corner. That's typical of our season so far, the goals we score are often beautifully crafted, whilst the one's we concede are often miscued rebounds.

Not long after another serious setback as Johan Berg Gudmundsson (JBG from now on, I'm not going to keep typing that lot!), goes down with what looks like a serious hamstring injury and his day is also over. His replacement is James Tarkowski who again will play in an unaccustomed midfield role.

Half time 1-1, and I think it's fair to say we are worthy of it.

I'm still soaking up the unseasonal sunshine but expecting a big push from the 'Blue Mooners' in the second half as they pursue maximum points in their title chase. Indeed the pressure does start to build and we seem to coping quite well defensively but with little to offer going forward.

Tragedy strikes again on the hour as our illustrious visitors scramble another extremely untidy goal that the scorer Aguero knows precious little about. Once again we have chances to clear the ball but defenders get in each other's way and the ball trickles in.

Now I'm sort of half expecting the flood gates to open but it doesn't happen. We keep our shape and with about 10 minutes to go we are going to 'go for it'. Off comes Steven

Defour, after what for him was a marathon stint, and on comes 'Basher' Barnes. Ashley's first action is of course to concede a foul - well they'll certainly know he has arrived.

We promptly throw the kitchen sink at them, not literally of course, and rein in crosses and long throws to our now twin spearhead of Vokes and Barnes. Unfortunately some desperate defending and a couple of good saves from the City keeper Bravo keep us at bay.

The game ends 1-2, and we are beaten but definitely not bowed! Team and manager leave the field to a standing ovation for a bloody good effort!

A special mention here for stand in keeper Paul Robinson who took his rare opportunity magnificently. He made some outstanding saves, exuded confidence, and proved an admirable cover for Tom Heaton.

Also, a tremendous substitute's performance from James Tarkowski. Once again played out of position but putting in a very influential stint. His impressive physique, here being a match for the visitors Yaya Toure, allied to no little skill may be just what we have been missing. I think 'Tarka' may well play an important role in the coming weeks.

Result - Burnley (Marney 14) 1 - 2 (Aguero, 37,60) Manchester City

Burnley Team

Robinson, Lowton, Keane, Mee, Ward, Marney (Arfield 40), Defour (Barnes 80), Hendrick, Gudmundsson (Tarkowski 43), Vokes, Boyd

Subs Not Used - Pope, Kightly, Flanagan, Gray

Manchester City Team

Bravo, Sagna, Otamendi, Kolarov, Clichy, Sterling (Sane 57), Fernando, Toure, Fernandhino, Nolito (De Bruyne 78) Aguero (Navas 89)

Subs Not Used - Caballero, Zabaleta, Silva, Iheanacho

Attendance - 21,794

Season To Date - Played 13, Won 4, Drawn 2, Lost 7, Goals For 12, Goals Against 21, Points 14

League Position after Game 13 - 13th

On Monday 28th I learn by email from Dotcom leader Bob Clare, that my walking buddy, Brian Higginson (Scouse Brian) has suffered a stroke on Saturday. That comes as a real shock and I hope that there is a positive outcome for a very popular and knowledgeable guy. Brian has been a great help and inspiration to me in producing these diaries in digital format. Once again, it's a timely reminder that we should live for today.

By Friday the 2nd December Brian's condition has improved sufficiently for him to be transferred to a stroke rehabilitation ward at Chorley Hospital. Initially his speech had been impaired to the point where he felt he was talking like a 'drunken Scouser'. It was then pointed out that he always talked like a 'drunken Scouser'. Hopefully he is now on the mend as he is blaming Brexit for his condition!

DECEMBER

Thursday 1st December provides another reminder of our advancing age, in the eyes of others that is, if not ourselves. A Burnley Contingent walk was planned from Nuttall Park, Ramsbottom, to Peel Tower taking in a stretch of the River Irwell through Stubbins. On arrival at the start point in the park, the usual requirement for a bunch of geriatrics is of course toilet facilities. Needless to say, Nuttall Park's public lavatories were locked up!

Just as we were about to head off all booted and weatherproofed, a minibus drew up consisting of driver, 'responsible other adult', and assorted teenagers dressed for a day in the open. The driver kindly asked if we wished to use the toilet facilities as he possessed the keys being a 'friend of Nuttall Park'. Whilst some of the group availed themselves of this godsend the driver went on to tell us how inspirational we were to the children! The kids on seeing our merry band had commented how good it was to see 'old people' getting out and enjoying the countryside. How touching!

It's funny though we don't see ourselves as old, in our heads we are about the same age as the kids. Is that dementia? Our walks always contain the same mickey-taking and personal abuse as I'm sure does any teenage gathering. Anyway, I bet we could teach those kids a thing or two about mental toughness if not physical fitness.

Once again an excellent wander and with the added relief of not being shot at on the army firing range on Holcombe moor and finished off with a beer stop at one of our favourite hostelries, The Griffin in Haslingden, home of the

Rossendale Brewery offering an excellent choice of beers, very reasonably priced and a very welcoming unpretentious pub.

December, sure to be an important month due to the high number of games to be played, kicks off with a tricky away fixture at Stoke City. Mind you with our away record any fixture is bound to be tricky!

According to the local press the injury situation which at the end of last week's game appeared serious, seems to be easing. Latest information is that both Tom Heaton and Dean Marney may make the Stoke game although JBG will definitely be out with his hamstring injury. I'm never quite sure whether these press leaks are to be believed or whether they are a ploy to con the opposition. Anyway, let's hope in this case they are true as we still have the best part of a month, and six fixtures to complete, before the transfer window re-opens. No less than four of these games will be against opposition currently involved in the survival struggle. That will take us to the end of 2016 and exactly to the mid-point of the season.

Game 14 – Saturday 3rd December, 15.00 – Stoke City v Burnley

Once again this is a difficult game for me to follow. Christmas comes but once a year and it would appear it is coming pretty quickly now in the Haworth household. My Saturday afternoon is mapped out for me by 'Wife Planner' with shopping trips scheduled for B&Q, Sports Direct and Sainsburys. I've switched mobile data on and also alerts on my phone's BBC Sports App.

The first notification comes through as we hit B&Q - it's the team line-up and there's certainly been some changes.

Paul Robinson continues in goal for the still injured Tom Heaton. In defence Jon Flanagan gets a start in his favoured right back role at the expense of Matt Lowton. In midfield Scott Arfield reclaims his place in the absence of JBG, George Boyd is the other wide midfielder and Jeff Hendrick and the fit again Dean Marney take the centre berths. Up front there's no Sam Vokes who drops to the bench and in come both Ashley Barnes and Andre Gray. Looks like not just a change of personnel but also a change of system back to 4-4-2 as Sean attempts to rectify our away day blues.

Unfortunately, there may have been many changes in personnel and formation but none in our travelling fortunes! We've left B&Q and fitted in an unscheduled stop at Boundary Mill before I get the next tingling in my trouser pocket. Yes, it's a phone alert as we enter Sports Direct! I hesitate to look, hoping for the best but fearing the worst. True enough my worst fears are confirmed as I see the dreaded 1-0 scoreline, and Walters 20' as the scorer. Not long to wait for the next trouser sensation which comes as I gaze at wall-to-wall pairs of trainers, whilst attempting to avoid tripping over unruly kids. Sure enough still 10 minutes short of half time and already two goals down.

That's it for shopping for me at Sports Direct, surely one of the most unlucky Clarets stores in town. I beat a hasty retreat to Sainsburys where at least we keep out our hosts till half time. I've lost my appetite for shopping now (not that I had one in the first place) and I'm off home for the start of Round 2.

Radio Lancashire commentator Scott Read and summariser ex Claret Paul Weller reckon Stoke had been pretty impressive first half. Paul however, not a man to mince his words, also feels that they didn't need to be! A rather subdued review of our first half efforts from the pair.

There's not much to say about the second half as the Potters satisfied that their day's work is done sit back to contain us and catch us on the counter. A better second half from us but still nowhere near enough, and we end once again with a pointless trip home. Our friend Mr Weller is pretty scathing about Andre Gray's contribution and Jon Flanagan also comes in for a slating. Don't pull any punches Paul, tell it like it is.

Oh dear, back to the drawing board!

Result - Stoke City (Walters 20, Muniesa 35) 2 - 0 Burnley

Burnley Team

Robinson, Flanagan (Tarkowski 81), Keane, Mee, Ward, Arfield (Kightly 90), Marney, Hendrick, Boyd (Vokes 77), Barnes, Gray

Subs Not Used – Pope, Lowton, Bamford, Defour

Stoke City Team

Grant, Johnson, Martins Indi, Muniesa, Pieters, Imbula, Adam (Whelan 87), Biram Diouf, Shaqiri (Allen 61), Arnautovic (Crouch 71), Walters

Subs Not Used – Given, Sobhi, Krkic, Bony

Attendance – 27,306

Season To Date – Played 14, Won 4, Drawn 2, Lost 8, Goals For 12, Goals Against 23, Points 14

League Position after Game 14 - 15th

Monday 15th December and once again I'm looking forward to a Dotcom walking day, an ideal opportunity to take the mind off the depressing sequence of away performances. Fortunately, tomorrow we shouldn't find the Preston mob in gloating mood as they also suffered defeat at Sheffield Wednesday on Saturday. What's more they even contrived to get two players sent off for fighting…each other!!!

This week will not be a scenic walk in the glorious East Lancashire hill country but can probably be best described as the 'Penwortham Plod'. Previous visits to this neck of the woods have given us the dubious delights of Penwortham Power station, and the litter strewn banks of the tidal River Ribble. The walk will be led by Chris 'One Direction' McCann, not so titled because of his youthful boy band looks, but rather for his ability to only lead walks that go in one direction. That is, straight along the river bank. Last time he took to 'leading' in tour guide fashion by holding up a placard which read 'Follow Me', God knows what tomorrow will bring.

Still there is one positive to the walk, a pub lunch! What's more at a Pensioners special price of £5.95! The down side is that it is in a pub called the Sir Tom Finney in which we will no doubt have loads of PNE memorabilia to endure.

Monday evening saw the draw for the FA Cup 3rd Round. The competition in recent years has not thrown up many favourable ties for us, i.e. one's at home that we can win easily against non-league opposition. Tonight's draw is no exception as we get Sunderland at the Stadium of Light! With our current away form I guess this means we can forget cup glory and concentrate on Premier League survival. The tie will be played only a matter of days after our New Year's Eve clash in the league with the Mackems. I know which one I'd prefer to win.

Well, it's Wednesday evening now and I have to report that Penwortham certainly lived up to its reputation. There were pylons aplenty, an occasional ramp (or what the Preston and South Ribble mob call a hill!), and a big river, though the tide was out. The North Enders did attempt to enlighten us with facts and trivia relating to Preston, but of course it went straight in one ear and out the other. 'One Direction' Chris managed to navigate the route surprisingly successfully, considering by his own admittance that he didn't know some of the paths existed! The icing on the cake however was the friendly welcome at the Sir Tom Finney, and an excellent choice of real ales. Today we opted for Jennings Cumberland Ale, pity there was only time for one. Best of all however was the fact that the price was £4.95 for lunch and not £5.95 as previously billed. That also included pre-walk tea or coffee, that's excellent value. If you ever find yourself in Penwortham (though why the hell you would) give the pub a look, don't be put off by the name.

Game 15 - Saturday 10th December, 15.00 - Burnley v Bournemouth

Today we welcome back our old friend and ex-manager Eddie Howe and his Bournemouth team, fresh on the back of a rousing comeback victory last week over Liverpool. Trailing 3-1 late in the game the Cherries managed a startling revival to take all three points with a 4-3 victory. Let's hope they've got that out of their system by now, but they are sure to come here full of confidence.

For December in Burnley it's an unseasonably warm day with the temperatures reaching a sub-tropical 12 degrees!

After the customary pre-match pints in an unusually less than crowded pub we make our way to the ground. Once again the streets seem relatively devoid of people and we wonder where everyone has gone. Surely not Christmas shopping! On arrival at the Turf the mystery is solved, they are all stood queuing at the turnstiles. Not to worry we manage to take our seats in time for kick-off.

It's squad rotation time again as fit again Tom Heaton reclaims his place, as do Matt Lowton, Steven Defour, and Sam Vokes. Dropping to the bench are Paul Robinson, Ashley Barnes, Andre Gray and Jon Flanagan.

The game starts with us playing in our favoured first half direction towards the Cricket Field end. Both teams are quickly into their stride, and our visitors in a high viz, luminescent lemon outfit are certainly catching the eye. I remark to my mate, John W that this looks like a game between two fairly evenly matched teams. I'm quite enjoying this one and feeling relatively confident.

That confidence is certainly boosted within three spectacular minutes early in the game. First off is a magnificent goal from record signing Jeff Hendrick, who it's fair to say has been coming in for some criticism on the fans messageboard. Jeff I think rammed some of his critics words back down their throats with this one. I think its best summed up in the words of Mail on Sunday reporter Jack Gaughan;

"The first came via Jeff Hendrick, the £10.5m record signing who pundits were claiming could find himself nestled inside a goal of the season list moments after Artur Boruc was beaten on 13 minutes.

And quite right too. This was a moment of absolute beauty, absolute quality. Hendrick killed Matthew Lowton's forceful pass dead in mid-air, used his knee to tee up the strike and then cut across the ball to send a crashing effort way into Boruc's top left-hand post"

What a stunner! The second followed quickly as our visitors reeling from the shock conceded once again, this time a goal of not such beauty but of equal value. It was the unmarked Ben Mee's header from a corner that deflected off a Bournemouth player to deceive the keeper - who could only fumble it into the path of a grateful Stephen Ward who prodded home. I bet Wardy enjoyed that, it was his first Premier League goal in 1804 days!

As our visitors slowly recovered from the shock and we took our foot of the gas, the game sauntered towards half time with no real alarms. The fourth official signalled one minute added time and this duly passed without incident. However, our friend the referee had his own idea of how long a minute was and deemed it to be more like 120 seconds than 60. Our lads clearly deciding it was time for the half time break promptly downed tools and allowed the Cherries a soft goal back right at the death. Just time to take the kick-off then the whistle blows for the end of the period.

What a disappointing and a deflating end was that. What should have been a comfortable half time lead had now shrunk to a narrow one and handed the initiative back to our opponents.

That late goal has, I must admit, taken the edge off what had been so far a thoroughly enjoyable Saturday afternoon. We can now look forward to an early onslaught from Bournemouth as they look to get back on level terms and maintain their momentum. As expected they do have the early upper hand, but then a crucial double substitution by Sean Dyche swings the game back our way. On 55 minutes Dyche introduces strikers Andre Gray and Ashley Barnes to replace Sam Vokes, and who else but Steven Defour. The visitors respond by introducing England man and Arsenal loanee Jack Wilshere, who up till this point had been bench warming.

In an attempt to stretch their defence and stem their attacking flow Sean has opted for the physicality of Barnes and the pace of Gray. The effect is felt immediately as we now start to take the game back to them and chances are being created. There are close calls from both Barnes and Gray, and then on 75 minutes it's surely game over. A move down the left flank breaks down but the ball is only cleared as far as Gray who backheels into the path of Boyd whose thumping shot is never going anywhere bar the back of the net.

Bournemouth can't repeat the comeback miracle from 3-1 down for the second week in succession, or can they? You just never know with the Clarets. With time running out and nothing to lose our visitors go for broke. But it's still the Clarets making chances as Gray outpaces the defence in a quick counter which comes to nought, and Arfield muffs a chance he should have done better with. Some nervous moments ensue, particularly as Afobe has the ball in the net but it's chalked off for handball. However, time rolls remorselessly on and we are entering the dreaded added time.

The fourth official signals four extra minutes, which to this referee probably means eight! To be fair he is probably being influenced by some pretty blatant time-wasting by our heroes. Just to make life a little more uncomfortable, early in the piece Bournemouth pull a goal back with a fierce shot following a short corner. However, there is insufficient time for another and a fifth precious home win is in the bag.

Just a word here for the lovely people at GM Fitted Furniture, an ex-employee of whom is a good neighbour of mine. Could they please in the interests of Claret's fans sanity stop sponsoring 'added time'. Don't they realise that in most cases we are perfectly happy to do without it. Save your money lads, and we can all go home relaxed. Ian Jones, be an even better neighbour and have a word with the powers that be!

Result - Burnley (Hendrick 13, Ward 16, Boyd 75) 3 - 2 (Afobe 45+2, Daniels 90+1) Bournemouth

Burnley Team

Heaton, Lowton, Keane, Mee, Ward, Arfield, Marney, Hendrick, Defour (Barnes 55), Boyd (Tarkowski 90+2), Vokes (Gray 55)

Subs Not Used - Robinson, Flanagan, Bamford, Kightly

Bournemouth Team

Boruc, Francis, Cook, Ake, Daniels, A. Smith, Gosling (King 72) , Arter, Fraser (Pugh 81), Wilson (Wilshere 59), Afobe

Subs Not Used - Federici, Mings, B. Smith, Ibe

Attendance - 19,680

Season To Date - Played 15, Won 5, Drawn 2, Lost 8, Goals For 15, Goals Against 25, Points 17

League Position after Game 15 - 13th

Ahead of the Bournemouth game I had been alerted by text from Chris 'One Direction' McCann that Dotcom leader Bob Clare had once again been reverting to his old tricks. Sure enough following soon after is an email from Bob entitled "In the LEP - again!" Attached to the email is a report published in the Lancashire Evening Post (LEP) of the recent Penwortham walk. The article was littered with Bob's fictitious trademark quotes attributed to various individuals, for example;

Walk leader Chris McCann (pictured fifth from right) said:

"It has to be said Penwortham does not have a big chapter in the annals of walking. But the route we took through to the river and back by Hurst Grange Park was varied and interesting"

Chris of course claims no knowledge of uttering any such nonsense. But worse is to come as I find I have also been talking to the press:

There was also a strong contingent from Burnley in the party. Peter Haworth (seventh from left) said: *"Aside from the fact of starting a walk named after Preston North End's most famous player, the true highlight was another chance to see Penwortham's National Grid Electricity station."*

He goes on to attribute further comments to soon to be crowned, 'Dotcom Moll of the Year 2016' Barbara Blackwell, and even the pub landlady gets dragged into the act.

Needless to say none of the above had been said, or if so not in those terms, but to make matters even worse Chris and myself had been identified in the picture making us even bigger targets of ridicule! Mr Clare will be receiving a communication from our lawyers presently.

Back to the football and in a hectic week next up come two away fixtures in far away London town.

Game 16 - Wednesday 14th December, 19.45 - West Ham United v Burnley

It's the first visit ever for Burnley to the London Stadium, the new home of West Ham and former Olympic Games stadium of London 2012. The Hammers seem to be having some problems adjusting to their new surroundings and poor home form has contributed to a slow start to their season. Let's hope we can take advantage of this and get some much needed away points.

I struggled to follow the first 25 minutes of this fixture as I had more pressing matters. My tea! I had to settle for goal alerts from my phone via the BBC Sports app. I don't have to wait long as within a minute of kick-off I get the first notification signal. Fearing the worst I check my phone but fortunately it's just an email offering to sell me tickets for UB40, The Christmasaurus, Alice Cooper....

I'm following the match stats also and it comes as no surprise to learn that we are having little of the ball. Twenty five minutes in and I'm now also listening to Radio Lancashire, where we don't seem to be doing as badly as the stats suggest. I don't know who is the live text reporter on the BBC app but it seems to be the most one-sided reporting I have ever seen. After 36 minutes he still hasn't managed to find one good word to say about the Clarets. It turns out the guy is Saj Chowdhury, I suggest he should consider a more detached approach.

Coming up to the end of the first period, the Hammers are whipping up the pressure, a Mark Noble shot cannons off the post and we are conceding corners too frequently for my liking. From one such and once again in 'added time' the inevitable happens. Two muscle bound Hammers take Tom

Heaton out of the equation and Ben Mee commits a foul to present our hosts with a penalty. Of course the correct decision was a free kick for the assault on our keeper, but this is the Premier League. For a moment a glimmer of hope as Heaton saves Noble's spot kick but this quickly evaporates as he nets the rebound. Half time trailing 1-0.

It's a different Burnley team that start the second half, not in terms of personnel but in terms of intent. We are at last taking the game to them. Our best chance so far falls to Sam Vokes on 50 minutes from a Ben Mee Knock down but he misses. The same pair are again involved in another close call on 54 minutes. It's a much better start to the second period as we are pushing men forward. Why do we have to wait till we are trailing before we do so!

The second half live text reporting is noticeably less verbose than the first half's. I wonder is this because good old Saj has been subbed, or could it be that we are gaining the upper hand, to his displeasure. From voluminous narratives we are now down to simple statements of fact:

Foul by Dean Marney.... Free Kick by...., you get the picture.

Another great chance goes begging as Sam Vokes who now could have had a second half hat-trick, contrives to head over from six yards with the net gaping. Wasteful!

Radio Lancashire are reporting we are all over them, but the BBC app is still not reporting any Burnley efforts. Who is biased? I'm gonna pack in reading that BBC crap (sorry app). Next, it's a brilliant save by West ham keeper Darren Randolph to keep out an excellent Scott Arfield free kick. Our radio friends can't believe we aren't level after three gilt edged chances for Sam, and now one for Scotty.

A substitution on 76 minutes as 'Basher' Barnes replaces George Boyd and we are going for it. With nine minutes left off goes 'Roughhouse' Andy Carroll, a 'bruiser' if ever there was one. Good riddance! We're close again on 83 minutes as the ball rolls along the goal line but the assistant referee is flagging, and so am I. We continue to press and the fourth official signals five minutes added time. Will there be more added time drama? Unfortunately, not for us and it's a sixth defeat from seven on the road. I bet Saj is happy.

Result - West Ham United (Noble 45+3) 1 - 0 Burnley

Burnley Team

Heaton, Lowton, Keane, Mee, Ward, Arfield (Bamford 90+4), Marney, Hendrick, Boyd (Barnes 76), Vokes, Gray

Subs Not Used - Robinson, Flanagan, Tarkowski, Defour, Kightly

West Ham United Team

Randolph, Kouyate, Reid Ogbonna, Antonio, Noble (Nordveit 89), Obiang, Cresswell, Lanzini (Ayew 69), Payet, Carroll (Fletcher 83)

Subs Not Used - Adrian, Fernades, Quina, Browne

Attendance - 56,990

Season To Date - Played 16, Won 5, Drawn 2, Lost 9, Goals For 15, Goals Against 26, Points 17

League Position after Game 16 - 13th

So, the terrible away run continues, seven games played, six lost, and one drawn. Only one goal scored and that from the penalty spot and a mammoth task coming up again on Sunday away at high flying Tottenham Hotspur. Fancy a bet on the Clarets anybody?

The only consolation on the night is that most of the fellow strugglers, with the exception of West Ham also lost. Defeats for Sunderland, Swansea, Hull, and Middlesbrough ensured none of these teams gained any advantage on us.

The other bit of personal good news was that thanks to a hat-trick by Salmon Rondon, I went top of the M&S Transfer Terrorism Fantasy Football League. Yippee! I can almost smell the prize money.

The Tottenham game marks the last away game of 2016 and I am praying that the 'God of away wins' is smiling beneficently down on us. In our last Premier League season, you may recall that somehow we had offended the 'God of goalposts' and he thwarted our attempts on a regular basis. It seems he must be pretty chummy with the 'away wins' guy as he is now very efficiently doing the same.

If he won't play ball then an early Christmas present from Santa Claus would be much appreciated!

Game 17 - Sunday 18th December, 16.00 - Tottenham Hotspur v Burnley

As I contemplate our chances in this fixture I realise one possible reason for the recent dire away run has been my forgetfulness in the sporting of the 'lucky charms'. However, once again I must confess that these have again been overlooked, temporarily at least. As the game kicks off I am in Clitheroe bidding a pre-Christmas farewell to daughter

Stephanie and partner Tom as they set off back after a brief visit to return to Darlington.

I miss the first 10 minutes radio coverage but as I leave the town I learn that we have one change from the West Ham game with Ashley Barnes replacing Sam Vokes up front. As I approach Read it appears we are doing OK and holding our own against our much-fancied opponents. Then a bolt from the blue! Yes, it's a Burnley away goal from open play as sloppy Spurs defending allows 'Basher' Barnes to prod home from close range. It's a scrappy one but who cares! Has the 'God of away wins' heard my plea?

Has he hell! By the time I reach the Padiham by-pass its 1-1 as Dele Alli slides in a Kyle Walker cross. A possible nasty moment coming up as I have to stop at a petrol station near home just before half time. Will it still be level when I emerge from filling up? Thankfully it is, and we get to the break all square at 1-1.

Thank God, not sure which one, but I'm now near home and can don the 'lucky charms' ahead of the second period. It's heartening to hear that at least this game we are 'giving it a go'. An hour gone and commentators Scott Read and Marlon Beresford's verdict is that it's a very good game and Burnley are competing well.

They spoke too soon and invoked the commentator's curse! On 71 minutes we are caught on the counter as Sissoko, who should have been red carded minutes earlier, sets up Danny Rose, who rifles home at the near post. It's Vokes for Barnes with about ten minutes to go, then the last throw of the dice, Kightly on for Boyd and Defour for Marney. Four minutes added time is signalled but there's no late drama on this occasion.

It's yet another pointless away trip despite a more encouraging performance. The result sees us drop to 16th and the noose is tightening as the 'drop zone' pack are hunting us down. So much for the bloody 'lucky charms'!

Result - Tottenham Hotspur (Alli 27, Rose 71) 2 - 1 (Barnes 21) Burnley

Burnley Team

Heaton, Lowton, Keane, Mee, Ward, Arfield, Marney (Defour 84), Hendrick, Boyd (Kightly 83), Barnes (Vokes 80), Gray

Subs Not Used - Robinson, Flanagan, Tarkowski, Darikwa

Tottenham Hotspur Team

Lloris, Walker, Dier, Vertonghen, Rose (Davies 77), Wanyama, Dembele (Sissoko 62), Winks, Alli (Son Heung-min 73), Eriksen, Kane

Subs Not Used - Vorm, Trippier, Nkoudou, Wimmer

Attendance - 31,467

Season To Date - Played 17, Won 5, Drawn 2, Lost 10, Goals For 16, Goals Against 28, Points 17

League Position after Game 17 - 16th

They have been two improved away performances on our London travels but unfortunately two more defeats have not helped the cause. We've dropped to 16th and the gap between ourselves and the bottom three is narrowing. The two home games coming up on Boxing Day and New Year's Eve now take on even greater significance.

On Tuesday 20th December it is announced that Joey Barton will be rejoining the Clarets on January 1st, subject to international clearance, until the end of the season. That was not totally unexpected following his disastrous episode at Glasgow Rangers but will still raise a few Claret's eyebrows. Let's hope he can continue for us in the same vein he left off. The Prodigal Son has returned, "Cry Joey, and unleash the dogs of war".

Thursday 22nd December is the date for the annual Burnley Contingent walkers group Christmas Bash. In a change with tradition this year we will not be visiting the Roggerham Gate Inn, no this time we are playing away at the Emmott Arms, Laneshawbridge. For the first time my wife Julie is able to join us though as she eyes the weather forecast she is beginning to wish she couldn't. Fortunately, the weather stays kind to us and a great day out was had by all. The day commenced with a bus ride decked out in Santa Hats and many of us brandishing bus passes, to Trawden. From there a short walk (4.25 miles) via Wycoller to the Emmott Arms. Splendid festive fayre served, and copious quantities of real ale supped. Then the usual thank you speeches and the much coveted (nonsense) awards, before a return to Burnley by bus. Many thanks to the staff at the Emmott Arms, I'm sure the venue will be high on next year's list of possibles.

There's certainly never a dull moment when Joey Barton is around. Only three days after we are informed he is returning with a half season contract, we learn that he is to be charged by the FA with misconduct. The charge relates to no fewer than 1260 instances of football match related betting between 2006 and 2016! Joey still has a one game ban to serve imposed by the Scottish FA for recent betting on games in

Scotland, and if as now looks likely he receives a further lengthy ban, his second coming at Turf Moor looks doomed.

It's now Christmas Eve and as I await my daughter Stephanie's arrival home for the festivities from her exile in Darlington, it's time to wish all my readers a VERY MERRY CHRISTMAS. Here's hoping a lovely time will be topped by a resounding home victory over relegation rivals Middlesbrough at the Turf on Boxing Day.

Game 18 - Monday 26th December, 15.00 - Burnley v Middlesbrough

As I believe I may have mentioned in previous tomes, I like Boxing Day home fixtures. After the confinement of Christmas Day it's good to get out and get some fresh air. Today 'fresh' is certainly the word to describe it as a fine clear December day is accompanied by a sharp biting wind. Fortunately, today I am equipped to deal with anything the weather can throw at me. I am sporting my new Berghaus Scaffell Hydrodown jacket which I have received as a Christmas present. It's brilliant, and in this cold it needs to be! As I reach the Talbot hotel I find my pint waiting for me, sat on a bench OUTSIDE the pub along with my 'hoppos'.

My BBC Sports app is soon into action with team news and I learn not unexpectedly that the only change will be Jon Flanagan at right back for the suspended Matt Lowton. The game is off to a pretty bad tempered start and the pattern is set with an early booking. The culprit Boro's Marten de Roon, for a bad foul on Stephen Ward within the first couple of minutes. The referee Craig Pawson, is no favourite of the Burnley fans following his failure to chalk off Arsenal's late winner at the Turf in October for a clear hand ball infringement. Still he is nothing if not consistent as he fails to award the Clarets an early penalty for another hand ball in the penalty area, this time by Callum Chambers.

It's soon apparent that we are in for an afternoon of frequent card waving by this extremely over-officious official. The early exchanges are scrappy but before long we are gaining some forward momentum bringing good saves from keeper Valdes from efforts by Barnes and Boyd. At half time we are comfortably in command although still level. The visitors have managed no shots on target, although an early miss from Stuani, who should have done better, could have proved costly. Frequent interruptions to the game for our friend Mr Pawson to produce his notebook, on no less than five occasions in the first half, coupled with a strong wind, are not helping the game to flow.

At the restart, with the stiff breeze now in our favour, I'm expecting us to push forward but the early action is contra to my expectations. For a spell we are on the back foot as Boro discover some attacking intent. Surprisingly, amid a further flurry of bookings, 'Basher' Barnes, who I thought was a candidate for 'Man of the Match', is replaced by Sam Vokes. Gradually our visitor's resurgence begins to run out of steam and the game is evenly balanced.

Then on 80 minutes, as we are starting to think we may be happy to settle for a point, comes our moment of Christmas magic. A free kick from keeper Tom Heaton is flicked on by Sam Vokes. The ball drops on the edge of the area to the lurking Andre Gray, who has been largely ineffectual for most of the afternoon. His instantaneous volley is struck firmly but a little too close to the keeper. Fortunately, the keeper - a butter-fingered Spaniard - gets to the shot but can't take enough 'sting' out of it and the ball creeps agonisingly slowly over the line. That's the cue for Christmas mayhem and a packed Turf Moor enthusiastically salutes a crucial strike. There's still time for even more bookings, but precious little threat from Middlesbrough and we comfortably close out the game. That's six wins and a draw from ten home games and that excellent form is giving us a real survival chance.

Well Mr Pawson certainly left his mark on the proceedings with a total of 11 yellow cards in the game. Six went to us and five to the visitors, one handed out to Jeff Hendrick now means he misses the next game under the 'totting up' procedure. It really was a dire performance by the referee as bad fouls which should have merited red cards received the same penalty as innocuous challenges that didn't really constitute a foul.

But at the end of the day, who cares! We have the precious points, bring on the Mackems.

Result - Burnley (Gray 80) 1 – 0 Middlesbrough

Burnley Team

Heaton, Flanagan, Keane, Mee, Ward, Arfield (Berg Gudmundsson 77), Marney (Defour 75), Hendrick, Boyd, Barnes (Vokes 66), Gray

Subs Not Used - Robinson, Kightly, Tarkowski, Darikwa

Middlesbrough Team

Valdes, Barragan, Chambers, Gibson, Fabio, Forshaw, Clayton, de Roon (Friend 87), Stuani (Traore 86), Negredo, Ramirez

Subs Not Used - Guzan, Bernardo, Leadbitter, Rhodes, Downing

Attendance - 21,562

Season To Date - Played 18, Won 6, Drawn 2, Lost 10, Goals For 17, Goals Against 28, Points 20

League Position after Game 18 - 14th

What fascinating facts emerge for Daily Mail readers on slow sports news days. Thursday December 29th the self-proclaimed 'SPORTS NEWSPAPER OF THE YEAR', leads on its back page with;

"Which Premier League manager wears a £45,000 watch – and whose cost £40 quid?"

Now without turning to pages 72-73, it seems highly likely to me that the £45k watch must be our friend Jose Moaninho's, and the £40 one will be Sean Dyche's, manager of perennial paupers Burnley. Imagine my shock on turning to the aforementioned pages to learn that the costly chronometer is in fact the property of our Sean. Fancy that, our manager owns a watch the value of which could buy a street of houses in some areas of Burnley. I can't somehow see Sean splashing his hard-earned cash on something like that, he's far too sensible and grounded. I'm assuming that the watch is probably a reward from Burnley FC for achieving the impossible of two promotions to the Premier League in three seasons, or possibly a part of a 'Golden Handshake' on his departure from Watford.

Anyway, Sean is in good company as we also learn that Queen Victoria and Prince Albert also purchased models from the Swiss watchmaker Patek Philippe at the Great exhibition in 1851. If I were him I wouldn't wear it on a night out in the pubs in Burnley!

The cost of Sean's timepiece, a Patek Philippe 5990/1A, eclipses that of the manager in second place Ronald Koeman (Everton), who chips in at £35,850. Other notables are David Moyes (Sunderland) £30,000, Sam Allardyce (newly appointed at Crystal Palace £27,700, with Moaninho a poor fifth at £25,000. The 'Wooden Spoon' went to Bob Bradley at Swansea with the £40 watch, a humble Timex Ironman 100 Classic. Probably just as well he's not a big spender as he has this week lost his job after a torrid run of results following his recent appointment.

It's now Friday December 30th and the eve of our final game in 2016. As I reflect on the year almost past it strikes me that it has certainly been an eventful one.

From a football perspective, it has been once again a monumentally successful one for my beloved Burnley FC. Following the Boxing Day defeat at Hull City in 2015, the Clarets embarked on that magnificent run of 23 Championship league games without defeat. That fantastic achievement not only took us back to the Premier League after only one season out, but did so as Champions! As I write now some tremendous home form has us nicely placed to make a 'good fist' of a Premier League survival battle. All that's needed is an improvement to the wretched run of away results which hopefully 2017 will bring. With the transfer window about to re-open in January, and presumably still with some funds to spare, some judicial strengthening of the squad can see us home and dry.

What a strange year politically with the EU referendum ending with a surprise win for the Brexiteers. Funny one that, in my many discussions with various groups of people I have so far only found two who admit to voting to leave! Oh well, about to take a leap into the unknown but with typical Bulldog spirit, we are undaunted. The EU shock was then 'trumped' literally by the victory in the US Presidential elections by a chauvinistic, former bankrupt businessman Donald Trump. Donald's racist outbursts and ludicrous statements, followed recently by a pronouncement to hugely increase nuclear arms spending, have certainly woken the peoples of the 'free world' from their stupor. Coupled with, the rise of 'right wing' factions in many EU states fuelled by mass immigration, terror attacks in many European cities and the ongoing disaster of Syria, the world in 2016 has become decidedly a more dangerous place.

On a personal note 2016 has been I would say a rather difficult year. I have seen at close hand the shock and life altering changes that sudden illness can bring to the families of many whom I would call good friends. Closer to home our small family has not been untouched, and it brings home the realisation that at my age, now is the time to 'live for today'.

Also on a personal note, my daughter Stephanie who has been our constant companion for almost 27 years left in the Spring to live in Darlington with her partner Tom. I must confess that both my wife and I were both a little concerned how this would work out for Stephanie, a real 'home bird'. We are both mightily relieved and proud at how well she has managed the transition, not only moving to a new job, but also a new house, and a new town. Much credit for this must also go to Tom, who is in the words of my wife Julie, 'a lovely lad'.

There have of course been some benefits to ourselves from her move. Toilet roll consumption has fallen by about 75%. What the hell had she been doing with it? My annual mileage and petrol bill has dropped by 50% as taxi duties are now a thing of the past. The noise level in the house has fallen by 80% and my tympanic membranes are slowly recovering. The house no longer needs tidying on a daily basis. Last, but not least, it has also afforded us the opportunity to make weekend visits to their new abode and discover the delights of Darlington and its environs.

I wish all those above and any that I have forgot to mention, a much happier 2017. Let's kick out the old year with a victory over Sunderland and welcome in 2017 on a positive note.

Game 19 - Saturday 31st December, 15.00 - Burnley v Sunderland

Our second visitors of the week from the North East, and the game which at its conclusion will mark the exact half way point in this our third tilt at the Premier League.

Ahead of the game as I plan my Fantasy football strategy to maintain or even better my current second place in the M&S Transfer terrorism league, I have a hunch. With my one available 'free' transfer in comes Andre Gray and out goes Salomon Rondon. I just have a feeling that Andre is the type of striker who scores goals in spurts. His goal against Middlesbrough will have given him confidence and Sunderland should be just the type of opposition where he can continue his run.

Our visitors have something of a hold over us and I believe we have only one victory against them since 1975, that coming in our first Premier League foray in 2009. After an appalling start to this season the Mackems are showing some signs of revival with four wins from the last eight games. With forwards of the calibre of Jermain Defoe, Fabio Borini and Victor Anichebe, they may pose something of a goal threat. However, a big loss for them is the absence through injury of promising young goalkeeper Jordan Pickford. The keeper played a major part in frustrating the Clarets in last season's local derby with Preston North End and has been in impressive form since his return to his parent club.

Two team changes for us, this time it is Steven Defour in for the suspended Jeff Hendrick, and Matt Lowton returning from his one match ban to replace Jon Flanagan. There's a bright start from the visitors which lasts for all of five minutes and then it is the Clarets pushing forward. Promising moves abound for the Clarets with Defour pulling the strings and Stephen Ward enjoying space down the left flank. There's a real physical battle developing between Ashley Barnes and the Sunderland central defenders Lamina Kone and Papa Djilobodji. However, this ends prematurely as Kone injures himself in a collision with the advertising hoardings and after a brief spell is unable to continue. A reshuffle means John O'Shea moves from a holding midfield position to fill the vacant centre back slot. Big mistake!

As Ashley Barnes jumps for a ball helped forward by Scott Arfield, he is challenged by both central defenders who impede each other in the process. The ball glances off the hapless O'Shea into the path of the lurking Andre Gray. Needing no second invitation Andre advances to the edge of the penalty area before unleashing a powerful shot, which for the second game in succession, is too strong for the stand in keeper Vito Mannone and is through him and in the net!

The next significant action sees the tireless George Boyd break up a an attack and as he accelerates away at speed he is pursued by a 'man mountain' Victor Anichebe. Unfortunately for Goliath the speed of Georgie Boy is too great and his desperate attempt to catch him leaves him stretched out on the grass nursing a pulled hamstring, and it's the end of his day. At half time it's a comfortable 1-0 lead and few concerns.

We start the second period as we left off and the visitor's central defensive pair of O'Shea and Papa (if you think I'm going to keep typing Djilobodji, dream on!) are looking decidedly dodgy. On 51 minutes Andre Gray pounces on a long ball out from Dean Marney, shrugs off a poor challenge from Papa and rounds the keeper Mannone who finds himself in no-man's land, before rolling home number two.

Not long to wait for number three as 'Blunderlander' Steven Pienaar, on as a replacement for Anichebe, inexplicably stands on the ball to concede possession. A slick passing interchange started by Defour finds Barnes hooking the ball between the two comedic centre backs for the now lethal Gray to side foot home his hat trick goal.

I knew it, they should make me a Premier League manager! My inspired inclusion of Andre Gray is reaping massive dividends and his hat-trick will net me a minimum 17 points in my Fantasy League quest. The enigmatic Andre is certainly on fire!

The Mackems are falling apart and it's no surprise as number four duly arrives. Scott Arfield moving sweetly onto a ball into the box is bundled over by Seb Larsson and it's a stonewall penalty. Scotty grabs the ball seemingly intent on a 'free hit' but 'Basher' Barnes is having none of it and relieves poor Scotty of the honour. Ashley fires home confidently in the corner, a just reward for his tireless battling. With about 20 minutes to go and a 4-0 lead I can at last start to relax and look forward to New Year's Eve at the Green Bangla.

Then in true Clarets fashion we contrive to concede what turns out to be just a consolation goal. A great run from Adnan Januzaj, followed by an accurate cross lands with ace marksman Jermain Defoe who makes no mistake.

The game, not unsurprisingly then starts to die a little as we conserve energy for Monday's visit to the Etihad and the challenge of Manchester City. After 90+3 minutes it's all over and mission accomplished. The only downside to the day, a booking for Dean Marney means he will now miss the City game, with presumably the returning Jeff Hendrick taking the vacant place.

What a fantastic Christmas period for the Clarets and Andre Gray. For the team six vital points from teams in the relegation dogfight, and for Andre four equally vital goals to give his confidence a real boost. The results open up a big gap between us and the bottom three. We now stand nine points above Sunderland, ten above Hull and eleven over Swansea. We now sit eleventh in the Premier League at the half way stage. Who would have believed that? What's more our improved survival chances can only be beneficial in negotiations with potential signings in the upcoming transfer window.

Result - Burnley (Gray 31,51,53, Barnes 67 pen) 4 - 1 (Defoe 71) Sunderland

Burnley Team

Heaton, Lowton, Keane, Mee, Ward, Arfield, Marney, Defour (Gudmundsson 68), Boyd, Barnes (Tarkowski 85), Gray (Vokes 78)

Subs Not Used - Robinson, Darikwa, Bamford, O'Neill

Sunderland Team

Mannone, Jones, Kone (Ndong 24), Djilobodji, van Aanholt, Larsson, O'Shea (Love 72), Januzaj, Anichebe (Pienaar HT), Borini, Defoe

Subs Not Used - Mika, Rodwell, Khazri, Manquillo

Attendance - 21,142

Season To Date - Played 19, Won 7, Drawn 2, Lost 10, Goals For 21, Goals Against 29, Points 23

League Position after Game 19 - 11th

JANUARY 2017

Game 20 – Monday 2nd January, 15.00 – Manchester City v Burnley

Following quickly on the heels of our latest magnificent victory was the daunting prospect of an away game at Manchester City. This was not an easy game to review as after the euphoria of the last two home games we returned to earth with a bump. A task made even harder as my wife declared a three day vow of alcoholic abstinence following the annual Christmas overindulgence. A very noble gesture I thought, until she pronounced 'that goes for you as well'!

An early morning walk in glorious winter sunshine taking in Worsthorne and Hurstwood was followed by removal of Christmas decorations and dismantling of the tree. As this coincided with kick-off at the Etihad it was a case of earplugs in and fingers and toes crossed. A quick dash up the stairs to get a full complement of 'lucky charms' and away we go.

A pretty uneventful start as the City slickers show four changes including resting Sergio Aguero and David Silva following the New Year's Eve defeat at Anfield. We are also showing changes as Johann Berg Gudmundsson comes in for the suspended Dean Marney, and Jeff Hendrick returns from suspension with Defour dropping to the bench. It's a puzzling situation with Steven Defour as he is probably the most talented midfielder in the squad but has not managed a full game yet, and is often dropped to the bench for away fixtures. Is there a fitness issue, or does Sean Dyche not consider his workrate sufficient?

There's an early scare for the Clarets as Ben Mee's sloppy pass is intercepted but 'Mr Reliable' Tom Heaton thankfully saves the day. From then on its fairly evenly balanced as the homespun Clarets compete equally as well as their mega-rich counterparts. On 32 minutes there's a potential turning point as City's midfielder Fernandinho, attempts to amputate Gudmundsson's foot with a reckless two-footed scissor tackle. Referee Lee Mason has no option but to send him off thus leaving City with the best part of an hour to play with ten men.

Half time is reached with the score remaining at 0-0, and the second half commences with changes in personnel for the home side as Aguero and Silva enter the fray. Disaster on 58 minutes as Bacary Sagna crosses only to see Michael Keane head clear, the ball falls to Gael Clichy whose right foot shot goes through Silva's legs and nestles in the corner of the net. Worse is to follow as the ten men go 2-0 up. A quick counter from City sees Mee stumble at a crucial time allowing Raheem Sterling a run on goal. Once again this is thwarted by the magnificent Tom Heaton but the ball falls to Aguero who manages to sneak the ball through the tightest gap between Keane and the near post.

How have we managed to concede twice in four minutes against ten men? All we can do is to continue battling and hope for some breaks. On 70 minutes a left wing corner from Defour, having replaced Gudmundsson, is flicked goalwards by Sam Vokes who has replaced Ashley Barnes. An almighty scramble evolves which sees home keeper Claudio Bravo flap it out only as far as Mee, who returns it via the underside of the crossbar only for the ball to bounce out! Did it cross the line? It has now as Andre Gray heads the ball out of Bravo's hands back into the goal. City claim a foul, but the referee has already credited the goal as the technology shows Mee's shot was indeed fully over the line. As George Boyd tries to wrestle the ball from Sagna in order to get the proceedings re-started the full back takes a kick at Georgie Boy. Surely a red card offence, but the referee bottles it this time in front of the partisan home crowd and it's just a booking.

Still twenty minutes to go can we do it? Time ticks on, Patrick Bamford replaces Scott Arfield with two minutes to go! Why? Strange one that, as Radio Lancashire summariser, ex Claret Paul Weller, has Scotty as his Man of the Match.

There's five added minutes, time to see a good save by Bravo from a skilfully improvised Keane shot. However, once again there's no fairy tale ending and another away game slips by, pointless.

Result - Manchester City (Clichy 58, Aguero 62) 2 - 1 (Mee 70) Burnley

Burnley Team

Heaton, Lowton, Keane, Mee, Ward, Arfield (Bamford 88), Hendrick, Gudmundsson (Defour 59), Boyd, Barnes (Vokes 69),

Subs Not Used - Robinson, Darikwa, Tarkowski, O'Neill

Manchester City Team

Bravo, Sagna, Otamendi, Kolarov, Clichy, Navas (Silva 45), Fernandinho, Y.Toure, De Bruyne, Sterling (Stones 89), Iheanacho (Aguero 45)

Subs Not Used - Caballero, Zabaleta, Nolito, Garcia

Attendance - 54,463

Season To Date - Played 20, Won 7, Drawn 2, Lost 11, Goals For 22, Goals Against 31, Points 23

League Position after Game 20 - 12th

Definitely a feeling of 'one that got away' here. City were there for the taking but some inspired half time substitutions by them, and a loss of focus by us, have once against cost us the game. The away jinx continues into 2017. When will we find the answer?

The news is confirmed on Monday 2nd January that Joey Barton has indeed re-signed and that the City game would serve as his one match suspension carried over from his Scottish adventure. He is now available for the upcoming FA cup tie at Sunderland this Saturday, if selected.

The transfer window is now open again and the early links see some familiar names being touted. Henri Lansbury from Nottingham Forest appears to be a continuing saga, and the Polish player who almost signed in August, Kamil Grosicki, is once more rumoured. A new name to add to the list is Barnsley centre back Marc Roberts but as yet there are no official foundations to the links. Clarets loanee Patrick Bamford is similarly rumoured to be a target for rivals Middlesbrough.

FA Cup 3rd Round - Saturday 7th January, 15.00 - Sunderland v Burnley

A break today from league action but not from recent opposition. Today's third round tie has us up against last Saturday's opponents Sunderland, this time at the Stadium of Light. With an eye on the main priority of Premier League survival Sean Dyche has rung the changes for this one. In come Pope, Darikwa, Tarkowski, Barton, Defour and Vokes, at the expense of Heaton, Lowton, Mee, Hendrick, Boyd and Vokes. That's a pretty drastic change of personnel and I think reflects the fact that we are not too concerned if we exit the competition at this early stage. Sunderland opt for a more regular line up and are clearly looking to progress.

It's a big day for goalkeeper Nick Pope who gets the nod above the much more experienced Paul Robinson, let's hope he can handle it (literally). No place even on the bench for Patrick Bamford which fuels the rumours that he is about to leave the club, either back to Chelsea his parent club, or as previously mentioned off to Middlesbrough.

I've decided today to conduct an experiment into the efficacy of the 'lucky charms'. Today I have decided to desist from sporting the accoutrements about my personage and see if that will break the away day hoodoo.

As I settle down to follow the game once again courtesy of Radio Lancashire I have my pen poised to record all the action. It's not long before I get some as an early chance falls to Andre Gray who however fails to work the keeper. Ace summariser Paul Weller reckons the Clarets are looking confident after the first 12 minutes, and shortly after my pen is called into action once more. This time it's a great through ball by Scott Arfield for Sam Vokes, but his weak shot is saved by Sunderland keeper Vito Mannone.

The next bit of action I record is the half time whistle and as this must be about 30 minutes since my last jotting, I conclude that I am wasting my time and abandon the pen. The first half can best be described as underwhelming!

The second half fares not much better. The nearest to a goal is a thumping header by Tarkowski from a Defour corner which unfortunately cannons back off the post with 15 minutes to go. Weller then tempts fate with the curse of the commentator by announcing that if there's going to be a goal it's coming Burnley's way! Fortunately, or unfortunately, whichever way you look at it, there are no goals and the game ends in a draw that neither side probably wanted.

There is a positive from the game in that Steven Defour manages, for the first time, to complete the full ninety minutes plus added time. However, there are also negatives in the loss of Scott Arfield and Johann Berg Gudmundsson who are both forced off with injuries. So, it's back to the Turf in just over a week's time to have another go. Meanwhile we maintain an interest in the 4th round draw coming shortly.

Result - Sunderland 0 - 0 Burnley

Burnley Team

Pope, Darikwa, Keane, Tarkowski, Ward, Arfield (Kightly 60), Barton, Defour, Gudmundsson (Hendrick 72), Gray (Vokes 72), Barnes

Subs Not Used - Robinson, Lowton, Mee, Marney

Sunderland Team

Mannone, Love, Manquillo, Djilobodji, van Aanholt, Denayer, Rodwell, Larsson (O'Shea 84), Januzaj, Defoe, Borini

Subs Not Used - Mika, Robson, Asoro, Maja, Honeyman, Embleton

Attendance - 17,632

The game was clearly not to the liking of Mail on Sunday reporter Craig Hope:

"It is early days, but this could rank as one of the most forgettable matches of 2017.

Not even two Premier League clubs, both fielding strong starting XIs, could produce anything bordering on entertainment. An advert for the FA Cup? It should only be shown after the watershed if so, for this was gruesome".

Don't pull any punches Craig will you!

By Friday 13th it's still slow, or should I say no, news on the incoming transfer front. The latest rumour is that we have tabled a bid for Norwich City midfielder Robbie Brady. According to the Daily Mirror the offer is worth up to £13m, a staggering amount but seemingly not-so in today's highly inflated market. Most fans would be extremely pleased if this came off as the player is seen as a good 'Dyche fit'. The general consensus seems to be that as a wide midfielder he is an upgrade on what we currently have available. Unsurprisingly there's no official confirmation of the offer and we await further developments.

One previously linked player who definitely will not be coming is Luciano Narsingh late of PSV Eindhoven who has joined strugglers Swansea in a deal reported at £4m. One player confirmed as leaving Turf Moor on a permanent transfer is full back Danny Lafferty who joins Sheffield United, after an initial loan period.

Tomorrow is a return to Turf Moor and a home league fixture with Southampton. This game will see the return of 'one of our own' as Jay Rodriguez hits town with the Saints.

Obviously, we wish Jay all the best, but definitely not tomorrow!

Game 21 – Saturday 14th January, 15.00 – Burnley v Southampton

There's good news coming from the club ahead of this fixture as it is announced that Season ticket prices for 2017/18 will remain at the current levels for people renewing in the 'early bird' saver period. I can state quite categorically now that I will be one of those, regardless of what the rest of the season brings.

No doubt this gesture has been helped by the fact that Burnley FC have been named amongst the ten most profitable clubs in Europe according to a Lancashire Telegraph report. This revelation comes from a UEFA Footballing Landscape report which included the financial state of clubs for the financial year ending April 2015. That covered the Clarets last Premier League season and showed an operating profit quoted of €54m placing us 10th in Europe. In terms of operating profit that places Burnley fifth in England behind Manchester United, Liverpool, Arsenal and Manchester City. Whilst in Europe only Paris St Germain, Real Madrid, Juventus, Barcelona and Zenit St Petersburg are the only clubs above us. Burnley are fifth in Europe for net profit for the 2015 financial year with a total of €40m. That is only behind, Liverpool, Newcastle, Real Madrid and Leicester City. Now that is sound financial management!

Anyway, that's enough of that, let's cut to the important stuff. Ahead of the match on a bitterly cold January day comes news that last week's casualties at Sunderland, Arfield and Gudmundsson have both failed to make the matchday squad. Reverting to a more normal line up, back come Heaton, Lowton, Mee, Marney and Hendrick. Defour retains his place but in an unfamiliar left sided midfield slot, outside of a central pairing of Marney and Hendrick.

It's a bright start by the Clarets against a strong looking Southampton side with Jeff Hendrick prominent in the early action. However, our early dominance is soon weathered by the visitors who start to assert some authority. The Saints, on a poor league run of three consecutive defeats, are definitely looking to end that sequence here. Although without the injured Charlie Austin they pose nothing like the same goal threat. It's a testing first half but as usual our magnificent defensive organisation sees us through to half time without too many scares. The media will point to goal line clearances but in reality they are routine stops by players doing defensively what they are paid to do.

The second half continues in the same vein with Southampton enjoying the lion's share of possession and the Clarets looking for a sucker punch on the break. As the game winds down and the substitutions start, a draw is looking at best what we can hope for. However, that did not take into account Sean Dyche's masterstroke, the introduction of none other than Joey Barton!

Coming on to a rapturous welcome on 73 minutes, replacing Dean Marney, Joey has only been on the pitch five minutes when a foul on George Boyd just outside the Saints penalty box presents Joey with his magic moment. With a wall that took minutes to assemble it looks like Joey will have to go up and over with his shot. But no, the Prodigal One shoots hard and true through what appears to be a rapidly crumbling wall and the ball nestles in the net.

What is it with Joey Barton and Burnley? A character for whom everywhere else he goes seems to be plagued by trouble and controversy, can in little homely Burnley do no wrong! He is, or seems to be our King Midas. The crowd are ecstatic, his teammates are ecstatic, but nobody is more ecstatic than Joey himself. He is a character that thrives on love, and that's what he gets in our small East Lancashire town.

Twelve minutes to hold out for another vital three points, and it's edge of the seat stuff now. The Saints, with Jay Rodriguez now on up front as a 68th minute substitute. are going for it. Once again the resolute home defence is holding firm and we still even pose a threat as our opponents commit men forwards in a desperate push. Then as time is running out, an incredible double save by Tom Heaton catches the eye. Firstly, he is at full stretch to push aside a goal bound effort from 'Jay Rod' and as the ball is pushed out to another Southampton sub Josh Sims, Heaton recovers to save again at the foot of the post. On this day he is not going to be beaten, and once again Fortress Turf Moor is impregnable to the opposition.

Result - Burnley (Barton 78) 1 – 0 Southampton

Burnley Team

Heaton, Lowton, Keane, Mee, Ward, Boyd, Hendrick, Marney (Barton 73), Defour (Vokes 74), Barnes, Gray (Tarkowski 87)

Subs Not Used - Robinson, Darikwa, Flanagan, Kightly

Southampton Team

Forster, Cedric, Yoshida, Van Dijk, Bertrand, Hojbjerg, Romeu, Ward-Prowse, Tadic (Rodriguez 68), Long, Redmond (Sims 80)

Subs Not Used - Taylor, Clasie, Martina, Reed, Stephens

Attendance - 20,254

Season To Date - Played 21, Won 8, Drawn 2, Lost 11, Goals For 23, Goals Against 31, Points 26

League Position after Game 21 - 10th

What a fantastic result, and that makes eight home victories from twelve games. I believe if only home form counted we would be third in the league! What is more it's the fourth consecutive home win equalling our record set in the first Premier League season 2009/10. The result takes us to the dizzy height of 10th in the Premier League. Poor home results for Swansea beaten 4-0 by Arsenal, and Sunderland going down 3-1 to Stoke further strengthen our survival prospects. Hull manage to climb off the bottom with a 3-1 home victory over Eddie Howe's defenceless Bournemouth, but remain 10 points adrift of us with a much inferior goal difference.

There's a real 'feel good factor' around the club at the moment and this is typified by Joey Barton's reaction to the win. In his post-match interview he states:

"It's a real collective effort and it's just fantastic to be a part of this group again, to be back playing football again and to be in the Premier League. This is a unique football club and a unique group of people.

You sometimes have to be not in the building to realise just how special that was and certainly I realised that in the summer. I'm very fortunate and feel very privileged to come back and be part of this again".

On the day of the Southampton game Sean Dyche also confirms that Patrick Bamford has been recalled from his unsuccessful loan spell with the Clarets and will sign for Middlesbrough in this transfer window. Very little seen of Mr Bamford and an impression that he may be a bit 'lightweight' for this ultra demanding league. Still we wish him - but not - Boro well.

Not much time for a breather now as the FA Cup replay follows shortly on the heels of this game, and we go again on Tuesday evening. I reckon we'll see some big changes for this one, particularly with a massive challenge coming up away at Arsenal.

My warm up for the cup tie replay is a Tuesday Dotcom walk, this time a shortish (5.19 miles, a very accurate estimate from Bob Clare which may or may not be true) circular from Hurst Green. Incorporated in the walk is a stroll through the grounds of Stonyhurst College, presumably to let us see how the other half live, or at least how they educate their children. It's another damp, dreary miserable day but enlightened with some cheerful banter with the North Enders. They are also in good humour following an excellent home victory at the weekend against promotion favourites Brighton. Poor old Blackburn John cuts a forlorn figure as the Rovers still languish in a Championship relegation spot following defeat at lowly Ipswich Town.

The walk mainly notable for the prolific amount of mud encountered, much to the chagrin of Steve Glover and his new birthday present boots, is topped off with a pub lunch at the Bayley Arms. The lunch billed as Soup, Sandwich and Chips, was I have to say rather disappointing. Insufficient sandwich provision meant some Dotcomers went home hungry, me included. Why is it that the swankier Ribble Valley hostelries invariably are 'stingier' than their urban counterparts? Last week's offering at The Crown Hotel, Colne was gargantuan in comparison and cheaper to boot! The one saving grace was a decent pint of Wainwright's to set us up for the cup replay. Interestingly despite the proximity of the pub to the esteemed college, the spelling on the notice boards left something to be desired. 'Janruary' instead of January, and 'Wainrights' instead of Wainwright's being two examples. 'Could do better' I think is the report here.

FA Cup 3rd Round Replay – Tuesday 17th January, 19.45 – Burnley v Sunderland

As expected, there are wholesale changes to the team from Saturday - seven in all. Once again Pope gets the goalie's jersey, and there are changes in both full back positions as Darikwa and Flanagan come in for Lowton and Ward. Mee is rested and Tarkowski comes in at centre back. In midfield there are starts for Barton and Kightly, whilst Vokes plays as lone striker as Barnes and Gray drop out. There are not so many changes for Sunderland as they are hampered by injuries and absentees on African Nations Cup duty. Notably their main threat Defoe enjoys a well earned rest on the bench.

It's a good start from the Clarets and visiting keeper Vito Mannone is kept on his toes almost from the off. In contrast Nick Pope is virtually a spectator as an excellent Burnley defence and a woeful Sunderland attack ensure he sees little action. We are moving the ball well and the full backs particularly Tenday Darikwa are getting forward at every opportunity. On the stroke of half time one such foray bears fruit. George Boyd feeds the overlapping Darikwa down the right and his exquisite cross is nodded home as Sam Vokes gets across his marker at the near post. A one goal half time lead is no less than this impressive first half display deserves, but our visitors are surely the worst side seen at Turf Moor this season.

It's more of the same in the second half, but the second goal that will surely clinch the tie is some time coming. However, inside the last ten minutes the tie is eventually put to bed, as Vokes heads on James Tarkowski's long ball into the path of the predatory Andre Gray on as a substitute for Michael Kightly. Gray must love the sight of Black Cats keeper Mannone as he fires unerringly past him for his fourth goal in a matter of weeks against the Mackems.

It's 88 minutes before redundant keeper Pope has his first save of the match to make, and this is followed shortly by an excellent tip round the post from a Sebastian Larsson free kick. However, it's much too little too late, and we comfortably take our place in Round 4.

An outstanding performance from Tarkowski, and good contributions from both stand in full backs. An excellent performance albeit against poor opposition, and a good run out for some of the fringe players. There's a growing confidence about the team, and I'm beginning to think that 2017 has all the makings of an excellent footballing year.

Result - Burnley (Vokes 44, Gray 83) 2 – 0 Sunderland

Burnley Team

Pope, Darikwa, Keane, Tarkowski, Flanagan, Kightly (Gray 77), Barton, Defour, Hendrick 72, Boyd (O'Neill 90), Vokes

Subs Not Used - Robinson, Lowton, Mee, Ward, Jackson

Sunderland Team

Mannone, Jones, Denayer, Manquillo, Djilobodji, van Aanholt, Larsson, Love (Defoe 63), Honeyman, Januzaj, Borini (Asoro 81)

Subs Not Used - Mika, E Robson, T Robson, O'Shea, Embleton

Attendance - 12,257

A break from the football again and time to reflect with the Burnley contingent walkers on a promising start to 2017. Thursday's walk is another excellent outing led by husband and wife team John and Judy W, the Alfred Wainwright and Julia Bradbury of Burnley walkers. This time it's a trip to Cowpe, up above Waterfoot, for an eight-miler taking in Cowpe Lowe and Waugh's Well.

I am quite looking forward to this one as I recall on a previous visit that there were a number of seemingly wild ponies roaming the area. Knowing John W's fear and dislike of our equine friends, I am hoping for some close encounters. John, as ever is very eager to educate us with background knowledge on the walk, most of which goes in one ear and out the other. Today we are informed at length by him that Waugh's Well is named after Edwin Waugh, a well-known Lancashire dialect poet. So, well-known in fact that nobody else in the group had ever heard of him! But I can assure you we have now!

Still despite John's attempt to educate, his recital of Waugh's poetry, and his occasional singing, we had a good day out, managed to not get lost, and retired to the Rifle Volunteer pub. The 'Rifle Vol' is establishing itself as a firm favourite with the Thursday group. A traditional street corner pub, close to St Stephen's church in Burnley, you can be assured of a warm welcome and great locally brewed ales. Today it was Filly Close Blonde from the Reedley Hallows brewery, an excellent way to finish the day.

Once again, this week we have no Saturday fixture, the away game at Arsenal being moved to Sunday for live TV screening. It gives us the opportunity to see what happens in the relegation battle before we face our daunting task. Fortunately, all the bottom three face tricky away fixtures so hopefully no ground will be gained on us.

What a shocker therefore as lowly Swansea start the weekend fixtures with a win away at Liverpool in the lunch time kick-off. Taking a shock two goal lead the Swans are then pegged back as the Reds level. At this point I'm confidently expecting the 'Pool to go on and win the game, but no the plucky underdogs unbelievably score again and hang on to take all three points. The victory takes them out of the bottom three and closes the gap between them and us to eight points.

Fortunately Sunderland, looking increasingly doomed, live up to all expectations and go down 2-0 at West Bromwich Albion. Crystal Palace, still winless under new manager Sam Allardyce, fall to a late goal at home to Everton and now find themselves in the relegation spots. Big spending Middlesbrough, who seem to be trying to buy every available player in the window, are comprehensively beaten at home by West Ham United. So, it's not too damaging a Saturday afternoon and there are still plenty of sides below us as we go into our game.

Game 22 - Sunday 22nd January, 14.15 - Arsenal v Burnley

There's only one word to describe my feelings after the events of this game, DEVASTATED!

On a cold but dry January Sunday my wife and I decide to head for St Annes to partake of some bracing sea air. Taking the precaution before leaving of setting up an information stream via text with PNE Ed, a man who always has his eye on the ball, we head for the coast.

It's certainly on the chilly side as we set off down the promenade in the direction of Lytham but it's a good day to be out as long as you're moving. As we hit Lytham I note it's around kick off time and my BBC Sports App furnishes me with the team line-ups. The Clarets reverting back to a more familiar team and formation following Tuesday's cup canter.

The text line is strangely quiet as I'm expecting the dreaded info of an Arsenal opener, but Ed's first effort is;

0-0 17 mins

Followed by;

0-0 30 mins

By now we have arrived back at St Annes pier and decide on a cuppa in the café to revive ourselves. I message Ed back to tell him to keep the texts coming. At which point I receive;

0-0 ht

Just as I am thinking that Ed is being very sparing with details the next one is more forthcoming;

Arsenal totally dominant, will the Clarets turn it round like Nob End yesterday? (A reference to Preston's comeback from being 2-0 at Aston Villa to draw the game 2-2).

Arriving back at the car I remark to Julie that we may be able to get commentary on the radio on the way home. I switch on just in time to hear the Gunners go 1-0 up and a text from Ed;

1-0 58 mins

An interesting and extremely frustrating episode then follows as Radio Lancashire decides it will alternate between commentary from Arsenal and Joe Wilson's Country music show! It's a battle and one that the music is clearly winning. My only hope is to get East as quickly as possible and hope the signal stabilises on the important news.

I've not got far, Blackpool airport in fact, when Scott Read interjects sufficiently for me to deduce that Arsenal are going down to 10 men as Granit Xhaka is red-carded for a bad foul on Steven Defour. By now my phone is in my pocket and I'm getting tingling sensations in my groin as Ed attempts to convey the news. I later learn from him;

Xhaka sent off 65 mins

1-0 71 mins. All Burnley, Barton comes on.

Onto the M55 now and the radio continues its little game of three minutes Country crap (apologies to Country Music lovers), 10 seconds football commentary. The farce continues as we hit the M6 southbound with just enough brief coverage to know that time is running out and the score stays at 1-0. Then suddenly approaching the M61 comes the announcement, seven minutes added time. Into the final straight now as I hit the M65 eastbound and the radio is at last behaving itself. Glory Be! A penalty awarded to the Clarets in the third minute of added time for a foul by Francis Coquelin on Ashley Barnes. Andre Gray makes no mistake with the spot kick and we are LEVEL AT THE EMIRATES. Can we snatch a winner?

Then the lowest blow of all, on 90+7 minutes unbelievably a penalty to Arsenal for a high boot by Ben Mee on Laurent Koscielny. Yes, the same Koscielny who robbed us of a point at Turf Moor with his hand-ball extra time winner. Needless to say, Alexis Sanchez despatches it, dinking it over Tom Heaton and incredibly we lose the game 2-1.

What have we done to offend the 'God of away wins' and how can we appease him (or her)? Once again we are bemoaning the injustice of it all, and once again it's a wasted away day. The last three away fixtures, against three of the top five, Tottenham Hotspur, Manchester City, and now Arsenal have ended in 2-1 reverses. Arguably we could, and maybe should, have taken points from all three but our extremely lopsided season continues.

The only good news on the day is the fact that Hull lose at Chelsea in the 16.30 kick off and remain in the bottom three. The points gap between ourselves and the bottom three remains at 10 which is still a healthy position. Champions Leicester City lose 3-0 at Southampton in the lunch time game and remain five points adrift of the Clarets, and their next fixture is… at the Turf!

Result - Arsenal (Mustafi 59, Sanchez 90+8 pen) 2 - 1 (Gray 90+3 pen) Burnley

Burnley Team

Heaton, Lowton, Keane, Mee, Ward, Boyd, Hendrick (Barton 73), Marney (Tarkowski 76), Defour (Vokes 77), Barnes, Gray

Subs Not Used - Robinson, Darikwa, Flanagan, Kightly

Arsenal Team

Cech, Gabriel, Mustafi, Koscielny, Monreal, Ramsey, Xhaka, Iwobi (Coquelin 69), Ozil (Bellerin 89), Sanchez, Giroud (Welbeck 87)

Subs Not Used - Ospina, Gibbs, Perez, Oxlade-Chamberlain

Attendance - 59,955

Season To Date - Played 22, Won 8, Drawn 2, Lost 12, Goals For 24, Goals Against 33, Points 26

League Position after Game 22 - 13th

Not surprisingly the aftermath of the game throws up a number of talking points. As I slowly assimilate more information it appears that apart from Granit Xhaka being dismissed, manager Arsene Wenger had also been sent to the stands. Dean Marney had suffered a potentially serious injury, and the Arsenal penalty should never have been as the player was offside before any contact was made. Not only that, it was dubious at best whether Ben Mee's 'high boot' was actually high, as the Arsenal man was ducking to head the ball. Oh dear! Undone again by poor refereeing decisions and once again at one of the top sides. Quelle surprise!

Mr Wenger it appears had been sent to the stands for abusing the referee for awarding (correctly) the Burnley penalty. Like all the Premier elite demi-gods, Wenger was clearly in the belief that this could not apply to him, refused to go and stood in the tunnel entrance. Being further instructed to leave he then pushed the fourth official twice. Wow! Laying hands on an official that doesn't sound too promising.

Wenger perhaps realising the seriousness of his offence was quickly into apologetic mode:

"I should have shut up – I apologise for not having done that"

"it was nothing malicious. I should have kept my control, even if it was in a hectic time"

"Look it was nothing bad, I said something that you hear every day in football. Overall, nine times out of ten, you are not sent to the stand for that.

"If I am, I am, and I should have shut up completely. I was quite calm for the whole game, more than usual."

Mmmm… doesn't sound all that contrite to me Arsene. The incident will be reported by the match officials and it looks like a touchline ban is on its way.

A calmer Sean Dyche - externally at least - was clearly unhappy about the Arsenal penalty. In his 200th game in charge of Burnley he felt that Koscielny was offside before being caught by Mee's high foot.

"It's a tough day for us in the end. To lose a game in that fashion, with an offside not given, is tough particularly when you come to tough places like this.

"We have never taken anything for granted. We know how tough this division is but you need officials to make the right decisions and that is the shame today."

I bet inwardly Sean is bloody seething!

Another worrying feature from the game is the injury to Dean Marney which some are suggesting may be a serious knee injury that could rule him out of action for some time. If this is the case, and if Joey Barton is facing a ban for his betting misdemeanours, we are once again seriously short in midfield. With the transfer window still open, but deadline day getting ever nearer, perhaps it's time to step up negotiations.

Away from the football again and it's another entry for the Good Pub guide. This time the Chetham Arms, High St, Chapeltown, Turton, Nr Bolton - a lovely community pub in a great walking location. This was the second Dotcom visit to the pub, and it was every bit as good as the first almost twelve months ago. Another fine day's walking en-route, taking in the scenic Entwistle and Wayoh reservoirs. Rag Pudding and a pint of Flat Cap ale (named in honour of Bolton's celebrity chimney destroyer, Fred Dibnah) - bliss! Definitely a pub to note in the Dotcom 'must return' diary!

At last! On 25th January, there is some firm news on possible incoming transfer activity. It transpires through the media that Crystal Palace have had a bid accepted by Norwich City for alleged Burnley target Robbie Brady. Strangely this bid is apparently £4m less than the Burnley bid. I can only surmise that this has something to do with the way in which the proposed bids are scheduled.

Following swiftly on its heels is news that Hull City have accepted a Burnley bid of £10m for Robert Snodgrass. Now if we could land one or other of those two targets, or better still both, that would indeed be good transfer business. As the day develops and the speculation mounts it seems we are indeed bidding for both players. However, there is reported competition from other clubs such as Crystal Palace, West Ham United, Middlesbrough, Bournemouth and Sunderland, for one or other of these targets. All the aforementioned clubs have greater financial punch, with perhaps the exception of Sunderland, and with the ability to offer bigger wages, the situation is far from straightforward.

Needless to say, the transfer saga rolls on into the 26th January, with increasing speculation as to who will end where. Nail biting times for the fans. The recent developments in transfer windows leave most Clarets fans pessimistic about our chances of landing our targets. Without naming names Sean Dyche reveals in his Thursday pre-match press conference that we are pursuing three or four possible targets, so it's a case of wait and see.

Bad news on the 26th as it is confirmed that Dean Marney's injury is once again a cruciate ligament in the same knee as his previous one. Poor old Deano! For the second time in his Premier League career he will have his season finished before the end of January. Best of luck Dean and we hope for a speedy and complete recovery. Dean's injury may well hasten the search for a central midfield replacement before the window closes on the 31st January.

Friday evening on the 27th January and still no incomings, and one target missed as Robert Snodgrass completes his move to West Ham United. Those 'in the know' reckon that 'Snoddy' was never really a primary target but our bid was more of a negotiating ploy to force Norwich City's hand regarding Robbie Brady. Time will tell but the latest reports are that Brady will be in the Norwich City squad for Saturday. That doesn't sound like he is Turf Moor bound any time soon. Predictably the 'Up the Clarets' messageboard is cranking up to fever pitch and finger pointing and recriminations are being fired in all directions. God knows what it will be like when we reach the 31st.

Fortunately, tomorrow we have a little diversion from league action as we look forward to a 4th Round FA Cup tie at home to Bristol City. I would anticipate a run out for the fringe members of the squad for this one and a line-up similar to the Sunderland ties is likely.

One further piece of news on the Friday is a four-game touchline ban for Arsenal manager Arsene Wenger following his 'contretemps' with last week's match officials. Perhaps that will serve as a lesson to our Mr Wenger to take a more dispassionate view, but somehow I doubt it!

FA Cup 4th Round – Saturday 28th January, 15.00 – Burnley v Bristol City

Just a small aside here relating to the purchase of cup tie tickets at Turf Moor. Being a season ticket holder for as many years as I can remember, I decided to avail myself of the opportunity to purchase my 'own seat' ticket for this game before they went on general sale.

On Friday 20th having a few moments spare I rolled up at the Turf in the early afternoon. On a quick recce I could see a large number of like-minded people had done the same. Not wishing to spend the bulk of Friday afternoon queuing in the cold outside the ticket office, I decided to leave it till Saturday. Minor grumble here. Why does the ticket office have to be served by outside counters?

Early Saturday afternoon I repeated the process and on arrival found no queue at all! A good reason for that, the ticket office was closed after 12.30. Undeterred I entered the Clarets Store which I am sure most of you will realise is the same building. There I was informed by a pleasant and efficient member of staff that although the ticket office was closed I could indeed purchase my ticket by visiting the Clarets Store in town! Now as they say in good dialect speech, 'that's a rum do'. Why can the store in town sell tickets but the store which is actually at the heart of the operation not? This is one for you more knowledgeable types to answer. Anyway, I was so impressed with our friend's advice that I promptly bought myself a new Clarets bob-cap.

Off into town I went to complete my purchase, a £5 Senior ticket, which was loaded to my season ticket card. Another minor grumble, no receipt was issued. Now I know it was only £5 but, just supposing on arrival at the turnstile my card was refused entry (it has happened before, cast your minds back to the August chapter), what recourse would I have? So, after all I got my ticket for £5 but with the added cost of the 'lucky (?) bob-cap my total spend was £15. So much for economising!

Would all my ticket trauma be worth the hassle? Of course it would. Our visitors struggling Championship outfit

Bristol City, on the back of seven consecutive league defeats, were hardly going to be a match for the Clarets.

As expected Sean Dyche rang the changes again, this time eight! The only survivors from the starting line-up at Arsenal were Michael Keane, Ben Mee, and Steven Defour. A formation change also as James Tarkowski came in to take up a central role in a midfield five, with Sam Vokes playing a lone striker role. Scott Arfield and Johann Berg Gudmundsson returned from injury to get some valuable game time ahead of another big night coming up on Tuesday.

The first half was a fairly tame affair with the Clarets comfortably in control without carrying much goal threat. Our visitors were certainly knocking the ball about nicely and making some pretty patterns but again without much punch. That is until approaching half time Nick Pope was called into action. A run down the right flank by the Bristol full back ended with a pinpoint cross onto the head of striker Milan Djuric, whose diving header was turned away brilliantly by our young keeper.

On the stroke of half time the vital first goal, a somewhat fortunate run of the ball gets Defour free on the right of the box and his pull back is turned into the corner of the net by Sam Vokes. Good timing that, we can relax now and enjoy the half time break.

The second period is much the same although the goal advantage has taken some of the anxiety out of both team and fans and we are settling into a comfortable rhythm. A decent effort from Defour goes wide of the post but on 68 minutes following a touch of absolute quality from the same player the lead is doubled. A free kick to Bristol City is punched clear, rather needlessly I thought, by Pope. The ball drops to Defour on the edge of the Burnley penalty area and he, accompanied by two fellow Clarets, sets off rapidly in the direction of the Bristol goal. Approaching halfway Defour pushes a pass out right to Gudmundsson and carries on his run. Gudmundsson repays the favour as Defour reaches the outskirts of the Bristol area. Spotting the giant City keeper, all 6'4", advancing off his line, our Belgian ace cool as a cucumber deftly 'dinks' the ball over him and it drops instantaneously to bounce into the net. A sublime moment in the words of Mr Dyche and once again an illustration of what this guy is capable of. Brilliant!

And that was that, game over! Substitutions by both sides but little else to report. Its job done and into the hat for Round 5 on Monday night. Wembley here we come.

Result - Burnley (Vokes 45, Defour 68) 2 - 0 Bristol City

Burnley Team

Pope, Darikwa, Keane, Mee, Flanagan, Gudmundsson, Barton (Hendrick 70), Defour (Kightly 78), Tarkowski, Arfield (Barnes 70), Vokes

Subs Not Used - Robinson, Lowton, Ward, Gray

Bristol City Team

Giefer, Vyner, Flint, Wright, Golbourne, Hegeler (Pack 76), Brownhill, O'Dowda, Reid, Bryan (Abraham 61), Djuric (Engvall 61)

Subs Not Used - Fielding, Magnusson, Paterson, Wilbraham

Attendance - 14,921

Round 4 of the FA Cup threw up a number of shocks, none bigger than the Vanarama National League sides (formerly the Conference) Lincoln City and Sutton United's victories against Brighton and Leeds United both high flying Championship sides. Millwall of League 1 disposed of Premier League Watford, whilst Oxford United similarly accounted for Newcastle United.

I always used to look forward to the FA Cup draws and the tension that surrounded who you were going to get. I must confess that I was similarly looking forward to this one as our recent good form had bred a real positive vibe about the club. Who did we want? One of the giants and an opportunity to give them a black eye, or one of the lowly ranked teams and a potentially easier progression to the last eight. Who did we not want? Without a doubt Blackburn Rovers, not because we wouldn't wallop them, but rather because of all the hassle associated with the bad blood between the two sets of fans. I personally preferred the option of a lower league side at Turf Moor.

Imagine my joy then as whilst watching the televised draw Gareth Southgate produced ball number 12, BURNLEY, as the first ball to be drawn. So, a home tie, great start. Then Robbie Savage's turn to draw the away team and to my great joy, LINCOLN CITY. I know all the stuff about not counting your chickens before they hatch, but surely this tie must give us a great opportunity to further progress. Predictably it's not long before Steve C, Burnley émigré to the Lincolnshire wastelands, is on the text. Now you may recall that Steve believes himself, for the purpose of wind-ups, to be a Hull City fan. That is, a Hull City fan who has never seen them play and couldn't name a single player. Well, would you believe it? He now professes to be a Lincoln City fan.

Obviously disgruntled, like all Hull City fans with the current sorry state of the club he is seeking to switch to a more successful outfit. How disappointed he is going to be when they become the next victims at Fortress Turf Moor.

January 31st marks the close of the transfer window and by the morning of that day, despite much speculation, there are still no incoming transfers. Three names are now prominent in the rumours, Robbie Brady from Norwich, Andrew Robertson from Hull, and Ashley Westwood from Aston Villa. Bids are believed to have been lodged for all three, Westwood being a late entry into the frame, presumably due to the season ending injury to Dean Marney.

I'm off to Sunderland Point for the regular Dotcom Tuesday walk but you can bet I'm checking the messageboards at regular intervals for any news. As we end the walk and settle down for lunch a quick check reveals Westwood has passed a medical and is at the Turf ready to sign. One done, two to go. Next comes the news that Hull City have dug their heels in on the Robertson transfer and he will not be allowed to leave. Oh well, just the long term on-off saga with Brady to resolve now. All the way back, and through tea time, reports indicate that the signing is going through but nothing is confirmed. Anyway, can't hang about any longer it's time to get to the ground for another mammoth challenge this time against current reigning Premier League Champions, Leicester City.

Game 23 - Tuesday 31st January, 19.45 - Burnley v Leicester City

The Leicester game brings to an end a very busy January this being the seventh fixture in the month. Once again we revert to a 'normal' league line up with just the one change from the Arsenal match, Joey Barton in for the injured Dean Marney.

I'm at the ground in good time and anxiously scanning the concourse TV's for any further news on the Robbie Brady signing, but to no avail.

An early departure for Steven Defour in this one, not even making it to half time, as he is replaced by Scott Arfield and heads straight to the treatment room. I can't help feeling that our Belgian Ace is carrying some long term injury and is having to be nursed very gently through games.

It's a fairly even first half but the game is marred by 'wrestling matches', holding and pushing at every set piece and aerial encounter. Referee Mike Dean's unwillingness to punish such offences purely resulting in further tussles. I was under the impression that referees were supposedly clamping down on this behaviour - the most blatant example being a clear push in the back by Danny Drinkwater on Michael Keane as he rose to head a cross in the Foxes penalty area. It was spotted by everybody in the ground except Mr Dean, and once again a clear penalty decision denied. Goalless at half time and I'm not too disappointed, we are giving as good as we get in what had the makings of a very tricky fixture.

Some great news during the interval as the stadium announcer reveals that Robbie Brady is now indeed a Claret. A record transfer fee paid to land the wide man but he was the target that seemed to be most desired. Welcome aboard Robbie!

The second half settles into a pattern of the Clarets pushing forward and our opponents looking to use the pace of Jamie Vardy to catch us on the counter. One or two penalty shouts from the visitors happen now. Firstly Vardy tumbles over Tom Heaton as he tries to latch onto a loose ball bouncing away from the keeper after a Riyadh Mahrez shot. No stranger to a dive isn't Vardy - and he repeats the performance colliding with Heaton as he moves onto a through ball. Fortunately Mr Dean is not falling for these pantomimes, perhaps realising his error from the push on Keane.

The Clarets are turning in one of their best performances of the season with great support coming from the stands. Barton has made a seamless reintegration into the side and is simply magnificent in this game as he wins every challenge. What a wasted first half season at Rangers! Similarly Andre Gray is troubling the gigantic Leicester City centre backs Wes Morgan and Robert Huth with his pace and power. Unlike his counterpart Vardy he stays on his feet despite being clearly held as he enters the penalty area but his shot is saved.

Entering the last ten minutes I remark to John W that the game is balanced on a knife edge and I'm settling for a valuable point. Then once again a late goal to send the fans delirious. Three minutes of normal time and a corner is awarded to the Clarets. Duly slung in by Arfield, then headed down by Keane, it is turned in by Vokes. Unbelievable scenes of joy.

It later transpired from TV footage that Big Sam may have handled the knock down to get it under control. But in view of the dodgy goals given against us, surely we were due one in our favour. Our friend Mr Dean clearly thought the handball was unintentional, how could I have doubted his outstanding refereeing ability!

Yet another home victory giving us now nine from thirteen fixtures. A great night, the only negatives being the injuries to Defour and Hendrick who hopefully has just sustained a knock.

Result - Burnley (Vokes 87) 1 - 0 Leicester City

Burnley Team

Heaton, Lowton, Keane, Mee, Ward, Boyd, Hendrick (Tarkowski 89), Barton, Defour (Arfield 34), Barnes (Vokes 79), Gray

Subs Not Used - Robinson, Darikwa, Flanagan, Gudmundsson

Leicester City Team

Schmeichel, Simpson, Morgan, Huth, Fuchs, Albrichton (Okazaki 77), Drinkwater, Ndidi, Gray (Musa 67), Mahrez, Vardy

Subs Not Used - Zieler, Chilwell, King, Mendy, Benalouane

Attendance - 19,202

Season To Date - Played 23, Won 9, Drawn 2, Lost 12, Goals For 25, Goals Against 33, Points 29

League Position after Game 23 - 10th

FEBRUARY

Our magnificent home form means we are getting closer and closer to our Premier League survival target. I am now beginning to think of our season as one of a league and cup double, that is league survival and an FA cup win. Steady lad, I think I'm getting a bit carried away!

Certainly, we are now entering a very interesting and challenging phase of our season. Fifteen games to go but due to the imbalance of home/away fixtures, owing to the early season switch of the Liverpool game, nine of these will be on the road.

On paper the home games look more challenging with Chelsea, Manchester United and Tottenham Hotspur still to come. In contrast the away fixtures look perhaps more 'winnable'. Starting from today we have away fixtures against seven teams currently below us in the table, and the remaining two are against the Merseyside teams. This of course looks easier on paper, but as Sean Dyche has reminded us only this week, games aren't won on a piece of paper.

Our away results have without doubt resulted in a large amount of pressure being put on home performances. From the ten away fixtures completed we have gleaned only one point from a possible thirty. However, recent performances on the road have been decidedly improved with only single goal defeats against three of the league's top teams. Surely by the law of averages we are due an away win. Today at Watford would be as good a time as any to achieve it!

Game 24 – Saturday 4th February, 15.00 – Watford v Burnley

Today's game marks a return to Watford for manager Sean Dyche who earlier in his fledgling managerial career was unceremoniously dumped by the Hornets. We are eternally grateful to them for that!

Early team news confirms my suspicions that new signings Robbie Brady and Ashley Westwood would have to bide time for their Clarets debuts. Dyche, loyal as ever to players who have served him well, goes with a tried and trusted line-up with both newcomers having to be satisfied with a seat on the bench.

As I may have pointed out previously, sometimes these match reviews are easier to write than others. This time I'm afraid it's one of the others. Looking forward to an afternoon where we may be able to garner further survival points, the wheels fell off before the bus even started rolling!

Watford determined to make their physical presence felt roared out of the blocks clearly intent on letting our lads know they were there. Watford loanee M'Baye Niang, clearly eager to impress, clattered into Stephen Ward and became the first man booked. Unfortunately, this physical approach was escalated to another level with a seventh minute two footed assault on Watford's Jose Holebas by Jeff Hendrick. The referee produced a straight red card and with 83 minutes to play with only ten men, the game was effectively over for us.

Within a matter of minutes Watford had the lead as Troy Deeney met a Niang cross to head the home side in front. It looked as though it was going to be a long afternoon ahead. Creditably the Clarets re-organised and gradually started to come into the game. As half time approached I was thinking how well we had performed to go in just the one goal down. Then the killer goal arrived in injury time as Niang headed home Holebas's cross.

Two goals down, 45 minutes to play, and a one-man disadvantage, wasn't exactly the scenario I had envisaged at 3pm. However, again to their credit the Clarets stuck doggedly to their task. By this point I had become somewhat disenchanted with proceedings and only half-heartedly followed the radio commentary whilst tuning into the BBC's Final Score programme. My ears did however prick up when I heard the award of a penalty to Burnley for handball in the box. Up stepped Ashley Barnes to convert and with 12 minutes plus added time surely enough to snatch an unlikely point. But this is Burnley and fairy tales rarely or never happen for us. Once again time runs out and it's a blank day on our travels.

Ironically Niang, who was rumoured to have been a loan target for ourselves, and who had made such a major impact on the game, could quite conceivably have joined Hendrick in the early bath. His goal celebrations following his header, joining with the fans to take the plaudits, should have incurred strictly speaking, a bookable offence. Coupled with his early booking this would have meant him seeing a red card. However, on this occasion the referee decided to overlook his over exuberance. A second half with an equivalent number of players on the pitch may well have been more favourable to our cause. Oh well! A day best quickly forgotten I think...

The result was made even worse to bear by the fact that Sunderland, who looked like 'dead men walking' pulled off a fantastic 4-0 win at Crystal Palace. Similarly, a reviving Hull City took maximum points from a current Liverpool side who couldn't win an argument at the moment.

Fortunately, other results were not so unkind with defeats for Middlesbrough, Bournemouth and Southampton ensuring they stayed below us. Sunday's fixtures also saw defeats for Swansea City and Leicester City against the two Manchester clubs. The gap between us and the relegation places remained at nine points. However, with the next match a home game against rampant leaders Chelsea, a likely 'nil pointer', alarm bells are starting to ring for me.

Result – Watford (Deeney 10, Niang 45+2) 2 – 1 (Barnes 78 pen) Burnley

Burnley Team

Heaton, Lowton, Keane, Mee, Ward, Boyd (Vokes 86), Hendrick, Barton, Arfield (Westwood 77) Barnes, Gray (Brady 55)

Subs Not Used – Robinson, Tarkowski, Flanagan, Gudmundsson

Watford Team

Gomes, Cathcart, Kaboul, Prodl, Holebas, Capoue, Behrami (Doucoure 65), Cleverley, Niang (Success 81), Deeney, Zarate (Janmaat 87)

Subs Not Used – Britos, Okaka, Arlauskis, Watson

Attendance – 20,178

Season To Date – Played 24, Won 9, Drawn 2, Lost 13, Goals For 26, Goals Against 35, Points 29

League Position after Game 24 - 12th

Wednesday February 8th gave me the opportunity to look up an old adversary from my previous life in the Textile industry. Needing to visit a pal in Blackburn Royal Infirmary, and being aware of the chaotic traffic and parking mayhem at afternoon visiting time, I hatched a cunning plan. I opted to cheekily email Anne Reid, Office Manager at Blackburn Yarn Dyers and request permission to avail myself of their parking facilities.

Anne I have known for many years through business, and for her sins she is a dyed-in -the-wool, (see what I did there with the textile dyeing connection? Clever eh!), Blackburn Rovers fan. Permission to park was no sooner asked than granted, along with an invitation to pop-in and see them. Well in view of the respective league positions and fortunes of our respective clubs, this was an invitation too good to miss.

After a few minutes of explaining the merits of being a Claret, and the obvious disadvantages of being a Roverite, I left for the hospital. Not before however being treated to a display of Rovers photographs that dated back to some far distant point in history, when I believe they may have bought the Premiership. Needless to say, these were covered in dust and I suggested the best place for them may be the skip in the yard. Foolishly before leaving the building I indicated which was my vehicle in case it was blocking an exit.

On returning from the hospital I once more called in to announce my imminent departure, thank them once again, and trade a few final insults. I should have known better. Upon reaching my car it was pointed out by my co-passenger and fellow Claret Mike McD that something was attached to the windscreen. Closer inspection revealed it to be something particularly nasty… a Blackburn Rovers club badge. Touché BYD! Not to worry, I will find another victim to deposit the offending article upon, a good suggestion from Mike being John W's swanky new motor…

There's no game for us Saturday as we are again the featured game on Sky Sunday, however there are seven Premier League fixtures, many featuring sides in the relegation battle.

The results certainly go in our favour as firstly Hull lose at Arsenal in the lunch time kick off. Surprise, surprise! Arsenal benefit from a first goal clearly hand-balled in by Alexis Sanchez, but of course not seen by the referee.

There's then a heavy home defeat for Sunderland, 4-0 to Southampton, tending to suggest their victory at Crystal Palace last week by the same score, was somewhat of a fluke. Palace are again losers, this time by a single goal at Stoke, whilst Middlesbrough manage a score-less draw at home to Everton.

The bottom three remain the same as they all lose, and the gap to the Clarets is still nine points ahead of our titanic task against Chelsea.

Game 25 – Sunday 12th February, 13.30 – Burnley v Chelsea

In the week ahead of this game I hadn't spoken to one Clarets fan who thought we would win the fixture. Our visitors, champions-elect Chelsea, were nine points clear of their nearest challengers, and in a rich vein of form. Their formidable attacking threat, with players of the calibre of Eden

Hazard and Diego Costa, and their speed on the counter attack made them a potent force.

Strangely enough the most confident view of our chances came from PNE Dotcomer Steve Glover who reckoned us good for a 1-1 draw. When asked if I would settle for that I told him that would be an excellent outcome. I'm sure that was a view that would be echoed by most Burnley fans.

So, once again on a most unlikely day and time for us more traditional football fans, that being Sunday 13.30, I set off for Turf Moor. It had to be one of, or perhaps the coldest day of the current season. With a raw easterly wind, a temperature not rising above two degrees and flurries of sleet and snow, just the kind of Burnley day to welcome the 'southern softies'.

In front of what looked like a packed Turf Moor, the game got underway with the Clarets showing two changes from the Watford defeat. In came new signing Ashley Westwood for the suspended Jeff Hendrick, and making a full home debut record signing Robbie Brady took over from Scott Arfield.

The early exchanges gave a taste of what we were likely to be in for as the visitors quickly transformed defence into attack, and the trickery of Hazard and the power of Costa were apparent. Not to be overawed though we pushed forward determinedly if not quite as skilfully. It was from one such quick counter that Chelsea took the lead, as our attack broke down and Chelsea shifted it swiftly and accurately upfield allowing Pedro to beat Heaton from inside the box. Seven minutes gone, and a goal down, not a great start.

Buoyed by their early success Chelsea continued to dominate possession but the Clarets retained their shape and gradually steadied the ship without sustaining further damage. On 24 minutes a possible way back into the game opened as Chelsea conceded a free kick outside the box. Burnley, now spoilt for choice with two 'dead-ball' experts Joey Barton and new man Robbie Brady, weighed their options as the Chelsea wall irritated the referee with their constant distance infringements. Who would it be, the right footed Barton, or left pegger Brady?

Not long to wait for the answer as up stepped Brady to mark his home debut with a stunning free kick goal. Starting just wide of the keeper's right hand post the shot curled beautifully to beat the despairing dive of Thibaut Courtois and hit the back of the net! What a fantastic strike, and what a lift for the Clarets.

Building on the confidence this equaliser had given them, the Clarets now start to take the game more to our illustrious opponents whilst still dealing admirably with their swift counters. A second goal almost arrives as Matt Lowton, running intelligently into the penalty area is picked out by Barton, only for his shot to be saved by the outstretched legs of Courtois.

In they go at half time all square with a very happy band of Burnley supporters in the stands. The big question was could we maintain that level of performance and effort for another 45 minutes plus? The possession statistics showed Chelsea on the ball for more than two thirds of the half. That means a lot of running for our guys to maintain shape and win it back. Still our fitness levels are becoming legendary under Dyche's regime, so no worries on that score.

The answer to the question was indeed a resounding yes! The early stages of the second period see us pushing for a second goal. It's nearly forthcoming as Andre Gray is put through one-on-one with Courtois from an astute break by Barnes. Unfortunately, Gray's shot lacks sufficient power and is saved comfortably. At the other end lots of endeavour, but as usual the magnificently marshalled rearguard is coping admirably with anything thrown at it. Multiple substitutions are made by both sides as tiredness creeps in, but the pattern of the play is now set - Chelsea pushing forward and Burnley still carrying sufficient threat on the break to discourage the visitors.

There are four minutes added time to be played and we are praying that our precious point is not going to be cruelly stolen away from us as in previous matches. There's no chance of that on this occasion and we rise as one to celebrate a tremendous, and at the outset, unexpected result. Fortress Turf Moor is once again impregnable and we edge yet closer to the survival target.

The lead over the bottom two teams now stretches to 11 points and third from bottom Hull City now trail by 10. Thirteen games to play and confidence is high!

Result - Burnley (Brady 24) 1 – 1 (Pedro 7) Chelsea

Burnley Team

Heaton, Lowton, Keane, Mee, Ward, Boyd, Westwood, Barton, Brady (Arfield 65), Barnes, Gray (Vokes 82)

Subs Not Used - Robinson, Tarkowski, Flanagan, Gudmundsson, Darikwa

Chelsea Team

Courtois, Azpilicueta, Luiz, Cahill, Moses (Willian 72), Kante, Matic (Fabregas 67), Alonso, Pedro (Batshuayi 87), Hazard, Costa

Subs Not Used - Begovic, Zouma, Ake, Chalobah

Attendance - 21,744

Season To Date - Played 25, Won 9, Drawn 3, Lost 13, Goals For 27, Goals Against 36, Points 30

League Position after Game 25 - 12th

I stopped up late tonight to watch it all again on MOTD2, well later than expected! There were only two games to show, both had two goals in them, guess who they put on last? Not to worry in my current mood of euphoria I'm not going to be put out by that.

It's been a long time coming but at last there seems to be a growing realisation, among the pundits at least, that Burnley are not just a team of 'long ball hoofers'. It is beginning to dawn on them that yes, at times we can be direct, but that this is part of a structured game plan that suits our players. When the opportunity arises we play our football as good as any team. Without the untold riches of the elite clubs this is how it has to be. As Dyche says, we have to find a way to win.

Of the MOTD pundits Danny Murphy is generally complimentary about our style, and judging by this evening's programme we have now won over Martin Keown. Compliments about our performance were plentiful and Keown even went as far as to say that he felt Antonio Conte and Dyche were currently the best two managers in the Premier League. High praise indeed!

You can get statistics about everything from a Premier League game these days, and as I suggested in my game review our level of physical exertion would be severely tested. This is borne out by after match statistics that reveal Burnley players covered a total of 75.1 miles in the game, compared to Chelsea's 71.1. That speaks volumes for our fitness levels and training regimes.

For those of you interested in statistics I thought I would just take a look at our comparative situation in the last Premier League season. On checking back I see that after 25 games last time we had amassed 21 points, nine fewer than our current total. We had won only four games against our current nine victories, but interestingly lost one fewer. I think this highlights the value of a win against that of a draw pretty emphatically.

Tuesday 14th February dawns and for all you romantics like my good self, it's Valentine's Day, and a celebration of love and affection. It's a long trip today for the Tuesday Dotcom walk which will take in the station buffet at Carnforth railway station. For those of you of a certain age you will recall that this is the station and buffet used in the David Lean directed romantic drama film of 1945, Brief Encounter. What better place for a Valentine's day stroll.

Starting on the shoreline at Bolton-le-Sands, the walk was to follow the coastal path up to Carnforth returning to the start via the Lancaster Canal, a distance of about 7.25 miles. Leader Bob Clare clearly intoxicated by the romantic mood had suggested that some of the Dotcomer's may wish to recite some romantic poetry under the iconic station clock at Carnforth. More on the clock to follow shortly...

Bob's idea was I believe, that he would get some poetry of the Roses are red, Violets are Blue variety. A little wishful thinking there, as this lot are about as romantic as a bucket of whelks. From approximately 30 walkers only two could be bothered to compose. Going first was Anne Luscombe, who recited a sincere and glowing tribute to her husband of 40 years Andy. I hope he was suitably embarrassed.

Next up the irrepressible Lesley Mcdevitt, who not content with composing a poem, went as far as to set it to music! Well her version of something that passed as music. The poem clearly aimed at husband Mike had a rather sinister feel to it, and could possibly have been taken as more of a threat than a token of love. Suffice it to say the best part of the recital was when the London Euston to Glasgow Central train flashed through at about 100mph making Lesley totally inaudible.

For my own part I did manage to have a couple of 'brief encounters' one with 'Moll of the Year 2016' Barbara, and the other with the love frenzied Lesley. These took the form of photo opportunities of re-enactments of the railway carriage scene from the film in a mock-up set. It was a lovely day out by the coast in unseasonable sunny weather for Lancashire in February. In the words of Lesley;

"a lovely day, full of fun, flirting....... and encounters! Thanks for the memories......."

On the matter of the clock, it seems some of the romance has gone from the tale. Apparently, the clock has been wound by a gentleman, voluntarily twice a week for the past 30 odd years. On a recent occasion a remark passed by the said gentleman, in conversation with a friend, was overheard by a member of the public and deemed to be racist.

This was reported to the station authorities who promptly suspended the gentleman from accessing various areas of the station. At this point the chap pointed out that, this being the case, he would not be able to wind the clock. The authorities then decided he could access the clock but not other areas, at which point I presume he made an appropriate non PC remark.

So, the station clock currently remains unwound, yes time has stood still at Carnforth Station. How sad, whatever happened to the principle of free speech?

Once again a break from Premier League action this weekend as we continue our march on Wembley. Saturday sees our Fifth round tie against non-league Lincoln City at the Turf, with a 12.30 kick off for live television coverage. Unfortunately, I am going to miss the tie as I head for Darlington and a reunion with daughter Stephanie. I had prayed that the game would be switched to Friday evening to make it accessible for myself, but alas it was not to be.

Following the game is going to provide major logistical problems as I drive to the north east inevitably losing contact with Radio Lancashire. Hopefully one of the national radio stations will also be covering the game. I'm hoping there's no repeat of the Wimbledon fiasco of 1975. I'm looking forward to a good night out in Darlington and don't want to have to spend it fending off 'witty' remarks from 'well-wishers'.

FA Cup 5th Round – Saturday 18th February, 12.30 – Burnley v Lincoln City

In the words of Victor Meldrew, I DON'T BELIEVE IT! What an unmitigated disaster! Who said lightening doesn't strike twice in the same place? In a re-run of the 1975 shambles, we have only gone and done it again!

Who would have thought it? Burnley beaten at their own game. The arch-battlers outbattled, outmuscled, outfought, outthought and finally ousted from the competition. Full credit however to Lincoln City who become the first non-league team to reach the last eight of the FA Cup for 103 years!

Showing six changes from the team that performed so admirably only last week against Chelsea, the Clarets should still have had sufficient quality and nous to see off their plucky challengers. There were major changes in defence with only Michael Keane retaining his place. Once again Sean Dyche took the opportunity to rest players ahead of Saturday's vital Premier League clash at Hull. Indeed, Tom Heaton in goal would also have enjoyed a rest day had Nick Pope not picked up an injury in training on Friday.

However, it wasn't the defence that were responsible for the defeat as they limited the visitors to only one attempt on target. One attempt on target - but one goal - and that was sufficient to end the lacklustre Clarets cup hopes for another year.

By all accounts the problem was down to our inability to handle a situation that was foreign to our normal game. In practically every Premier League game we have started as underdogs and built a game plan around defensive stability and minimal possession. On this occasion the opposite was the case, we were expected to blow our opponents away, but what happened was a reflection of our failure to handle the greater possession and effectively break down a resolute opposition.

A large and physical Lincoln team had clearly done their homework well, and unfortunately we got sucked into something of a physical battle. A prime culprit on this occasion being Joey Barton, who in contrast to his usually exemplary behaviour at Burnley, got himself involved in a number of unsavoury incidents with various adversaries. A long running niggling feud with Lincoln's massive striker Matt Rhead, (for whom the term 'brick sh**house' could have been coined), not only got him a yellow card but also negated his more customary constructive contribution.

Some may point to an early over robust challenge by a Lincoln defender on Johann Berg Gudmundsson which terminated his involvement in the game as a reason for our downfall. His replacement however, the enormously experienced George Boyd, could not really be seen as weakening the team. Up front strikers Sam Vokes and Andre Gray enjoyed the occasional half-chance but neither carried sufficient threat to worry a determined and unflappable rearguard.

Toward the final period, and following Ashley Barnes's introduction, there was at last an increased sense of urgency as we started to force the visitors back. However, just as I contemplated a poor afternoon's work would mean an unwanted replay, the final blow.

With nothing to lose and the game entering the final minute the Red Imps broke out of their defensive fortress to force a couple of corners. From the second, a well-rehearsed dead ball routine, defender Sean Raggett rose to head home through a ruck of Burnley players on the goal line. Tom Heaton's desperate attempt to claw the ball out was overruled, rightly so as confirmed by the goal-line technology, and the disaster was complete.

Oh the humiliation of it, beaten at home by a team ranked 81 places lower in the league structure. The only top tier team to TWICE be knocked out of the competition by non-league teams. What a few days ribbing am I going to be in for. It doesn't take long for the aforementioned 'well-wishers' to appear and start the gloating. Not to worry, I will switch off my phone, avoid the newspapers, and put my foot through the telly!

As the fans of all beaten cup teams say, now we can concentrate on the league!

Result - Burnley 0 – 1 (Raggett 89) Lincoln City

Burnley Team

Heaton, Darikwa, Keane, Tarkowski, Flanagan, Gudmundsson (Boyd 20), Barton, Westwood, Arfield, Vokes (Barnes 73), Gray

Subs Not Used - Robinson, Lowton, Ward, Mee, Agyei

Lincoln City Team

Farman, Wood, Habergham, Waterfall, Muldoon (Southwell 64), Power, Rhead (McCombe 90+1), Hawkridge (Ward 81), Raggett, Arnold, Woodyard

Subs Not Used - Walton, Long, Marriott, McMenemy

Attendance - 19,185

And that's another thing, whose daft idea was it to let the team be led out by Senior Citizen mascots? Totally wrong idea that, it gave the opposition the idea that we were best suited to playing walking football. You don't see boxers entering the ring behind some old dodderers. No, they come bouncing in behind some young, blonde, nubile young ladies who sure as hell scare the life out of me! I think this was one experiment that needs to be put to bed, along with the mascots. Let's get back to using the kids whose youthful exuberance should serve as a livelier entrance. Can I just say here to forestall any accusations of ageism that I too fall into the category of 'old dodderer'.

Tuesday 21st February sees a blank day in the Dotcom walkers calendar; yes, it's half term once again. Not wishing to be incarcerated for the day, I mentioned at last Thursday's Burnley contingent debrief that perhaps we should organise something ourselves for this date. The 'Wandering Weirs', rapidly assuming the mantle of expedition leaders confirm that they have a route planned and are ready to go. It was decided that in the time honoured fashion the route would be circulated on Monday and all those 'up for it' would confirm their availability.

The infamy of John W's routes are such that of 15 people canvassed, there was only one acceptance…me! So, on a dry Tuesday morning but with heavy rain forecast for early afternoon, three intrepid hikers set off from Clough Bottom, Widdop. The route planned, an 8.5 mile circular taking in Rodmer Clough and Reaps Cross on Heptonstall Moor, it was decided that it would be by way of a reccy for Thursday's meander.

Having received the GPX file of the route, entitled rodmer2 (sic), I loaded it on my fancy Garmin SatNav ready to demonstrate my mastery of the route. I might have suspected something afoot from the title, it transpired that John W had more than one variant of the route, and it soon became apparent that he and I were tracking different versions. Unperturbed I gave up the idea of following my version and sat back for the ride. All went well till after lunch when John obviously becoming bored with his pre-rehearsed route decided to go 'off piste'. His impeccable reasoning being that we would take a short cut!

What followed was the most horrendous trek across moorland bog, risking life, limb and sanity. John seemed largely unconcerned by his, and our flounderings across by now a rain sodden Heptonstall Moor, but did however conclude that perhaps next time we would stick to the route! To cap it all, eventually we arrived at Reaps Cross which through the passage of time has lost some of its glamour. In fact, it is no longer a cross and could probably be more aptly named Reaps Stump.

A gentle return through driving rain via Gorple reservoir to Clough Bottom rounded off an interesting day, and the prospect of a repeat on Thursday to enthral a larger gathering. Little did we know that twas all in vain as Storm Doris would ensure that nobody would venture forth this particular Thursday.

On return from the outing I was greeted by the news that old 'friend' Owen (Judas) Coyle had once again lost his job. Having successfully managed to maintain Blackburn Rovers in a relegation spot for almost the whole season so far, the owners had decided that with 15 games to go drastic action was required. We can only thank Owen for his splendid effort at Ewood but even that will not go far to ingratiate himself with we Burnley fans. Within 24 hours Tony Mowbray is appointed to the 'hot seat' at Deadwood. We wish him all the best in his efforts to maintain their position in the bottom three.

Thursday evening brings news that stuns the football world as Premier League Champions Leicester City terminate the contract of manager Claudio Ranieri. What a way to treat a guy who not twelve months earlier had masterminded a miraculous title win for the 5000/1 outsiders. On days like this the game stinks! The affable Claudio has paid the price for a lacklustre season for the Foxes that now leaves them facing a relegation fight. Last season everybody was willing Leicester City to win, after this action I'm sure most fans will be hoping they fail.

Hull City away coming up next as we return to the more serious business of Premier League action. It's probably best not to get too hung up about last week's little hiccough in the cup. Forget it and move on.

That certainly seems to be what old 'oppo' Steve C has done. Yes, he who changes colour (or allegiance) quicker than a chameleon, is already starting to attempt to wind me up regarding the forthcoming fixture. Steve for some strange reason seems to think that now is he not only a Hull City fan, but also a Lincoln City fan. I presume his allegiance switches depending on who is most successful at the time. Anyway, in view of the fact that he has never seen either team play in his life, I shall continue to treat his jibes with the contempt they deserve. I shall be employing every 'lucky charm' at my disposal this weekend, and heaven help him when we torpedo the sinking ship that is Hull City below the water line. They will then become hulk city, not Hull city.

Game 26 – Saturday 25th February, 15.00 – Hull City v Burnley

Returning after a good overnight stay and trip to Harrogate Theatre, I'm back in Burnley and fully kitted out in good time for this vital fixture. This is the first in a run of consecutive away games that can go a long way in deciding our Premier League survival chances. Anything but a defeat for us here will put a severe dent in rivals Hull's prospects. A victory would really give us a boost, failing that a point would edge us closer and maintain a 10 point gap over the opposition with another fixture 'eaten up'.

Returning to a more normal league line up, we welcome back, Matt Lowton, Stephen Ward and Ben Mee in defence. Robbie Brady who last week was cup-tied replaces Scott Arfield, and George Boyd is back for the injured Johann Berg Gudmundsson. Up front Ashley Barnes is preferred to Sam Vokes in the starting line-up and we go with the familiar 4-4-2 formation.

A bright start to the game sees us enjoying the early exchanges and setting up camp in the hosts half as we press forward. However, there are no real early chances and slowly but surely Hull start to get a foothold in the game. With goalmouth action at a premium the best chance of the first half comes from a Mee header which hits the woodwork following a 'flap' by the home keeper. At the other end Hull's best chance falls to one time Clarets target Kamil Grosicki who fires over. A fairly comfortable opening period sees the teams in at half time all square.

I am feeling fairly relaxed at the interval and results elsewhere seem to be going largely in our favour with most of the strugglers trailing, with the exception of Crystal Palace.

The half time team talks seem to have done the trick and the action is moving up a gear. Sensing a real chance of an away victory we are again looking the more likely scorers. A near miss by Barnes is followed by an even better chance not taken by Andre Gray, and I am confidently awaiting the arrival of the first goal.

On 72 minutes it duly arrives, but not for us! Defending a City corner, Michael Keane is adjudged to have handled and a penalty awarded. It can't be that clear cut as the radio commentators can't see any infringement until their third video replay. In the aftermath of the dubious decision, Barnes who all afternoon had been walking a tightrope, picks up an unnecessary booking for dissent. Tom Huddlestone steps up to take the kick, Tom Heaton guesses correctly and gets a hand to the ball, but can't prevent it going in.

Once again we are behind away from home, time now to see what we are made of. These Clarets though are nothing if not resilient; within four minutes we have proved our battling qualities once again and have drawn level. Keane is left unguarded in the Tigers penalty box as a Brady corner is swung across. Taking the ball down on his chest, he lets it drop and as it sits up off the turf fires home low into the net. Taken more like a top-notch striker than a centre half, the young man is delighted and no doubt mightily relieved.

The stuffing has now been knocked out of our hosts and it takes them time to recover their momentum as the clock ticks down. Entering stoppage time another disaster occurs as Barnes feels the wrath of the referee for a challenge and picks up a second booking and the inevitable sending off. It's too late though to make any difference and we see the game out to earn a second away point of the season and more importantly deny City a further two.

A satisfactory afternoon's work indeed with only Palace managing a victory over fellow strugglers Middlesbrough. Their victory lifts them out of the bottom three ironically dropping Leicester City, without a game, temporarily into the drop zone.

Result - Hull City (Huddlestone 72 pen) 1 - 1 (Keane 76) Burnley

Burnley Team

Heaton, Lowton, Keane, Mee, Ward, Boyd, Westwood (Tarkowski 85), Barton, Brady (Arfield 89), Barnes, Gray (Vokes 85)

Subs Not Used - Robinson, Flanagan, Darikwa, Agyei

Hull City Team

Jakupovic, Elabdellaoui (Hernandez 82), Rannochia, Maguire, Robertson, N'Diaye, Huddlestone, Elmohamady, Maloney (Meyler 67), Grosicki, Mbokani (Niasse 67)

Subs Not Used - Marshall, Diomande, Tymon, Bowen

Attendance - 20,156

Season To Date - Played 26, Won 9, Drawn 4, Lost 13, Goals For 28, Goals Against 37, Points 31

League Position after Game 26 - 11th

Tuesday February 28th sees the first Dotcom walk of the new term (don't ask again!) and is billed as a walk on the West Pennine Moors. The plan is an ascent of Great Hill (not that great) followed by a walk along the ridge to Belmont. However, on arrival at the car park we are greeted with snow, sleet, and rain. A wise decision is swiftly made to abort that route and go for a more sheltered ramble through Roddlesworth Woods, which is appreciated by all.

Of course, this being the first walk since the catastrophic cup exit to Lincoln I am expecting a fair amount of 'stick'. Fortunately, this seems to be fairly low key, perhaps due to the fact that the ten-day gap between the fixture and the walk has obliterated it from most of the ageing memory banks. Group leader Bob Clare does however take every opportunity to keep raising the subject, using any tenuous link possible. Our resident 'Latics' fan Nigel however is disinclined to join in, unsurprisingly as the Red Imps also put out Oldham Athletic at an earlier stage.

I think I may have got away lightly with this one and retribution is at hand as I later learn that Bob Clare has misplaced his mobile phone. He does however locate it as his washing machine cycle comes to an end with some meaty clunks. Yes, his phone has gone in with the walking gear and been 'cleansed'. That'll teach him to stir it with the Burnley Boys!

MARCH

March it's often said, comes in like a lion and goes out like a lamb, this being a reference to stormy wintry weather early in the month fading to more docile conditions by the close.

As we head for our second away fixture of this crucial run we must hope that the Clarets will come in like lions, and by the end of the month with safety assured, go out hopping and frolicking like lambs. Swansea City are the next opponents and under new manager Paul Clement are making a remarkable comeback from down among the dead men. They're not totally out of it yet, but in a much healthier place than before, and playing with confidence and style. They are going to be extremely difficult opponents. We owe this lot one, having gone down to a late goal in the first game of the Premier League season back in August.

Can we improve on last week's away point and this time take all three, or will it be a return to the familiar away day blues?

Game 27 - Saturday 4th March, 15.00 - Swansea City v Burnley

Well it's that time again and I'm settling into a regular Saturday afternoon away game routine. This usually consists of tuning the radio, opening the BBC Sports App, sweating, pacing the floor and quite often the use of foul and abusive language. Today will be no exception.

First comes a bit of a shock with the news that Tom Heaton will miss the game and is replaced by veteran keeper

Paul Robinson. Suggestions are that he was having difficulty kicking last week at Hull City, although he seemed to make a good job of kicking the post in frustration at his near penalty save. Sean Dyche later confirms his absence as due to illness on the evening before the game. Other team news sees Jeff Hendrick, returning from a three-game ban, replacing Ashley Westwood who drops to the bench. Sam Vokes comes in for Ashley Barnes as the latter serves his one game ban following his dismissal last week.

A slow start from both teams according to the live text on the BBC, but that doesn't last long as the action starts to come thick and fast. Before the game has even reached the ten minute mark the hosts centre back Alfie Mawson has hit both crossbar and post. Is it going to be our lucky day?

Apparently not as on twelve minutes Fernando Llorente heads the Swans in front and that familiar sinking feeling starts to set in. However, on twenty minutes my faith in the 'God of Good Luck' is restored as referee Anthony Taylor awards us a completely unwarranted penalty. Challenging for a corner Sam Vokes clearly handles the ball, but not in the eyes of the referee who sees it as a Swansea hand. Should have gone to Specsavers! An opportunity to level which is too good to miss and we don't, as Andre Gray's free shot hits the back of the 'onion bag'.

Clearly incensed by the injustice of it all our hosts set about righting the wrong and we are pinned back for the rest of the first half - although we almost go behind again but are saved by another woodwork intervention, phew! We make the sanctuary of the dressing room at half time with the scores fortuitously level.

If I wasn't nervous at the start, I certainly am now. If the referee has got the penalty decision as wrong as the commentators believe, there's surely one coming at the other end at the first opportunity. Also, with Stephen Ward on an early yellow card, he'd better watch out.

The half time break seems to have settled us down somewhat and then on sixty minutes the unbelievable! Yes, Burnley have an away lead, with a smart finish from Andre Gray giving us the advantage with 30 minutes to play. Can we hold out? What do you think? Can we hell! The lead lasts nine minutes before Martin Olsson finishes comprehensively levelling the scores.

For a brief spell I thought we might break our away day hoodoo, but alas it was not to be. As the clock ticked on towards full time, I am so nervous I am forced into several diversionary tactics. One of these is to put my wife's car in the garage to eat up precious time. This is however not without hazard as she has the radio tuned to Radio 2 and I suffer a few minutes radio silence. Back on station the game enters added time, and I enter the kitchen. Just in time to hear Fernando Llorente climb to head his second goal of the day and once again cruelly deny us of our point. I have to confess at this point I start to utter a shocking profanity, stifled only by the presence of my wife.

There's nothing for it but to pour a restorative gin & tonic and settle to watch Final Score to see if the other results have inflicted major damage on our survival chances. Swansea move to within four points of us and Crystal Palace manage a second win on the trot to go six points behind. Leicester City, at last recovering some momentum, beat strugglers Hull City and ten man Bournemouth hang on for an unlikely point at

Manchester United. Hapless Middlesbrough lose again at Stoke City and drop into the bottom three, nine points adrift of us. Hull's defeat leaves them 10 behind and Sunderland's expected loss at home to Manchester City in the Sunday fixture has them 12 off.

A quick look at the match stats and reviews of the Sunday paper reports confirm that we came away with what we deserved...nothing. Outplayed by the fast improving Swans, even with the aid of a non-penalty, assistance from the woodwork on three occasions and two goal line clearances, we still lost. Our away form now sees us with two points from a possible 39 - and is nothing short of embarrassing. What's worrying is that with away fixtures still to come at Sunderland, Middlesbrough, Crystal Palace and Bournemouth - all in the dogfight - I'm not confident of gleaning points at any of these. Although the gap to third bottom is still nine points I am becoming increasingly edgy. With our next fixture an away game at Liverpool, on paper for us a wasted journey, things look like getting even more 'hairy'.

Result - Swansea City (Llorente 12, 90+2, Olsson 69) 3 - 2 (Gray 20 pen, 60)) Burnley

Burnley Team

Robinson, Lowton, Keane, Mee, Ward, Boyd, Hendrick, Barton (Westwood 80), Brady (Arfield 66), Vokes (Tarkowski80), Gray

Subs Not Used - Pope, Flanagan, Darikwa, Agyei

Swansea City Team

Fabianski, Naughton (Rangel 89), Fernandez, Mawson, Olsson, Cork, Carroll (Amat 90+5), Fer, Narsingh (Ayew 73), Llorente, Sigurdssson

Subs Not Used - Nordfeldt, Britton, Routledge, Borja

Attendance - 20,679

Season To Date - Played 27, Won 9, Drawn 4, Lost 14, Goals For 30, Goals Against 40, Points 31

League Position after Game 27 - 12th

To round off a thoroughly depressing Saturday afternoon, Blackburn Rovers (spit), win at home to fellow strugglers Wigan. New manager Tony Mowbray's haul of seven points from a possible nine takes them out of the drop zone. Why, oh why did they have to sack Owen Coyle!

Sunday 12th March and almost ready for round three of our four match away day challenge - so far it's one draw and one defeat. Does that mean today will complete the set with a, from where I'm sat, highly unlikely away win? Today should prove to be the sternest challenge of the four as we come up against a Liverpool team currently in fourth place and pushing for a Champions League spot.

This game was originally scheduled for Turf Moor but due to the early season fixture switch sees us once more on our travels. Early team news suggests that Tom Heaton will be fit to return in goal, and Ashley Barnes may well return following suspension. Fortuitously Joey Barton's FA hearing to answer gambling charges on the 8th March was cancelled due to illness of the chief investigator, and so he is once again available to play. Joey will be returning to his home city, hopefully he can once again turn in a masterclass in front of his fellow Scousers.

This weekend has seen a dearth of Premier League fixtures as it has been FA Cup Quarter Final day. Only three fixtures yesterday and the Anfield game today. Saturday saw Hull City's narrow victory over Swansea City cut the gap between ourselves and the bottom three to seven points. Bournemouth recorded a last-minute victory over West Ham United to move them just one point behind us. The other fixture between Everton and West Bromwich Albion was meaningless as far as our position is concerned.

It's all getting mighty nerve wracking as I keep looking back over my shoulder at the other teams coming up on the rails. I'm sure there'll be many twists and turns before the race is over. Once again, I find myself dreaming that today could see a major boost to our chances if we could somehow magic that elusive first away victory. I think it depends very much on which Liverpool team turns up. Will it be the team that comprehensively took Arsenal apart last week, or the side that has struggled on a few occasions this season against lesser lights. Not long now before we find out!

Game 28 - Sunday 12th March, 16.00 - Liverpool v Burnley

Sunday afternoon at 4.00 o'clock, what a bizarre time to play a football match, still the clubs do what their paymasters, the TV companies, demand. Can't say I'm a big fan of Sunday football at all, it seems totally alien to me.

Anyway, Sunday it is, and the Clarets line-up is as suspected but with one further change, Scott Arfield replacing record signing Robbie Brady, who drops to the bench.

Presumably Sean Dyche sees this as a backs–to-the-wall type game and feels Scotty is better equipped in the defensive arts.

A good start by the Clarets who are posing early problems suddenly becomes much more as on seven minutes we take the lead. A ball to Matt Lowton, enjoying acres of space in the midfield area, allows him to advance a couple of yards before threading a sublime low cross into the box. Andre Gray can't quite get on to it but Ashley Barnes sliding in at the back post certainly can. In an instant the ball is in the net and we have just reward for a fluent attacking move.What a fantastic start and the first Burnley goal at Anfield since Peter Noble's in 1975.

Following our fine opener our hosts are clearly rattled and the game continues with us in the ascendancy. The locals are not enjoying the spectacle one little bit, and with the half time break looming it looks like harsh words will be the order of the day in the home dressing room. Then as so often happens, the curse of the added time goal strikes again. On 45+1 minutes and with their first shot on target the Reds are undeservedly level.

I blame the bloody radio commentators who seconds before the goal had said we were 'looking comfortable'. This follows comments indicating we might be on target for our first away victory of the season. Why can't they just keep their mouths shut and their hands together in prayer as we fans certainly are! Still I doubt it would make for very good radio coverage if they kept their mouths shut…but please stop tempting fate! If we are relegated I will personally be holding Radio Lancashire responsible and blacklisting the station.

There's for me a growing predictability about what is going to happen next. Yes, we all know it, once we have conceded one there is an inevitability that others are going to follow. And, true to form, on 61 minutes a fine long range effort from Emre Can nestles in Tom Heaton's net and we are in our familiar position of trailing away from home.

The fluency of the first half seems to have evaporated as we seem to resort more to long-ball tactics. Robbie Brady is introduced at the expense of George Boyd but tasked to play an unfamiliar right wing role. Andre Gray's tiring pace is replaced by Sam Vokes more aerial presence as route-one becomes the order of the day. On 89 minutes a Premier League debut for youngster Daniel Agyei. Anfield - what a place to make a first team debut!

Plenty of huff and puff, and jitters from the home crowd, but Matt Lowton manages to miss with the best late chance and once again we end the game pointless. It's another fixture against one of the top teams, on their own turf, from which we could and should have had some reward, but again reel in nothing. If ever there was any truth in the saying, 'there's no place like home' then Burnley FC are that living proof.

At home 29 points from a possible 42, away from home two points from a possible 42. Incredible and almost unbelievable! An interesting statistic is that from seven of the last eight away fixtures, barring the draw at Hull, all have been decided by a single goal. However, a much more damning statistic is that all seven have still ended in defeat. No, we are not getting battered on the road but the points tally is no better than if we were. When will it end? Surely, we can't go the whole season without an away win...or can we? Five games to put that right and in the process avoid the lowest away points total in a Premier League season, currently held by Derby County with a paltry three.

<u>Result</u> - Liverpool (Wijnaldum 45+1, Can 61) 2 - 1 (Barnes 7)) Burnley

<u>Burnley Team</u>

Heaton, Lowton, Keane, Mee, Ward, Boyd (Brady 73), Hendrick, Barton, Arfield (Agyei 90), Barnes, Gray (Vokes 80)

<u>Subs Not Used</u> - Robinson, Tarkowski, Darikwa, Westwood

<u>Liverpool Team</u>

Mignolet, Clyne, Matip, Klavan, Milner, Wijnaldum, Can, Lallana, Mane, Origi (Lucas 79), Coutinho (Woodburn 60)

<u>Subs Not Used</u> - Karius, Gomez, Moreno, Wilson, Alexander-Arnold

<u>Attendance</u> - 53,145

<u>Season To Date</u> - Played 28, Won 9, Drawn 4, Lost 15, Goals For 31, Goals Against 42, Points 31

<u>League Position after Game 28</u> - 12th

Spring is coming, but you wouldn't have thought it on Tuesday 14th as we assemble for the Dotcom walk. It's a circular from Thornton-in Craven taking in Kelbrook, led by Burnley Contingent stalwart Ed 'Sherpa' Walton. Starting from St Mary the Virgin church, 27 hearty souls set off in weather more akin to November than March, topped off with incessant drizzle. However, the vagaries of the British climate are soon demonstrated as within an hour we are walking in lovely spring sunshine.

It's the same again on Thursday as 13 (unlucky for some) Burnley lads and lasses, and Button the dog, meet for their weekly wander. The weather starts damp, overcast and miserable, and soon deteriorates further on the approach to Keighley Moor reservoir. Today's walk, once again led by husband and wife team John and Judy W, the 'Bogfinder Generals', is from the little known village of Goose Eye, Oakworth. **Where?** I hear you say.

Now the best thing about this walk is that it starts and finishes at a pub worthy of a special mention, The Turkey Inn, Goose Eye. This is a truly outstanding example of a British pub at its finest. I would recommend anybody with foreign visitors who want to sample a proper Inn to visit this place. Needless to say after an 8.2 mile trot via the aforementioned reservoir and back via Oakworth Moor and Newsholme, (which John W informs me **constantly**, is mentioned in the Domesday book) a visit was definitely called for. Roaring log fires, and an excellent choice of real ales, lagers and ciders, complemented by a proper pub food menu. What more could you want?

Goose Eye is a lovely little village and its relative inaccessibility only adds to the charm of both it and the pub. 'Google' the pub if you are interested and give it a try - you won't be disappointed!

Even the weather improved after the lunch stop, as we huddled down behind the dam wall of Keighley Moor reservoir to shelter from wind and driving rain. Super optimist Ian Mckay ventured at this point, not without some ridicule, that the sun was coming out. Within 30 minutes this rare phenomenon had indeed occurred, and we were all blow-dried before we hit the pub. Well done Ian, the Michael Fish of Worsthorne! An interesting discussion ensued over the beer, about the relative merits of Penis Pipes as worn by some tribal residents of Papua New Guinea, but that is for another day.

By the way, I had Goose Eye Bitter which was outstanding, but there are several more offerings to try, a few from the Settle Brewery Company, which I believe is based in Keighley. A pub and walk which will be undoubtedly repeated.

Another massive game coming up for the Clarets as we complete our four match away trek, this time with a visit to bottom club Sunderland. It's a must win game for our hosts and for us really, in view of our abysmal away form, a must not lose one. This game if all the results go right for us, i.e. wins for ourselves, Manchester United at Middlesbrough, and Everton at home to Hull City could go a long way towards seeing us safe. Fingers and toes crossed, lucky charms donned, nerves jangling. Here we go again!

Game 29 – Saturday 18th March, 15.00 – Sunderland v Burnley

Well Middlesbrough and Hull City admirably fulfilled their part of the bargain going down 3-1 and 4-0 respectively. For us though only partial success as we have to settle for a share of the spoils at the currently inappropriately named 'Stadium of Light'. At the moment it would be more aptly named 'The Stadium of Gloom'.

For the hosts, desperate for a win to haul them back into contention, it's a poor first half performance. From the unchanged Clarets it's a confident and capable opening period. As half time approaches I'm in a relatively relaxed mood. This is aided by the laconic style of new Radio Lancashire match summariser ex Claret, Michael Phelan. Mickey, currently unemployed after a distinguished playing career and successful coaching spell at Old Trafford under Sir Alex Ferguson, has a laid-back style that oozes calmness. Let's keep him for the remainder of the season!

There's almost a perfect half time boost as 'Basher' Barnes could and should have converted Scott Arfield's incisive pass from close range. Not this time for our Ashley as he prods a great opportunity wide of the post.

Unsurprisingly, it's a better second half from the now desperate Black Cats. Two or three decent chances are created and then a glorious one, missed by Billy Jones with a close range header that should really have been in.

The Clarets remain fairly comfortable and in control settle for a point that proves far more valuable to us than our hosts. Another point gained in our survival quest, but for them a dire result leaving them anchored at the bottom, still 12 points adrift of ourselves. Even the massive home support expresses their disapproval amid a growing realisation that they are as good as doomed.

I'm not so sure they are yet, but to be honest they are the poorest side we have played this season. Four league and cup matches have resulted in two Burnley home wins and two away draws. The point gained enables us to draw level with Derby County's record number of away points in a Premier League season. With four more away fixtures to come surely that record will stay with the Rams.

Result - Sunderland 0 - 0 Burnley

Burnley Team

Heaton, Lowton, Keane, Mee, Ward, Boyd (Brady 74), Hendrick, Barton, Arfield, Barnes (Vokes 65), Gray

Subs Not Used - Robinson, Tarkowski, Flanagan, Westwood, Defour

Sunderland Team

Pickford, Jones, Denayer, O'Shea, Oviedo, Gibson(Ndong 74), Rodwell, Larsson (Khazri 78), Januzaj, Defoe, Borini

Subs Not Used - Mannone, Djilobodji, Lescott, Manquillo, Honeyman

Attendance - 41,518

Season To Date - Played 29, Won 9, Drawn 5, Lost 15, Goals For 31, Goals Against 42, Points 32

League Position after Game 29 - 13th

Wednesday 22nd March marks a momentous day for young central defender Michael Keane who makes his full England debut in a friendly versus Germany in Dortmund. Playing on the right-hand side of a back three, Keano enjoys a mightily impressive start to his international career - so much so that the Daily Mail make him their 'Man of the Match'. It's also a memorable day for Burnley FC as Michael becomes the first Burnley outfield player to start for England since Martin Dobson in 1974!

There's no Premier League action on the weekend of 25/26th March due to the international break. The foul weather in the week leading up to it is replaced by a weekend of unbroken sunshine. This is perfect timing as we are celebrating my wife's parents Diamond Wedding anniversary with a weekend break at Nidd Hall, near Harrogate - a lovely setting for a much-enjoyed short stay.

Michael Keane's impressive debut in midweek is rewarded with a further full cap, this time a World cup qualifier against Lithuania at Wembley. This time Gareth Southgate reverts to a standard flat back four formation with Keano partnering Manchester City's John Stones in central defence. It's another faultless performance from our young stopper and he is rapidly establishing himself as an important member of the full England squad.

This is of course not without benefit to Burnley FC as his growing reputation further enhances his transfer value. I think most Clarets fans realise that this is probably his last season with us as he is strongly rumoured to be on the shopping list of most, if not all, of the Premier League's top clubs. I'm sure when the time comes, and assuming we land the big fee that is now a realistic valuation of the player, all at Turf Moor will wish him well in what has the makings of a glorious career.

Hooray! At last! After 46 days, a return to home turf. Our four-away game stint eventually yielded two points from a possible twelve. A frugal return, one could say, but double what we had amassed from the previous 22 possible. Not only that, the two points gained denied relegation battlers Hull City and Sunderland much needed victories and maintained our points advantage over them.

It's time now to push on and claim the few extra points that are required to ensure survival with two home games now in quick succession, Tottenham Hotspur, and Stoke City.

Neither are easy games but with our impressive home form we should fear nobody, particularly after the highly encouraging performance last time out against Champions elect Chelsea.

As March comes to a close the football club's accounts for the year ending June 2016 are published. Following the big profit showing from the last Premier League season (£30.1m), these accounts for the following Championship campaign not unexpectedly show a net loss of £3.7m. However, on closer inspection it transpires that this loss is sustained after payment of 'promotion bonuses' to players and staff of £11.3m.

Forecasts for the current financial year are indicating another substantial profit. Maintenance of our Premier League position is clearly paramount to further enhancing our financial stability and cementing a bright future for the club.

APRIL

Game 30 - Saturday 1st April, 15.00 - Burnley v Tottenham Hotspur

April 1st, All Fools Day, and there's no prizes for guessing who were the fools today! It was a bad day at Turf Moor with a poor performance, a defeat - and to put the tin hat on it - victories for our rivals in the relegation scrap. A sharp reminder here to those who were already behaving like a Venky and 'counting chickens' that the relegation issue is far from over.

A lacklustre display, admittedly against a very strong Spurs side who still have ambitions of stealing the crown from Chelsea, made for a rather depressing afternoon. I think the die was cast when I broke with tradition and only had a single pint pre-match instead of the customary matching pair, ahead of a big evening celebrating my in-laws Diamond Wedding anniversary. Note to self, don't do that again!

The first piece of unsettling news arrived as I made my way to the pub, my phone alerted to me to the selected line-ups. Unsurprisingly the Clarets named an unchanged eleven, but Tottenham sprang a surprise omitting regular England full back Kyle Walker to include former Turf Moor favourite Kieran Trippier. Well aware of the damage that 'Tripps' can cause from an attacking full back role I was fearful that his desire to impress his former employers might prove costly. It wouldn't be nice to see our former hero inflicting damage on his former team mates and fans. Good old 'Tripps' received a great reception from the crowd and had a nice hug from all his former team mates, a lovely gesture.

There were no immediate signs of the impending doom as the game got underway. Our visitors opting for a 3-5-2 formation with Trippier and Davies pushed high up on the flanks, whilst we favoured, as usual, the now rather predictable 4-4-2. A fairly tame start, with Tottenham playing a smooth passing game, whilst we countered with our more direct approach using the pace of Andre Gray. A first half of few chances, and one glaring miss from Spurs England 'media starlet', the talented but temperamental Delle Alli, was fairly evenly balanced.

Worryingly, creeping into our play was some pretty sloppy passing, the biggest culprit being the usually ultra-reliable Joey Barton, but the visitors were unable to gain advantage at this stage. Both Clarets full backs, Matt Lowton and the impressive Stephen Ward were on top form and nullifying any threat from the wings. During this first period Tottenham were rocked by two injuries forcing substitutions. Firstly, Victor Wanyama seemed to suffer some form of spinal injury and after a couple of attempts to continue succumbed to the inevitable. Then promising youngster Harry Winks, twisted an ankle while being completely bamboozled by Ward. Sickeningly colliding with a drinks cooler in the technical area, he was stretchered from the pitch and straight to hospital.

So, half time arrived and the job half done, still a long way to go yet though to keep the points tally ticking over. Obviously, the injuries forced Spurs boss Mauricio Pochettino into some serious thinking and a reshuffle. Unfortunately for us this resulted in a reversal to a 4-4-2 formation and a more potent attacking unit.

From the off the visitors seized the initiative and play became largely concentrated in our half. This is not an unusual scenario for us and Andre Gray, despite his somewhat 'hit-and-miss' style, still proved a distraction for the Spurs rearguard and a useful 'out-ball'. Rather strangely, manager Sean Dyche decided on 56 minutes to remove this threat and replaced him with the more physical but less pacy presence of Sam Vokes.

A goal was coming and it duly arrived on 66 minutes as Eric Dier, benefitting from some poor defensive work following a corner, calmly slotted home. The visitors, now totally in control, continued to look threatening and on 77 minutes the killer goal duly arrived. Good work by the highly talented, but lamentably arrogant and unlikeable Alli, created a cross giving the substitute Son Heung-min a simple tap-in. Game over and realistically the visitors could and should have had more!

A very disappointing effort from the Clarets and made more disturbing by Hull City's late winner at home to West Ham United, and Crystal Palace's unbelievable away win at Chelsea. We slip to 15th and the gap between us and third bottom is now down to just five points. A big game is looming on the horizon, Stoke City at home on Tuesday, bringing with it time for a re-think by the manager perhaps? Stoke are comfortably placed in mid-table and will again present a formidable challenge. We have to find a way to incorporate our more creative players into the starting eleven.

Result - Burnley 0 - 2 (Dier 66, Son 77) Tottenham Hotspur

Burnley Team

Heaton, Lowton, Keane, Mee, Ward, Boyd (Brady 74), Hendrick, Barton, Arfield (Defour 78), Barnes, Gray (Vokes 56)

Subs Not Used - Robinson, Tarkowski, Flanagan, Westwood

Tottenham Hotspur Team

Lloris, Dier, Alderweireld, Vertonghen, Trippier, Wanyama (Dembele 44), Winks (Sissoko 45+2), Eriksen, Alli, Janssen (Son 73)

Subs Not Used - Vorm, Walker, N'Koudou, Carter-Vickers

Attendance - 21,684

Season To Date - Played 30, Won 9, Drawn 5, Lost 16, Goals For 31, Goals Against 44, Points 32

League Position after Game 30 - 15th

At least Sunday's goalless draw between Swansea and Middlesbrough at the Liberty Stadium didn't do too much damage to our prospects. The result left 'Boro second bottom and still trailing us by nine points, albeit with a game in hand. Swansea remained four points adrift of us with a much inferior goal difference and a home game coming up against our conquerors, Spurs.

Saturday's defeat and the despondency that followed it certainly impacted on my next-door neighbour, Albert. He greeted me with forecasts of doom and claims that we would be relegated. However, I think his despair may have been alcohol fuelled, and we will soon see him back on the road to recovery.

There's no doubt though that the recent run of no victories in seven games is causing some alarm bells to ring with the fans. Granted five of the seven have been away fixtures and the two home games have been against the top two clubs. We need to quickly get a victory to settle the nerves. At the risk of repeating myself, I would suggest that Tuesday's game against Stoke would be as good a time as any. Following this match is another away game at Middlesbrough and two defeats in these fixtures will surely see us right in the mire!

A lovely Dotcom walk in beautiful Kingsdale, near Ingleton preceded the Stoke fixture. Once again we had received Papal dispensation to venture outside our Lancashire boundary and attempt missionary work on the lost souls of Yorkshire. A splendid sunny day following a cool overcast start added to the pleasure of a great walk in limestone country.

One incident seemed to greatly amuse North End Dotcomer Chris McCann who took great delight in relating the tale to myself. Shortly after lunch, taken in the vicinity of a nearby quarry, two of our lady Dotcomers, who shall remain nameless to preserve their anonymity, felt the need to answer a call of nature. Taking the opportunity to distance themselves discreetly from the throng, they headed off for cover in the rocks. At this time the quarry sounded it's siren, which we all assumed meant a blast was imminent. However, no explosion was forthcoming but Chris did overhear the returning ladies proclaim one to the other, that she had "expected a louder noise than that"! Really, whatever did she mean?

This so tickled our Chris that he found it difficult to suppress his laughter every time the quarry was mentioned for the rest of the day. Only one thing brought a wider smile to his face, and that was North End's subsequent 5-0 demolition of Bristol City at Deepdale that evening. This result takes them to within three points of a play-off place. Perhaps the Prestonians may be regretting their cowardice at not taking on our annual bet!

Game 31 - Tuesday 4th April, 19.45 - Burnley v Stoke City

Not for the first time this season I am approaching Turf moor in a rather apprehensive mood. Saturday's defeat has potentially increased the chances of our being caught by the stragglers significantly and so tonight is once again a 'must win' game. The team sheet shows two changes from Saturday. There is a welcome start for fit again Steven Defour, although once again being played wide left which is not where he is most effective, It seems mighty strange that in January we pay out a record transfer fee for a specialist left winger in Robbie Brady, then leave him bench warming and play our most creative centre midfielder out of position there! The other change sees Sam Vokes replacing Ashley Barnes in a like-for-like swap.

What follows is an ugly, ugly victory, which thankfully ends the winless run! A game for the football purists it certainly was not! Our visitors' set-up in a 3-5-2 formation similar to Spurs in the previous game and for us it's once again 4-4-2. Stoke as ever are heavily populated with players from the 'land of giants', although the tallest of the lot, Peter Crouch only makes the bench. A physical encounter is on the cards and as expected the ball is taking one hell of a bruising as it is battered from end-to-end. An imminently forgettable first half ends unsurprisingly goalless, notable only for the not so friendly antics of referee Kevin Friend. The official is completely blind to the blatant pushing and shoving that is apparent at every aerial challenge, but is quick to caution both Stephen Ward and Joey Barton for the Clarets, whilst ignoring similar offences notably from the visitor's Charlie Adam.

Indeed, Barton and Adam, clearly both players who enjoy a physical challenge, are embroiled in a battle royal in the midfield, both giving as good as they get. I'm quite impressed by Adam who it was rumoured was a pre-season target for the Clarets. His meaty frame gets around the pitch surprisingly swiftly and he is making a significant impact for the Potters. Well done that man!

My half time prediction was that we were probably going to lose this game, as I couldn't see how we were going to manage a goal. Surely though the second half couldn't be as bad as the first, or could it?

It opened with a lovely comedic moment as pantomime villain for the night Adam stepped up to take a corner. As he went to take the kick he slipped and fell, his knee nudging the ball out of the quadrant. Quick as you like he tried to redeem his gaffe by grabbing the ball to re-spot. Not so quickly though that the assistant referee hadn't spotted his manoeuvre and signalled for the referee to award a free-kick for handball. No doubt a clip that will be shown for many years on 'bloopers' outtakes.

Once again Steven Defour taking a knock in a challenge failed to make the hour-mark and was substituted, Robbie Brady coming on to thankfully take up a left wing berth, instead of being wasted on the right. Quickly following this substitution came the one moment of real quality of the night.

The move started with Barton playing the ball to Ward on the left flank, he then found Brady further down that side. Robbie's ball in-field was into the path of Jeff Hendrick who for once drove positively into the box. With great skill he avoided two challenges, before cutting a ball back to Boyd whose excellent finish gave former Burnley keeper Grant, not a sniff. You could feel the relief reverberate around the stadium. What a fantastic goal, that left me thinking why does Hendrick not try these powerful surges more often.

Only 58 minutes gone though and still a long way to go. Fortunately, our visitors had neither the desire nor the guile to break down our magnificent resolute rearguard. With 12 minutes left, Dyche pulled off a masterstroke as he introduced Ashley Barnes at the expense of Andre Gray. Barnes then enjoyed a typical cameo, breaking the game up and drawing fouls aplenty, particularly from the previously impressive Bruno Martins Indi.

The Clarets clearly deciding one goal was enough took to playing the ball into the corner to 'eat up' time. It was all rather negative, even when a good free-kick situation presented a shooting opportunity for dead-ball specialist Brady, we again took the time-wasting option. Six minutes added time were signalled and consumed with no real scares and an immensely valuable three points were ours. Thank God!

The points gained took us to 35 meaning we had surpassed our previous best Premier League points haul, and this with seven games still to go. More importantly the result heaped further pressure on our nearest rivals whose fixtures were next up on Wednesday evening. On the same night bottom club Sunderland lost again, this time at Leicester, and now trail us by 15 points, surely an impossible task.

Result - Burnley (Boyd 58) 1 - 0 Stoke City

Burnley Team

Heaton, Lowton, Keane, Mee, Ward, Boyd, Hendrick, Barton, Defour (Brady 57), Vokes (Tarkowski 85), Gray (Barnes 78)

Subs Not Used - Pope, Arfield, Westwood, Agyei

Stoke City Team

Grant, Shawcross, Martins Indi, Muniesa, Diouf, Cameron, Adam, Pieters, Allen (Afellay 85), Arnautovic, Berahino (Crouch 71)

Subs Not Used - Given, Johnson, Whelan, Imbula, Sobhi

Attendance - 19,881

Season To Date - Played 31, Won 10, Drawn 5, Lost 16, Goals For 32, Goals Against 44, Points 35

League Position after Game 31 - 14th

Wednesday 5th April provided a very nervy evening following Premier League scores on the BBC Sports app. Several teams both below and around us were in action, and the early scores were looking decidedly dodgy. Crystal Palace led at Southampton, Swansea City were in front against Spurs, Bournemouth were ahead at Liverpool and Hull City after an early shock, had got in front of Middlesbrough. Even Arsenal were being held at home by West Ham United. It was unbelievable that all this could be happening.

Not to worry though, most of those results were to change in our favour by full-time. The Saints overcame Palace 3-1, Arsenal came good to the tune of 3-0, Liverpool drew with Bournemouth, the Cherries snatching a late equaliser. Unfortunately, 'Boro capitulated at Hull where for us a draw would have been the ideal result. Biggest downer of the night though came at Swansea, 1-0 up after 88 minutes they fell apart to lose 1-3 to Spurs sending them crashing into the drop zone.

The result of all this meant that we remained seven points clear of Swansea in 18th, 12 points clear of Middlesbrough, and 15 ahead of bottom placed Sunderland, the latter two having a game 'in-hand'. Effectively the gap above Swansea is three wins as their goal average is much inferior to ours, and if the worst came to the worst, a draw and two wins would be insufficient to lift them above us. It's an intriguing situation with Southampton in ninth position on 37 points only four clear of 15th placed West Ham. A lot of teams can still drop but Sunderland and Middlesbrough are now looking 'odds-on'. A win for us at the Riverside on Saturday would probably seal both our fates, for us survival and for them the drop. Come on Clarets finish them off!

Away game 16 coming up, will this be the one? I've got a good feeling about this one. If I cast my mind back to our first ever Premier League away win it came in April 2010. What's more it was almost to the day coming on the 10th April, a further coincidence being that it was also Grand National Day. More cause for optimism is that it was a lovely sunny day in 2010, and the forecast for tomorrow is 16° and sunny!
The result also came against a team who were ultimately relegated, Hull City. How can we fail?

Interestingly our first away victory in that debut season came in away fixture 17, so victory tomorrow would put us ahead of the game.

Game 32 – Saturday 8th April, 15.00 – Middlesbrough v Burnley

Well the omens were good but unfortunately the result was just not quite as good. However, a goalless draw at the Riverside kept the Clarets well on track for Premier League survival.

On a lovely sunny Spring day, and after a quick trip to the bookies to place my Grand National bets, I took up a suitable position in the back garden. The team news soon filtered through from the North East, and surprisingly Middlesbrough caretaker manager Steve Agnew decided to bench his most potent strikers in what for them was a 'must win' game. Opting for a 3-5-2 formation Alvaro Negredo and Adama Traore both found themselves, like myself, taking up a sunbathing position.

Burnley, as you may well have guessed, favoured a 4-4-2 system, but did make two changes from Tuesday evening. Coming in up front was Ashley Barnes for Sam Vokes whilst substitute Robbie Brady replaced the injured (yet again) Steven Defour.

Once again a pretty unforgettable first half, between two of the league's most goal shy attacks, produced a goalless score line at the break. Boro were neat and tidy in their approach but totally lacking any bite up front. The Clarets appeared content to absorb the home team's pressure and draw the sting from them. The most notable chance of the half was Brady's free kick from outside the penalty area that grazed the top of the home crossbar.

However, a lively second period followed, as our heroes realising they had nothing to beat upped the tempo, and took the game to the increasingly desperate hosts. Predictably on came Negredo and Traore, and to complete the set late on Patrick Bamford. Poor young Patrick had poured his heart out to the press about how wicked Sean Dyche hadn't given him much of a chance during his loan at Burnley. Would this be the opportunity to settle his grievances?

Well in truth it very nearly was, a bright cameo performance from the reluctant violin playing striker almost earned him hero status. Latching onto a long ball he was clear on goal until felled by Michael Keane who slipped in his pursuit and sent him tumbling. The crowd bayed for a red card but referee Atkinson produced only a yellow and the chance was gone.

A great save by Tom Heaton, from a tremendous Negredo effort, and two goal line clearances from Matt Lowton ensured the hosts frustration was complete. At the other end a great chance set up by Stephen Ward and a Barnes dummy saw Brady fire wide. After four minutes added time the referee's whistle signalled another valuable point for the Clarets, and a disastrous one for the home team. 'Boro remained second bottom - 12 points adrift of ourselves. Hull City lost at Manchester City and Swansea City went down at West Ham United leaving the Clarets now eight points above the drop zone. With six games left for us, we are slowly but surely edging towards safety.

Unfortunately, the Grand National horses, also edging slowly, couldn't complete a highly satisfactory afternoon.

Rogue Angel, after challenging for most of the race, ran out of steam at the end. Pleasant Company turned out to be a bit too pleasant and lacked the 'killer touch' trailing in ninth. My wife's horses for all we know could still be running, probably taking a wrong turn at the Canal Turn or held up in traffic at the Melling Road!

Result - Middlesbrough 0 - 0 Burnley

Burnley Team

Heaton, Lowton, Keane, Mee, Ward, Boyd, Hendrick, Barton, Brady, Barnes (Tarkowski 90=4), Gray (Vokes 62)

Subs Not Used - Pope, Flanagan, Arfield, Westwood, Agyei

Middlesbrough Team

Valdes, Bernardo (Bamford 83), Ayala, Gibson, Barragan, Leadbitter, Clayton, Forshaw, Downing, Stuani (Negredo 58), Gestede (Traore 69)

Subs Not Used - Guzan, Fischer, de Roon, Fry

Attendance - 29,543

Season To Date - Played 32, Won 10, Drawn 6, Lost 16, Goals For 32, Goals Against 44, Points 36

League Position after Game 32 - 12th

Easter weekend is coming up, and unusually or so it appears to me, only one fixture scheduled in the Premier League. Once again we are on our travels as we head to Goodison Park, a ground where we seldom seem to do well. Seventeenth away game this one, and if we are to record an away victory we'd better get a move on; only three left now.

Game 33 - Saturday 15th April, 15.00 - Everton v Burnley

A different away day experience for me today as I have the opportunity to watch the match live via an internet stream, although I am dubious that it will work. I seem to be engaged in a running battle with BT over internet speeds and dropped connections, and it's a battle BT are winning!

There's no place for Andre Gray in the starting line up as we go with Sam Vokes and Ashley Barnes as the front two. It's going to be a difficult one today as our hosts are on the back of a run of seven successive home wins, and victory today can move them up to fifth in the table.

With fingers crossed I tune into my live stream and miraculously it is working and with a perfectly acceptable picture quality. The Clarets are making a good start and surprisingly pushing back the fancied 'homesters'. Almost ahead on 16 minutes as Michael Keane gets a good head on a Robbie Brady corner only to see it cleared off the line by Ross Barkley. It's been quite an eventful week for young Ross, involved in a late-night altercation in a Liverpool Bar, and then the subject of some pointless and malevolent journalism from a Sun newspaper reporter.

We are close again as Robbie Brady just can't get his head on a teasing Matt Lowton cross. At the other end not too much to worry about so far, Tom Heaton making a routine save from a good opportunity for Romelu Lukaku.

Then my fears are proved justified as on 22 minutes my internet stream is on the blink. A quick shift to my back up plan, i.e. turn on radio Lancashire match commentary! After several stuttering attempts to revive, the stream eventually returns. Strangely enough though the radio commentary has the teams off for half time, whilst in front of my very eyes and in supposedly live-time, the game at Goodison continues. Still I can watch it calmly as I know from the radio that the half time score is 0-0!

It's been a good first half for the Clarets and the match stats show we have had four attempts on target to the Toffee's three. More impressive action by my stream as it now shows first half highlights - my missing moments coinciding with two excellent chances for Vokes, both unfortunately saved by Everton keeper Joel Robles. I remark to my mate John W by text that I would have put away both chances.

A big start to the second half by the hosts who have clearly had a tea break rollocking! We are immediately under pressure and that pressure tells as on 49 minutes Everton take the lead as Phil Jagielka heads home following a corner. All of a sudden we are in familiar territory away from home, behind!

Not for long though as Vokes beats Robles to the ball he is brought down in the box by the keeper, needlessly so as he was heading away from goal. These two guys have certainly seen a bit of each other in this game, and on this occasion Sam is triumphant as he slots the resulting penalty away, 1-1 and game on!

It's not long though before the Toffee's regain their momentum and a let-off on 64 minutes as a Kevin Mirallas effort hits the post. They're pushing hard now and it's no great surprise as they regain the lead on 71 minutes. A cruel one this as our friend Mr Barkley takes a pot at goal, the ball hits Michael Keane and looks to be going wide, only to then hit Ben Mee and bounce into the net. A double deflection!! That just about sums up our luck away from home. Good old

Ross does his best to claim the goal, managing to get himself booked for his celebrations, but it goes in the record book as a Mee o.g.

That goal is the cue for the introduction of Gray but it's academic as on 74 minutes the game is all over as a contest. Lukaku does what he does, using power and pace as he turns Keane and fires home. The Clarets continue to battle valiantly but, without a sharp enough cutting edge, it's meat and drink to the home defence as they play time out.

Seventeen away games played now without a victory... Once again a good performance but with no end result. Oh, how costly were those first half misses! Fortunately, the gap to the relegation spots remains unscathed, Hull City and Swansea City both lose away from home and as we enter the last five fixtures the safety gap is still eight points. Surely we can't blow it from here. No worries, it's only Manchester United to come next!

Result - Everton (Jagielka 49, Mee o.g 71, Lukaku 74) 3 - 1 (Vokes 52 pen) Burnley

Burnley Team

Heaton, Lowton, Keane, Mee, Ward, Boyd, Hendrick (Westwood 86), Barton, Brady, Barnes (Agyei 83), Vokes (Gray 74)

Subs Not Used - Pope, Flanagan, Tarkowski, Defour

Everton Team

Robles, Holgate, Jagielka, Williams, Baines, Gueye (Valencia 45), Schneiderlin, Davies, Barkley (Lookman 90), Mirallas (Barry 76), Lukaku

<u>Subs Not Used</u> - Stekelenburg, Calvert-Lewin, Pennington, Kenny

<u>Attendance</u> - 39,328

<u>Season To Date</u> - Played 33, Won 10, Drawn 6, Lost 17, Goals For 33, Goals Against 47, Points 36

<u>League Position after Game 33</u> - 14th

Easter week provided a good opportunity for some decent walking. Firstly, on a wet Easter Sunday, wife Julie and myself headed for the good footpaths and tree cover afforded at Bolton Abbey. Having said that the tree cover might have been better if they had some leaves on, but mid-April in North Yorkshire is a bit early for that. Julie, glad of the opportunity to escape her deskbound office environment was undeterred by the weather, and once again good waterproof clothing proved that rain need not be an obstacle.

On Tuesday an outing with the 'Wandering Weirs' had us heading for Littleborough and an excellent walk from the White House pub on the A58 Rochdale to Halifax road. Starting from altitude the route took in Blackstone Edge, White Holme, Light Hazzles, and Warland reservoirs on well defined paths over the moor. Having said that, as seems to be the case with most reservoirs these days, there is extensive work being carried out and path diversions may be expected. After the reservoirs the route drops down to the Rochdale canal at Warland, a pleasant canal stroll follows before a steep ascent back to the pub. The White House, a pub I had not previously frequented did not disappoint and there are excellent views from the room at the rear.

Thursday saw the Burnley Contingent head for pastures new, well new to me, as we enjoyed a circular walk from Hetton. A route billed as 8.2 miles taking in Rylestone, Flasby, Eshton, and Friar's Head, which as usual ran out a bit longer at a distance of 8.7. Again, another new pub for me, The Angel at Hetton - lovely, if a little pricey. A nice pint of Craven Brewery Bitter finished off another great day in the countryside.

It's just as well my week had lifted the spirits as an article in Friday's Burnley Express reported that Burnley was hitting back at an 'unhappy town' slur. Apparently a survey by the Office of National Statistics had us as the third unhappiest place to live in the U.K. Corby, I assume in Northamptonshire, took the somewhat dubious honour of coming first, followed by West Lancashire.

Bit of a strange one this coming hard on the heels of the survey that revealed we were the 'friendliest town' in the country. Just goes to show what an absolute load of meaningless bollocks these surveys are. And before any of the Preston mob think of gloating, unfortunately for them, Preston ranked fourth!

Another big weekend looms up in the quest for survival. Once again a big ask for the Clarets as we host Moaninho's Reds in a televised game on Sunday. The two teams that pose a threat to our chances, Hull City and Swansea City, (I have already written off Middleborough and Sunderland), both have 'winnable' home games on Saturday ahead of our fixture. Let's hope that Watford and Stoke City can take points off those two and make for a more relaxed

Sunday afternoon. I have my doubts, and am looking forward to another nerve shredding experience.

Game 34 - Sunday 23th April, 14.15 - Burnley v Manchester United

Nothing ever comes easy if you're a Claret. In Saturday's fixtures both Watford and Stoke both failed miserably in their task of taking points off fellow strugglers. Watford even contrived to lose at Hull whilst playing against 10 men for 65 minutes. Stoke were equally inept at Swansea, managing to miss a penalty that would have levelled the scores. Middleborough sank without trace at Bournemouth going down 4-0. That meant we went into this match with the points gap now reduced to three over Hull and five over the Swans. Squeaky bum time indeed!

A fixture we didn't really expect to get much out of didn't confound our expectations. Injuries to key players at United, particularly Zlatan Ibrahimovich, had 'Moaninho' whingeing about how difficult it all was pre-match. What a bugger! He had to replace Ibrahimovich with Wayne Rooney and still have the luxury of leaving Marcus Rashford on the bench! We are without the injured Sam Vokes and have to rely for striking options from the bench on the hugely inexperienced youngster Daniel Agyei. Once again on paper at least, it's a mis-match.

A lovely sunny Spring day again and as I walk to the Turf I'm once again feeling more than a little apprehensive. Sure, our home form has been excellent and we have been able to compete with even the 'elite' teams, but recent form is not great and we look completely devoid of goals.

It's a fairly even start against an extremely strong looking United team and we manage the opening minutes fairly comfortably. Then on 21 minutes, a lightening quick counter attack by the Reds, once again pulls the rug from under us. Rooney, Anthony Martial, and Ander Herrera combine before Martial tucks the ball home and the visitors have the lead. There was a moment as Martial broke over the halfway line where Joey Barton had the opportunity to 'down him' and 'take one for the team'. This was a course of action that I vociferously advised much to the disgust of John W, who deemed it exceedingly unsportsmanlike. Unfortunately on this occasion Joey sided with my pal and we paid the full price.

John W's take on it was that a booking at this stage would have left Barton, no stranger to referees, walking a tight rope for 70 minutes. My view was that it would have kept the score at 0-0, and as we are not the most prolific of scorers to say the least, kept us in the game.

Further disaster struck on 39 minutes as Rooney doubled the advantage. A somewhat streaky affair this as Tom Heaton managed to keep out Martial's effort only for Rooney's scuffed shot to trickle over the line. This left a veritable mountain to climb now - and no real evidence to suggest that we were going to miraculously find three goals to win the game.

More bad news at half time as Ben Mee failed to return after the break, giving the opportunity for James Tarkowski to get some much-needed game time in his favoured centre back position.

There was an improved second half performance, with some encouraging signs of a more attractive attacking style, but still no real goal threat. Robbie Brady had probably his best game since his January move looking much more like a record transfer signing. A much more confident performance as he made himself available for the ball at every opportunity, earning him the sponsors 'Man of the Match' award. Another positive was a lively cameo from the returning Johann Berg Gudmundsson who replaced the largely ineffective George Boyd. Andre Gray battled and ran hard but we look sorely impotent up-top.

Incredibly in the later Sunday game fellow strugglers Crystal Palace come back from a goal down to win 2-1 at Liverpool. Palace after defeating Chelsea, Arsenal, and Liverpool in the space of a couple of weeks, are showing the kind of form that makes a mockery of their lowly position. Indeed, many of the strugglers have hit some sort of form when it matters. In contrast, we now have only one victory in the last 11 games and we are dropping rapidly towards the danger zone! Next up - Crystal Palace away....

Result - Burnley 0 - 2 (Martial 21, Rooney 39) Manchester United

Burnley Team

Heaton, Lowton, Keane, Mee (Tarkowski 45), Ward, Boyd (Gudmundsson 62), Hendrick, Barton, Brady, Barnes (Agyei 75), Gray

Subs Not Used - Pope, Flanagan, Westwood, Defour

Manchester United Team

de Gea, Young, Bailly, Blind, Darmian, Herrera, Fellaini, Pogba (Carrick 90), Lingard (Rashford 70), Martial (Mkhitaryan 80), Rooney

Subs Not Used - Romero, Shaw, Fosu-Mensah, Tuanzebe

Attendance - 21,870

Season To Date - Played 34, Won 10, Drawn 6, Lost 18, Goals For 33, Goals Against 49, Points 36

League Position after Game 34 - 16th

On a personal note Monday 24th April marks a rather sad day for myself. It is the day of the funeral of an old friend whom I have known since my first day at primary school. It is also the day a more recent acquaintance and walking buddy passes away. Both fine people who have been taken by cancer way ahead of their time. Turf Moor will miss another two staunch Clarets. It's once again a sobering reminder that we only pass this way once and we are now reaching an age where it's time to crack on with the things we want to do.

Wednesday 26th and finally the FA rule on the betting charges levelled against Joey Barton. The outcome is a stinging 18 month ban and £30,000 fine. At the age of 34 this is most definitely a career ending punishment for Joey. I can't help feeling that the severity of this ban is influenced by Joey's controversial character, and a chance for the FA to make an example of a high-profile figure. I'm sure there are many more footballers out there who are guilty of similar misdemeanours. Will they receive the same harsh sentence? I doubt it!

So, it looks like we now face the final four fixtures of the season without a very influential player both on and off the pitch. Joey's leadership qualities and will to win have proved invaluable in his short second spell with the club and he will be sorely missed. In the time-honoured Burnley fashion we will just roll up our sleeves and get on with it. Four games to go and probably three or four points needed to see us safe, let's get them quickly.

It's now Friday the 28th and in keeping with my new philosophy of living life to the full I have decided to change my car. Yes, I am about to dispense with the services of a loyal servant, my 2006 Honda Civic will be traded for a 2016 Hyundai i30. After almost 11 years and 107,000 miles the ever-reliable Honda is being retired from active service, well by me that is! As I head for Motorpoint I am praying that the car will behave itself on its final journey and not flash up any warning indicators. No need to fear we make it in pristine condition and we part company on good terms. I only hope that the Koreans build cars as good as the lads in Swindon!

Game 35 - Saturday 29th April, 17.30 - Crystal Palace v Burnley

Are we about to snatch defeat from the jaws of victory in our survival quest? It is beginning to feel that way, and the mood is not helped as Hull City grab a point with an impressive performance at Southampton to narrow the gap to three points on us. Hull's form under their new manager has been remarkable and they are certainly full of self-belief. Swansea City play at Manchester United on Sunday, so it now becomes important that we get something at Palace to heap the pressure on. Not the easiest place to go when the recent form of both sides is considered.

The team news shows a number of changes for the Clarets. Joey Barton is history and Ashley Westwood gets the nod as his replacement. The returning from injury Scott Arfield and Sam Vokes are preferred to Robbie Brady and Andre Gray. Another enforced change is James Tarkowski in for the injured Ben Mee at centre back.

I can't say that I'm over impressed with the selection. It looks to me like a team set up to try to not lose, rather than one to win. With big money signings such as Brady, Steven Defour, and Johann Berg Gudmundsson left bench-warming, will this be costly against a very dangerous attacking side.

My initial fears are almost proved well-founded as the Eagles tear into us from the start. It's difficult to keep count of the corners conceded in the opening few minutes but I believe it's four. I'm just tucking into my Saturday tea when I almost choke! On seven minutes Ashley Barnes gets a second bite at the cherry from a low Stephen Ward cross and fires home left footed from close range. That's just the start we wanted, but obviously not one that a Palace fan did. As the Clarets celebrate the goal poor old 'Tarks' is hit on the head by a cigarette lighter thrown from the crowd. A nice gesture but I doubt that James smokes, and if he did, surely not seven minutes into a game!

The rest of the first half then evolves into a Burnley masterclass as we dominate our hosts who ahead of the game must have fancied their chances of an easy three points. 'Basher' Barnes has the ball in the net again but it's overruled for handball in the build-up. Sam Vokes and Ashley are giving a first class demonstration of dominance over the Palace centre backs. Stephen Ward is enjoying acres of space to get forward on the left, Ashley Westwood and Jeff Hendrick are dominating centre midfield, and 'Tarks' and Michael Keane are dealing imperiously with any Palace forward threat.

The only 'downer' of the half comes just before the interval as Ward, a pre-match injury doubt, succumbs to several knocks and is replaced by Jon Flanagan. A difficult one for 'Flanners' as he comes up against the extremely dangerous Wilfried Zaha, and at left back on his least favoured side.

An excellent first half though and we probably should have gone in more than one goal to the good. This is more like it!

What follows is for me an extremely nerve wracking second period which seemingly goes on for eons. A tremendous Tom Heaton save from a Damien Delaney shot ensures we maintain our advantage. A penalty claim, correctly denied for an alleged foul by Flanagan on Zaha, continues to keep the tension at fever pitch. Then Sean Dyche's final masterstroke - as Palace's desperation increases, with time running out, Sean introduces Gray to replace Barnes who has given his all. Palace now pushing further forward, and with defenders tiring, are vulnerable to a quick counter. And that's just what they get as George Boyd's exquisite outside of the boot pass is perfect to set free the pacy and fresh Andre Gray. As he bears down on goal he hits a venomous right footer that beats Palace keeper Wayne Hennessey low down at his near post. Eighty five minutes gone and the Clarets 2-0 up away from home, it doesn't get better than that!

The remaining few minutes are played out without too much trauma and at last, at the eighteenth attempt, we have our first away victory of the season. It couldn't have come at a better time or place either. It's a performance that the Burnley Express's Chris Boden describes as MONUMENTAL.

We are surely now, as we hit 39 points with three games to play, on the brink of Premier League survival. That will be an achievement as great as, if not greater than, the two Premier League promotions that Sean Dyche has masterminded. How could I have questioned his team selection? What an idiot I am, it just shows what I know!

The victory produces two rare and precious things. Firstly, a first Premier League 'double' of the season, with home and away victories over Palace. Then secondly and equally rare, glowing praise from Match of the Day pundit Alan Shearer, from whom I can't recall a good word about the Clarets all season. Mr Shearer even goes on to say that if Antonio Conte of Chelsea is not named Manager of the Season, then it should go to Sean Dyche or Eddie Howe.

Result - Crystal Palace 0 - 2 (Barnes 7, Gray 85) Burnley

Burnley Team

Heaton, Lowton, Keane, Tarkowski, Ward (Flanagan 45+1), Boyd, Hendrick, Westwood, Arfield, Barnes (Gray 79), Vokes

Subs Not Used - Pope, Long, Defour, Brady, Gudmundsson

Crystal Palace Team

Hennessey, Ward, Delaney, Kelly, van Aanholt, McArthur (Campbell 71), Milivojevic, Puncheon, Zaha, Benteke (Remy 71), Townsend

Subs Not Used - Speroni, Flamini, Lee Chung-yong, Sako, Schlupp

Attendance - 25,013

Season To Date - Played 35, Won 11, Drawn 6, Lost 18, Goals For 35, Goals Against 49, Points 39

League Position after Game 35 - 14th

Whilst not being one to count chickens before they hatch, I believe that the weekend's results virtually guarantee Premier League football at the Turf next season. With three matches still to play who would have thought that possible way back in August? Not me for one.

Sunderland's narrow home defeat to Bournemouth meant relegation to the Championship for the Wearsiders. What a miserable campaign this has been for them and I'm sure their fans will be glad when it's all over. On Sunday, Middlesbrough fought their way to a creditable draw against Manchester City. An unexpected point but for them not enough, with three fixtures remaining they trail the Clarets by 11 points and cannot catch us. Similarly, third bottom Swansea City came away from Old Trafford with a priceless point but with nine points to play for are still seven adrift of us, and with a much inferior goal difference. This means they must win all three remaining fixtures and hope that we fail to collect two more points. Surely too much to ask…

Bring on the Baggies, let's put it to bed at Turf Moor this coming Saturday!!!

MAY

Two separate but interesting articles contrasting the present-day fortunes of local rivals Blackburn Rovers and Burnley appear in the Daily Mail sports pages of 5th May. Firstly, in an 'exclusive' by writer Laurie Whitwell, he reveals; *'Burnley to hand stars £8m bonus for survival.'* It is described as one of the most generous schemes in the Premier League, and this from a club with one of the smallest wage bills. It reminds me of a similar scheme that was explained to me when I asked a former MD for what in my opinion was a totally justified pay rise. His response on that, and many other similar occasions was; *"You don't give elephants buns till after they've performed."*

Players who have made the most frequent starts stand to benefit by about £650,000. This eclipses the bonus pay-out awarded to Leicester City players on winning last season's Premier League which was reputedly £6.5m. Survival for the Clarets, which would be guaranteed by victory over West Bromwich Albion tomorrow, will be worth a further £95m injection of TV money. Staggering isn't it!

Tucked further into the paper was the second article entitled; *'Jack Walker must be turning in his grave.'* It was an article highlighting the decline of our once haughty neighbours on the eve of a crucial battle to avoid relegation to League 1. The article goes on to claim that Rovers' debt now stands at £100m, and that cleaning staff were laid off at Ewood Park after the final home game against Aston Villa. How the 'mighty' are fallen! Failure to match Nottingham Forest's result tomorrow will bring relegation and surely an even worse financial outlook. As usual, Indian owners the Venky's take all the blame, but the truth is that our 'friends' have for too long spent what they didn't have. The day of reckoning looms!

Game 36 - Saturday 6th May, 15.00 - Burnley v West Bromwich Albion

The weather in the week preceding this game had been, for Burnley at least, unusually sunny but with a cold easterly wind. Typically, as we hit the weekend we keep the wind but lose the sun. Shame that as I was looking forward to pre-match pints outside the Talbot without the need for coats and gloves. This being the penultimate home fixture, and the last Saturday game, it seems that will have to wait till next season.

As I take my first sip of Moorhouse's Premiership Bitter the team news comes up on my phone. Neither of our stalwart central defenders, Michael Keane and Ben Mee, have made the squad. James Tarkowski gets the chance to build on his growing reputation and he is joined this time by the almost forgotten man, Kevin Long. I bet Kevin didn't think he'd be starting a Premier League fixture this season. I must confess to being a little nervous at the thought of an untried pairing, but one piece of good news is that left back Stephen Ward has been declared fit and plays.

It's a bright start by the Clarets in front of a good crowd swelled by a large turnout of vociferous 'Baggies'. The Albion always seem to bring a decent crowd and this for a fixture that is largely meaningless for them. Following our early season battering at The Hawthorns I'm conscious of their strength from set-piece situations and am hoping we don't present them with too many of those opportunities. They always seem to be a big physical side, perhaps it's the striped shirts that visually elongate them. Today is no exception as they line up with four hulks occupying the defensive positions, and our 'tormentor' or is he a 'dementor' Salomon Rondon up-front. It's not very reassuring to learn that the visitors are on the back of a winless run and haven't scored for something like eight hours. The perfect cue for the 'law of averages' to intervene.

The first half whilst short on goalmouth action is being keenly fought, and from a confident looking Burnley side we are seeing some pleasing attacking forays. A snap shot from Sam Vokes brings a save from visiting keeper Foster, but probably the best chance of the first half falls to Scott Arfield. A flowing attack sees the ball played in from the left wing, then fed expertly by Ashley Barnes into the path of the onrushing 'Scotty'. As he pulls the trigger James McClean gets back in the nick of time to block what would surely have been the opener. It's goalless at half time with the visitors barely troubling Tom Heaton; I'll settle for that but a winner would be nice.

If the first half was short on excitement the second certainly proved to be a different tale. The Clarets take a precious lead on 56 minutes and amazingly I miss it! Ashley Barnes makes inroads into the box in the inside right channel, the Baggies defender decides to halt his progress by grabbing him with both hands round his waist and hauling him down. I scream for the penalty, as the assistant referee is flagging vigorously, but the referee is pointing not at the spot but to the centre circle! The crowd are cheering wildly but I assume for the award of the penalty. How wrong I am. Whilst distracted by the flag waving assistant I failed to notice that Barnes had managed to extricate himself from the illegal challenge, got to his feet and squared the ball for Vokes to tuck home from close range. A typical Barnes 'never-say-die' effort - the guy is a hero!

The crowd sensing that Premier League survival was now firmly in our grasp are about to get the party started. How fatal is that? On 66 minutes our balloon is deflated as Salomon Rondon takes advantage of a luckily deflected pass to turn and rifle home an equaliser. If that was a deflation, the balloon was well and truly burst on 78 minutes as one time Burnley target Craig Dawson scored with a diving header from a Chris Brunt corner. No goals in eight hours and then two in 12 minutes. What did I say about the law of averages?

It's time for some drastic action now and Sean Dyche goes for a double substitution. On come wide men Robbie Brady and Johann Berg Gudmundsson to replace Scott Arfield and George Boyd. Once again it's a tactical masterstroke, (or just plain lucky), as Robbie makes a quick impact. As Albion concede a free kick our own set piece expert steps up to curl a cross into the centre of the box. Goalkeeper Ben Foster hesitates fatally before coming for it and is beaten to it by Vokes whose header loops over the hapless custodian and into the net. That's the cue for more delirium and ecstasy for the home crowd. We hope for a winner but have to settle for a draw. That is job done I think, the forty point mark reached, the usually accepted target for survival, and still two games to play!

As news come through of a shock home defeat for Hull City by already relegated Sunderland, our position though not mathematically impregnable, must be unassailable. With two games to go, Hull trail us now by six points and a goal difference 19 worse than ourselves. Effectively we could lose our last two fixtures both 5-0, and Hull win both theirs 4-0, and it would still not be enough.

Furthermore, we could still be mathematically safe if Swansea failed to beat Everton in the 5.30 kick off game. Typically, that didn't happen with the Swans scraping a 1-0 win to lift them above Hull who now look favourites to drop.

Result - Burnley (Vokes 56,86) 2 - 2 (Rondon 66, Dawson 78) West Bromwich Albion

Burnley Team

Heaton, Lowton, Long, Tarkowski, Ward, Boyd (Brady 83), Hendrick, Westwood, Arfield (Gudmundsson 83), Barnes (Gray 79), Vokes

Subs Not Used - Pope, Darikwa, Flanagan, Defour,

West Bromwich Albion Team

Foster, Dawson, McAuley, Evans (Nyom 51), M.Wilson (Yacob 88), Fletcher, Field (Morrison 54), Livermore, McClean, Brunt, Rondon

Subs Not Used - Myhill, Chadli, Leko, K.Wilson

Attendance - 20,825

Season To Date - Played 36, Won 11, Drawn 7, Lost 18, Goals For 37, Goals Against 51, Points 40

League Position after Game 36 - 14th

On Sunday 7th May, an already highly satisfactory weekend for all followers of Burnley FC, suddenly gets even better. Arch rivals Blackburn Rovers become the first team ever to win the Premier League and become relegated to

League 1, the third tier of English football. A dire season comes to a disastrous end for our near neighbours, despite a 3-2 away victory in their final fixture. Wins for Nottingham Forest and Birmingham City mean that it's all too little, too late. Goodbye Rovers, perhaps we may meet again sometime, but not in the near future I hope!

Burnley safe, Rovers relegated, it can't get better than that! And what is more, the sun is shining again!

The following Tuesday's Dotcom walk on the West Pennine Moors, a circular including Great Hill and Belmont, provided the perfect opportunity to 'congratulate' our token Rovers fan 'Blackburn John'. Despite for various reasons, a poor turnout by the Burnley Contingent, there were still sufficient sundry North Enders plus myself to form an orderly queue to rub salt in his wounds. I almost felt sorry for him but it didn't last long and I soon recovered my senses!

Game 37 - Saturday 13th May, 15.00 - Bournemouth v Burnley

Not much to say about this one for two reasons. Firstly, I didn't manage to follow much of the action, and secondly because there's not much to say about it. Strange as this may sound to some of you, other things sometimes take precedence over football. A visit to my daughter in Darlington is certainly one of these occasions. So, as the Clarets headed south, my wife and I headed north-east for an excellent weekend in Durham and North Yorkshire.

Dropping my wife and daughter in the town centre for some 'retail therapy', I made my way for a circuit of Darlington's South Park, a venue that would keep me well away from the perils of parting with any of my own cash in the shops. A pleasant stroll in the sunshine ensued before making my way back to meet the girls for coffee and cake.

My internet connection was variable to say the least but I did manage to glean before leaving the park that the team was unchanged from last week. Once again, there would be no Michael Keane and Ben Mee, but another chance for their patient deputies James Tarkowski, and Kevin Long.

As we sit down in the coffee shop the first bad news of the day, Junior Stanislas has put the Cherries ahead mid-way through the first half. This is quickly followed by a wifely rebuke for studying the internet whilst enjoying social discourse! Discretion being the better part of valour, and the internet connection being hit-and-miss, I decide she is probably right. Aren't they always?

No more coverage for me till daughter departs for home and we check in at the Premier Inn. As we reach our room I'm just in time for BBC's Final Score programme. No change yet we are still trailing 1-0. At this point, Julie makes an excellent suggestion that we should perhaps head down to the bar of the adjacent pub and sample the wares. Needing no second invitation I decide to utilise the bathroom facilities before we leave. I'm no sooner through the bathroom door than news comes through of another goal at the Vitality stadium. On 83 minutes, good old Sam Vokes has equalised!

Note to self - must spent more time using toilet facilities when the Clarets are losing. Quick as a flash I am texting daughter Stephanie to give her the good news. However, alas and alack, before I've even washed my hands, Bournemouth have taken the lead again. Almost two minutes we managed to stay level! I suppose with our away record that shouldn't have come as a surprise.

I'm not expecting a comeback from that so we hit the bar for a pre-dinner consolation pint. News comes through that Swansea City have won away at Sunderland to heap massive pressure on Hull City. The Tigers are not scheduled to play till Sunday, now trail the Swans by four points and face a difficult away fixture, from which they must take something, from Crystal Palace. A point for us would have seen us home and dry but it was not to be, however Hull's plight is such that it's only a matter of time.

On the following day, our Premier League status for 2017-18 is confirmed as the Tigers tamely drop out the league following a 4-0 demolition by Palace. Glory be! Time to knock off a quick text to my old pal Steve C, the Lincolnshire émigré and would be Tigers fan. Of course, Steve currently holidaying in Greece, claims to be on the beach and knowing nothing of their disastrous day. Never mind Steve, you'll have to take your head out of the sand at some point!

Result - Bournemouth (Stanislas 25, King 85) 2 - 1 (Vokes 83) Burnley

Burnley Team

Heaton, Lowton, Long, Tarkowski, Ward, Boyd (Brady 55), Hendrick, Westwood, Arfield (Gudmundsson 75), Barnes (Gray 45), Vokes

Subs Not Used - Pope, Darikwa, Flanagan, Defour,

Bournemouth Team

Boruc, A Smith, Francis, S Cook, Daniels, Stanislas (Ibe 87), Arter (Gosling 81), L Cook, Pugh, King, Mousset (Fraser 66)

Subs Not Used - Allsop, B Smith, Mings, Gradel

Attendance - 11,388

Season To Date - Played 37, Won 11, Drawn 7, Lost 19, Goals For 38, Goals Against 53, Points 40

League Position after Game 37 - 15th

Tuesday 16th May is both my wife's birthday and a second attempt for the Dotcomer's at a Waddington Fell walk. Earlier in the year this proposed ramble had been abandoned at the start point owing to extremely inclement weather. This time, after some weeks of lovely weather and dry conditions, what happens? Yes, true to form we arrive at the rendezvous, the lay-by close to Waddington fell quarry, in lashing rain and with zero visibility! There's no way we can tackle this in these conditions so for the second time we postpone and head for the lower levels of Slaidburn.

Kitted out in full waterproofs we are a match for anything the weather can throw at us. After starting the walk in steady rain it's not long before it stops! There's not much wind and the temperature is rising and by half-way we are shedding layers faster than a racing snake. Isn't that just typical of England in Spring time. A good walk, with some dispute about the projected distance between myself and walk leader Nigel Hext, but as always I am right. A quick debrief over a pint of 'No Eyed Deer' at the Higher Buck, Waddington, rounds off another splendid day in the country.

The Waddington Fell walk seems to be truly ill-fated for me as it is rescheduled for July 11th, coinciding with my holiday in Menorca. Oh well, perhaps one day!

Aren't handheld GPS Sat Nav's a wonderful gadget for walkers? Well yes, they are if you are following the correct track! Ahead of the Burnley Contingent Thursday trek on

Ilkley Moor (baht 'ats) I ask walk leader John W (he of the 'Wandering Weirs'), to forward me the proposed GPX file of the route. No sooner said than done and I import it onto my Garmin device. I'm a bit disconcerted as discussion en-route to Ilkley between the happy 'Wanderers' seems to suggest there may have been some tampering with the proposed route over breakfast.

It's not long after starting the walk that my fears are confirmed. After a brief visit to the 'Swastika Stone', my device is directing me on a route following a wall-side path. At the same time, John W is heading uphill at an angle of 45°. The party splits in two as the routes continue to diverge. As both groups blunder on their separate paths it becomes apparent that somebody will have to yield.

In deference to John W, the walk leader, that I suppose must be me. Making a rapid detour which takes me completely off-screen from my forwarded route we eventually re-combine. Harsh words are spoken, but in a light-hearted fashion, and I decide to place little faith in my trusty device for the rest of the day. This decision is well founded as it is not the only deviation encountered during the walk. I should have known better, John W has previous for this sort of thing. In his defence, he blames his wife! Well you would, wouldn't you? Still it didn't mar a great day's rambling on 'Yarkshire's' most famous moor, and we will be back - hopefully, both singing from the same hymn sheet.

Coming up it's the last game of another highly successful season, for that's what survival in the Premier League is for us. We round off our fixtures with a home game against West Ham United, in what is effectively a 'dead rubber'. It should make for a more relaxing afternoon at Turf

Moor, and I'm hoping for once to be able to sit back in my seat rather than on the edge of it. Just pride and place-money to play for, let's go out on a high!

Game 38 – Sunday 21st May, 15.00 – Burnley v West Ham United

It's the last game of the season and a bit of a dilemma for me. Sunday being one of my 'dry days' - do I break with tradition and go for pre-match pints or not? As it's a nice sunny day I decide to forsake the beer in favour of a spot of gardening. That could be mistake number one.

In the absence of the pub stop I'm at the Turf in good time and seated with ten minutes to spare. Not so my match day amigos who are, as usual, finding it difficult to extricate themselves from the ale house. The team news shows once again no Michael Keane, who it's possible we will never again see in a Claret's line-up as he pursues his ambition of a tilt at the Champions League with one of the 'big boys'. Ben Mee is also again absent and I'm hopeful that his absence is down to injury and not anything more sinister. Also missing from the squad is George Boyd, a loyal servant now coming to the end of his contract, and seemingly unlikely to re-sign on the terms offered. Ashley Barnes drops to the bench and his place up front goes to Andre Gray.

It's a promising start and we should take an early lead, but Gray makes an absolute hash of an early golden chance. The early exchanges are littered with defensive errors from both teams and it looks like a high scoring encounter could be the order of the day. Another opportunity goes begging as Sam Vokes agonisingly fails to get a touch on an inviting cross. Whilst we are looking decent going forward, defensively we are decidedly shaky. As the half wears on the action on the pitch is becoming increasingly feisty. There are bookings for the Hammers', James Collins, and our own Ashley Westwood. Most of the niggling seems to involve Sofiane Feghouli, who is displaying a liking for the 'dive', and some superb play-acting that Richard Burton would be proud of.

However, on 27 minutes we have the lead as Gray is put clear down the right flank, his low ball in is missed at the near post by Scott Arfield but not by Vokes, coming in behind him to slot home from close range. That's better - now let's turn on the style.

Unfortunately, the lead is short-lived, and from a well worked move by the Hammers, the villain Feghouli calmly levels the scores. There's not much further incident before half time, although Gray almost puts us back ahead with a 'cheeky' backheel that just goes wide following a mazy Robbie Brady dribble. Westwood is lucky to escape a second booking and inevitable red card as he catches Collins with a high challenge, and West Ham's influential playmaker Manuel Lanzini also becomes a yellow card victim. Half time 1-1.

The second half turns out to be somewhat of a disappointment. West Ham, sensing a victory, step up a gear and play is now predominantly in our half. A decent headed effort from Vokes, another free-kick attempt (much too high) by Brady, are our early highlights. Not long after record signing Brady makes way for Johann Berg Gudmundsson, but before he can make any impression we are behind.

On 72 minutes Edimilson Fernandes hits a powerful right foot shot which Tom Heaton does well to touch onto the crossbar. Unfortunately, the rebound falls straight onto the head of Hammers striker Andre Ayew who can't miss from almost on the goal line. A double substitution on 78 minutes as Barnes comes on for Gray, and an almost forgotten Steven Defour replaces Westwood.

The substitutes are unable to materially affect the game and we lose the final fixture of a long, sometimes difficult, but ultimately successful season. Time for the usual tiresome pitch invasion before the players take their lap of honour, and we fans at least, can all relax for a few months before it all starts over again.

Result - Burnley (Vokes 23) 1 - 2 (Feghouli 27, Ayew 72) West Ham United

Burnley Team

Heaton, Lowton, Long, Tarkowski, Ward, Brady (Berg Gudmundsson 67), Hendrick, Westwood (Defour 78), Arfield, Gray (Barnes 78), Vokes

Subs Not Used - Pope, Darikwa, Flanagan, Agyei,

West Ham United Team

Adrian, Byram, Fonte, Collins, Ogbonna, Cresswell, Lanzini, Fernandes (Rice 90+1), Snodgrass (Fletcher 84), Ayew, Feghouli

Subs Not Used - Randolph, Quina, Makasi, Kemp

Attendance - 21,634

Season To Date - Played 38, Won 11, Drawn 7, Lost 20, Goals For 39, Goals Against 55, Points 40

League Position after Game 38 - 16th

JOURNEY'S END

Well dear reader, how was that for you? For myself I think I can best describe it as exciting but exhausting! A Premier League season should come with a government health warning for Clarets fans. The nervous tension inflicted during the course of a game, let alone a season, is surely detrimental to the heart - and probably the head.

Yet on reflection why should that be? In the whole season we only occupied a relegation spot once, and that following the first fixture, a narrow home defeat to Swansea City. Indeed, had I been a 'Swans' fan after the season they had seriously dicing with relegation, I would by now have been a gibbering wreck.

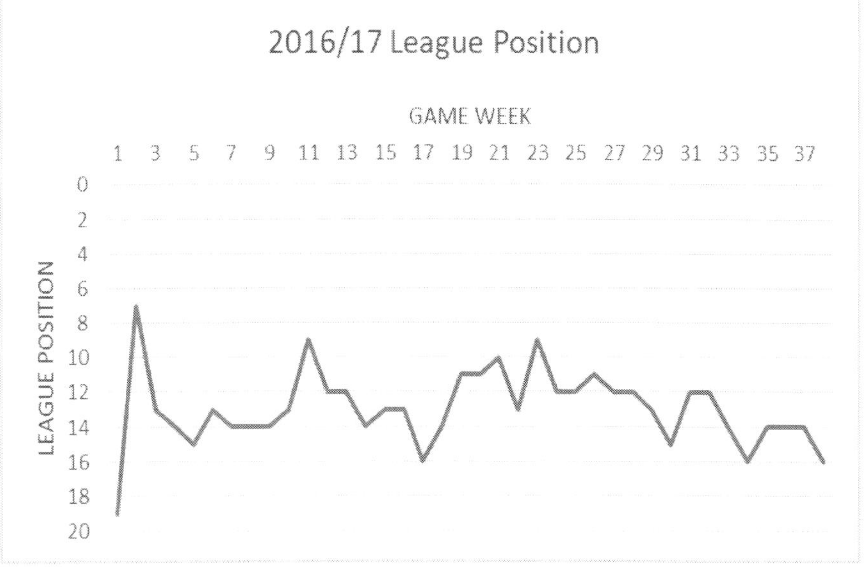

We had brief flirtations with the top half on three occasions, but spent the bulk of the season respectably above the drop zone. Why did it never, to me at least, feel all that comfortable?

I think some of the answer to that is down to the fact that we were unable to match our first half season points tally in the second period. At the halfway point, 19 games, we had acquired 23 points, from seven victories, two draws and 10 defeats. From the end of December on we managed, four victories, five draws and again 10 defeats, netting 17 points. Obviously, the fact that in the first half season we had played 11 home games, and only eight away, had a significant bearing. As this statistic reversed itself in the second period, particularly considering our less than impressive away points tally, consternation increased.

On the subject of home and away form, what a sharp and alarming contrast! Nineteen fixtures at Turf moor yielded a total of 33 points, with a magnificent 10 victories for us to cheer. Added to that was a very creditable draw with Champions Chelsea, and points also taken from Hull City, and West Bromwich Albion.

Regrettably the points gained on our travels came nowhere near this level, bagging us a meagre total of seven! A solitary away victory coming at Crystal Palace, and that in the penultimate fixture. Additionally, there were four draws, the first coming unbelievably at Manchester United, followed by invaluable points at Hull City, Middlesbrough and Sunderland - all three teams being subsequently relegated.

Never was the old saying **'there's no place like home'**, more relevant.

Defensively we were pretty tight, conceding 55 goals at an average of approximately 1.5 per game. That's not an unreasonable amount being bettered only in the bottom half of the table by Middlesbrough - who ironically were relegated.

The major problem was at the other end of the pitch where goals were in short supply, 39 goals from 38 fixtures, as good as one per game. This tally was surpassed by every other team bar the three relegated ones.

As Sean Dyche continually reminded us, games are decided on fine margins. Unfortunately, on most occasions we were on the wrong side of those margins. No less than 12 matches were lost by one goal, if we had just managed another goal in those games we would have been edging towards qualification for Europe. Both fixtures against Arsenal, and Manchester City resulted in single goal defeats, and on all four occasions we could count ourselves very unlucky.

Following a rather worrying early season spate of heavy away defeats, results had by the second half season become much closer. However, we were still on most occasions unable to bring home any reward. The away goals total for the season was a paltry 13, only two of which came from eight games before the new year. Things did improve subsequently with 11 in 11 fixtures. Only twice on our travels, at Swansea City and Crystal Palace, did we manage to find the net twice.

Our adventures in both cup competitions ended disappointingly, although it's fair to say that these games were treated as a diversion from the main event - Premier League survival. Multiple team changes were the order of the day in these fixtures as we looked to reduce fatigue and injury risk. They also provided opportunities for some of the 'fringe' members of the squad to get some meaningful action.

Firstly, an early exit in the League Cup, or EFL or whatever they call it now, to nearest neighbours Accrington Stanley. A dour game decided by a goal in the last minute of extra time. Still, who would deny little old Stanley there moment of glory.

The FA cup seemed, for a while, to bring some hope of a possible Wembley outing. Victories over Premier League Sunderland, after a replay, and the Championship's Bristol City, landed us a plum fifth round home tie with non-league Lincoln City A banana skin if ever there was one, and yes, who slipped and fell on their a***s? With it came the dubious distinction of being the only top-flight team to exit the tournament twice to non-league opposition. Next time can we have Chelsea away please!

However, having said all that, we were successful in what we set out to do. Survival at Premier League level, against the mega-rich city clubs, who can pay agents more for a single transfer than we can spend on our total transfer budget, is nothing short of a miracle! In fact, Mr Dyche God bless him, has now worked the miracle three times with two promotions and now this. Where would we be without him?

Once again, we had a manager who was a model of professionalism, and his team both on and off the pitch, reflected this. No whingeing and moaning here about too many games to play, albeit we did it with a smaller squad than most. No surrounding and harassing match officials at every decision that went against us. No badmouthing of rival managers or players, and all the other mindless word games employed by some of the 'elite' bosses.

We are Burnley, we may be unfashionable and small town, but we are honest (often to our detriment) and the club is run on sound and sustainable business principles. We don't 'bet the ranch' here, we take the sensible route and try to build gradually. My dad always told me never to spend money I hadn't got, an adage that should be the business model adopted by the more profligate clubs.

Three times in the season the club's transfer record was broken as the strengthening of the squad got underway. The money spent on solid, dependable performers that fit the team's profile and manager's psyche. I don't think we'll be seeing any 'Flash Harry' types down Turf Moor way. With a second Premier League season now assured I'm sure our policy of gradual improvement will once again be in evidence this summer.

So, finally another momentous season has come to an end, but has it? Does it ever really come to an end? As soon as the last ball is kicked the planning starts for the next challenge. The fan's thoughts turn to which players may be leaving the club, and who might be coming. As the players and management team take a well-earned break until pre-season training begins again in July, the fans continue to scour the media for news. Then of course there is the clamour for next season's fixture list. Due out in June we will anxiously wait to see who we meet first, what are the Christmas games, and do we have an easy finish?

One thing is for sure, next season will be as difficult and challenging as the last. However, with the club in the capable hands of the Directors, management team and players, there is no reason why we cannot again prosper against all the odds.

Keep the Faith!

Up the Clarets!

P.S. For those who have managed to keep going and are wondering. The ukulele still lies abandoned, hidden from view in the spare bedroom. Fear not George Formby your status remains unthreatened.

There was better news on the Fantasy Football front however, a solid finish and a bagful of goals from Harry Kane, earned me fourth place. I am advised that this puts me in the money, M&S here I come to collect my winnings!

26661329R10175

Printed in Great Britain
by Amazon